ENGLISH GRAMMAR AND WRITING SKILLS

Paul F.M. Ai-Gbahan Lahai & Saidu Challay

authorHOUSE

AuthorHouse™
1663 Liberty Drive
Bloomington, IN 47403
www.authorhouse.com
Phone: 1 (800) 839-8640

Published by AuthorHouse 5/27/2020

ISBN: 978-1-7283-5782-9 (sc)
ISBN: 978-1-7283-5781-2 (e)

Library of Congress Control Number: 2020906337

Print information available on the last page.

CONTENTS

PART 1
PARTS OF SPEECH

PART 2
SENTENCE STRUCTURE

PART 3
ENRICHING VOCABULARY

PART 4
PUNCTUATION MARKS AND MECHANICS

PART 5
ESSAY WRITING

PART 6
COMPREHENSION AND SUMMARY EXERCISES

ACKNOWLEDGEMENTS

We have been assisted tremendously in various ways by several colleagues in the process of putting our ideas together to work on this book. We are particularly indebted to Mr. Michael Hamadi Secka of the Curriculum Research Evaluation Directorate of the Gambia for voluntarily proofreading our manuscript. We also highly appreciate the contributions of Mr. Olawuyi Mutiu who painstakingly reviewed our manuscript and shared his thoughts on our efforts. His comments, criticisms and suggestions greatly helped to improve the quality of this book.

We are also very grateful to staff of the West African Examinations Council (WAEC), who assisted us in accessing past examination questions in English Language and also making available comments of Chief Examiners for the West African Senior Secondary Certificate Examination (WASSCE). The past papers, coupled with the Chief Examiners comments gave us an insight into some of the key areas that need to be addressed in the teaching of English Language at the secondary school level. The past papers also proved to be very useful in planning some of the essays in this book. We thank them very much for making these invaluable resources available.

We also want to thank Andrea Lunsford and Robert Conners, Leslie C. Perelman, James Paradis and Edward Barret, Madeline Semmelineyer and Donald O. Bolander, Diana Hucker and Kinneavy Wariner for their books which we used as reference materials. The following books, *The New Webster Grammar Guide, Writing and Grammar (Rube Level), Rules for Writers (6th edition), Elements of Writing and Oxford Advanced Learners Dictionary (8th edition)*. These books served as sources of reference while working on this book.

We are also very grateful to the many instructors at the secondary school level as well as the tertiary level for their useful comments and suggestions. We engaged colleagues in focus group discussions about the challenges students face in learning English Language. Their inputs in those discussions helped us in shaping our work to address the key issues they raised. In order to give us an idea of the difficulties students encounter in writing essays, we also requested the instructors to make available some scripts of past examinations which they readily made available. We went through some of these scripts and in the process we were able to identify some errors in grammar as well as in essay writing. Those errors guided us in developing exercises that will help students overcome their difficulties.

INTRODUCTION

English Language is used as the medium of instruction as well as subject of instruction in the educational system of the former colonies of British West Africa. This policy has remained to be in existence even after independence. There are a lot of challenges in the teaching and learning of English in Sierra Leone. This has been partly as a result of poor preparation of students and partly because of lack of appropriate teaching and learning materials. Even where the requisite materials may be available, lack of the required pedagogical skills on the part of teachers of English also poses serious problems.

Although English Language remains to be very important in the educational system of Sierra Leone, the performance of students at both the Basic Education Certificate Examination (BECE) and West African Senior School Certificate Examination (WASSCE) has been very poor. Chief Examiners' reports of the West African Examination Council (WAEC) over the years have indicated that students lack the necessary skills in writing essays and answering comprehension and summary questions. Although the reports often focus on these areas, it is also evident that grammar poses serious challenges for learners of English Language. It is possibly as a result of their poor grasp of the grammatical rules that they makes them not to be able to present their ideas in clear and grammatical sentences. Most students cannot construct simple sentences in English as they do not have a firm grip on the grammatical rules.

The main focus of this book is to address the problem of lack of grammar texts in simple and straightforward language that students will find less difficulty in understanding. Although this book is designed for students preparing for the West African Senior School Certificate Examination, it can also serve as a useful resource material for students studying English Language in tertiary institutions, teachers of English Language and other people who may want to improve their skills in the use of English Language.

This book comprises five parts as follows; parts of speech, sentence structure, enriching vocabulary, punctuation marks and mechanics, essay writing and comprehension and summary.

What Does Grammar Mean? Grammar simply put means the systematic description of the structure of a language. It deals with the study of the rules that govern the use of language. The use of language means putting related words together in order to convey a complete idea or thought. Any word that is used in communication/sentence makes an important contribution to convey a complete idea. Words are grouped according to the roles they play in communication. The main focus in the grammatical description of a language is to explain the relationships among parts of a sentence. Words combine to form phrases and phrases combine to form sentences. The rules governing how words combine to form phrases and phrases to form sentences encompasses part of grammatical description.

"Part of speech" refers to the classification or grouping of words according to the role they play in a sentence in the process of communication. The role a word plays in a sentence, in most cases, determines the *word class* (part of speech) to which it belongs. There are generally eight parts of speech and these include noun, pronoun, verb, adjective, adverb, preposition, conjunction and interjection.

Part one deals with parts of speech, and it entails those aspects of English grammar that fall under the traditional eight parts of speech, namely nouns, pronouns, verbs, adjectives, adverbs, prepositions, conjunctions and interjections. For learners of English, the parts of speech constitute a very important aspect in understanding how words are arranged to make meaning in the language. All the key aspects related to the parts of speech are covered in this part of the book. In order to guide learners, the definitions of these parts of speech are given with ample examples in each case. Emphasis has also been placed on how these parts of speech are interrelated in making meaning.

In part two, which covers sentence structure, some explanations have been provided on how words combine together to make phrases and clauses. Thus, in an attempt to learn English, there is need for learners to be familiar with how grammatical sentences are constructed in English. Some of the key aspects discussed in this part include phrases and clauses, sentence structure, subject verb agreement, common sentence errors, active and passive sentences and direct and indirect speeches. We combine words to make phrase, and phrases to make sentences. The rules of how to combine words to form phrases, and how these phrases are combined to make meaningful sentences in English is explained in chapter five. Furthermore, the functions of phrases and clauses are also dealt with in this chapter. In chapter two, the basic sentence structures are explained, including their functions and types. Chapter seven covers subject verb agreement, an idea that poses a lot of difficulties for learners of English as a second language. The rules of subject verb agreement have explained with suitable examples in each case. Chapter eight present some common errors in the use of sentences. The arrangement of words within a sentence can in most cases lead to ungrammaticality or in some cases ambiguity. Thus, aspects such as parallelism, fused sentences, sentence fragments, and the wrong use modifiers are elucidated. Chapter nine deals with the basic rules of changing sentences from the active voice to the passive voice, and chapter ten deals with how sentences are changed from direct speech to indirect speech.

Part three of this book covers developing vocabulary in English Language. In order for learners to be comfortable in the use of any language, they need to be familiar with a variety of lexical items of that language. Learners need to know how words are composed. In this regard, learners have been provided with some techniques on enriching their vocabulary with distinguishing between roots, prefixes and suffixes in English. We can increase our stock of vocabulary by being familiar with prefixes or suffixes that could be attached to root words to give us new meanings.

Part four covers an important aspect in writing which has to do with the use of punctuation marks and mechanics. Much of what one writes can be misunderstood because of the use of wrong punctuation marks. Chapters twelve and thirteen deal with punctuation marks and chapter fourteen with mechanics, mainly focusing on the use of capital letters.

In part five, readers have introduced to continuous writing. This has been broadly categorised under essay writing and letter writing. In each case, the different types of essays and types of letters are explained.

Part six deals with reading comprehension. In the West African Senior Certificate Examination, candidates are always tested in these areas. It is expected that candidates should be able to read a given passage, which is based either on comprehension or summary. Some guidance has been provided on how to answer comprehension and summary questions, after which some passages on both comprehension and summary have been provided for readers to practice.

In order to enable readers to practice, some questions have been provided on both essay writing and letter writing. This is intended to make readers confident in their writing, which they could prepare them for examinations. At the end of this book, answers have also been provided for most of the exercises. Readers are encouraged to try the exercise first before comparing their answers with those provided in the book. Answers were not provided for some of the exercise for which no one answer suffices. For these exercises, readers are encouraged to be creative in providing the correct answers which can be compared with others readers.

As a way of helping learners to practice, exercises have been included in every chapter covering grammatical areas. These exercises are aimed at consolidating the readers' understanding of the grammar rules discussed.

PART 1

PARTS OF SPEECH

CHAPTER 1

NOUNS AND PRONOUNS

A noun is a naming word. All words that name people, animals, places, things, or ideas are nouns, and all human languages have systems or patterns of naming The following are some common examples of nouns: *table, decision, love, football, family, Kailahun, Ngo Blama, Jarju, goat, Banjul, classroom, dining table.*

EXERCISE 1

Underline the nouns in the sentences below.

1. My best game is politics.
2. Timoh, Joseph, and Amina are best of friends.
3. Evolution is part of nature.
4. The enthusiasm is in the air.
5. Sunday was the coldest day of the month.
6. My brother is a prominent lawyer.
7. Is it time to go, Fodeiwa?
8. The horse is in Fandu.
9. The chair is old and has a missing leg.
10. When will the boys arrive?

EXERCISE 2

Underline all the nouns in the passage below.

On my way to school this morning, I witnessed a serious fight between two in-laws; both were elderly men. It was in Bakau car park, and a huge crowd were excitedly watching, shouting, laughing, and clapping for the fighters. They fought for some money that was given to them by a driver.

The two men had helped the driver to load his vehicle, so he gave them some coins and leones as compensation for their effort. According to one bystander, the man who handled the cash attempted to hide with it. He was later found behind one of the abandoned cars in the corner of the park, eating *nyebeh* and bread he had bought with the money. When he failed to produce the money, the other man hit him with an iron bar. He was bleeding and swimming in the pool of his blood. Police officers were immediately called to the scene. The bleeding man was taken to the hospital, while the other man was arrested and taken to the police station for investigation.

Types of Nouns

There are six different types of nouns: proper, common, concrete, abstract, collective, and compound.

Proper Nouns

A proper noun is the particular or specific name given to a person, place, animal, or thing. Proper nouns always begin with a capital letter. Some examples include: *Sierra Leone, Banjul, Kailahun, John, Fatoumatta, Omar, Blacky, Bundung, House of Assembly, God, Gabriel, Serrekunda, Gambia, Monday, August, Easter.*

EXERCISE 3

Underline all the proper nouns in the passage below.

On Friday morning, Alfred left for Kailahun to go play football for his club, Kailahun United. Kalahun United played the match with Kambo Warriors, the most famous club in the country. Kailahun United has Amara, Osman, Tommy, and Sahr as its star players. The Head of State donated Le 500,000 to each of the teams. Mr John Jusu from Nyandehun, was the referee for the match. When he blew his whistle to start the game, Modou of Kailahun United passed the ball to Lamin. From him the ball went to Mustapha, who crossed it to Tamba.

Bubakar of Kambo Warriors, the man of the match, scored the first goal in the tenth minute. At the end of the ninety minutes, it was Kambo Warriors 3, Kailahun United 2. The National Stadium was jam-packed with jubilant fans from all corners of the country. Among them were Muslims, Christians, ChrisMus, and freethinkers, all sitting together to watch the match.

Common Nouns

Common nouns do not refer to any specific person, animal, place, or thing. A common noun is a general name for kinds of people, animals, places, things, or ideas; for example, *boy, father, goat, town, village, government, month, building, country.*

EXERCISE 4

Underline all the common nouns in the passage below.

The youths nowadays have no patience about life. This impatience may be one of the reasons many young people act in ways that cause them regret. Let us imagine that a young man and a young woman run into each other today, propose marriage tomorrow, and the next day are a couple. They do not ask for any parental advice or blessing, nor do they give themselves enough time to observe each other. Such marriage is always temporary. My brother engaged in one such marriage in the past. He met the girl in a nightclub when he was celebrating his eighteenth birthday. Two weeks after, he informed the family that he had met a woman he loved and wanted to marry. To our greatest dismay, he did not even know the actual name of the girl, her tribe, her home, or a single member of her family. Realizing this, our father thanked him and asked him to lead us to the girl's family, which he was unable to do. He was ridiculed.

Compound Nouns

A compound noun is formed from two or more words. **Closed compound** nouns are written as single words and are often formed from two nouns:

classroom, playpen, bookcase, software, firewood, tablecloth. **Hyphenated compound** nouns are formed from two or more words, usually including at least one noun but often other parts of speech as well: *brother-in-law, passers-by, merry-go-round.* **Open compound** nouns are written as two or more separate words that function grammatically as a single noun: *high school, city hall, head of state, secretary general, state house, dining table.*

EXERCISE 5

Underline all the compound nouns in the passage below.

Nowadays, football is the best game in the world. It is written about in every newspaper around the globe. The grandchildren of my brother-in-law have vowed to have it as their future career. Their late grandmother loved to play volleyball and basketball. She had many playmates when she was in the game. On the Merry-Go-Round Day in Kailahun, she won several prizes. Among them were toothbrushes, a tablecloth, gunpowder, a teacup, and a penknife. When these grandchildren decided to play football, I expected they would be famous in future, especially since their landlords have constructed a pitch for them and bought them a cupboard full of the necessary textbooks about the game. Among the books were some with teaspoons and baseball pictures on the cover. They were the most important ones for their training. Now Kailahun hopes to produce world-class footballers. Fodei Lahai told us that he saw these promising boys last year on Tobaski Day, Christmas Day, and Easter merrymaking in and around Fandu Neiwuibu in Nyadehun Mambabu, Kailahun District, eastern province of Sierra Leone.

Collective Nouns

A collective noun is a name for a group or collection of animals, people, or things which act or are referred to as single unit. All collective nouns are singular in number but plural in meaning: *family, congregation, audience, crew, flock, class, mob, band, committee.*

EXERCISE 6

Underline all the collective nouns in the passage below.

Most communities in the world today are prone to violence. Youths these days can be easily fashioned into destructive weapons that will destroy their own society and even their own lives. For instance, two days ago, a mob of youths attacked and killed a trader for not selling to them what he hadn't in his shop. In another incident, some groups among the spectators attacked one another after an argument had broken among them. The audience in Community Centre in Kailahun set fire on the building when one of the actors left the stage earlier than expected. Why is the world so violent these days? Is it because of the way families bring up their children? Psychologists and sociologists must work hard to find out how peace in society must be maintained. One thing we must do is to ask the congregations in the churches and mosques to pray for world peace.

EXERCISE 7

Underline all the collective nouns in the sentences below.

1. My family is part of the congregation that worship in St Pius Parish X in Bo.
2. The violent mob demonstrated against the act of the crew.
3. The team did not play to the expectation of their fans.
4. This community set up the committee to monitor the work.
5. The destruction of the swarm was the staff's decision.
6. I was part of the band that entertained the harem of the king.
7. The light from the galaxy exposed the gang of thieves in hell.
8. Maintaining groups within the club may lead to division.
9. I saw our couple in the huge crowd that came to welcome us.
10. A herd of cattle destroyed the colony of termites.

Concrete Nouns

A concrete noun names physical objects—including things, animals, people, or places—that we can see or touch: *Paul, city, school, chair, table.* It is the opposite of an abstract noun.

EXERCISE 8

Underline the concrete nouns in the sentences below.

1. The action of the actors did not please the audience at the theatre.
2. The consumption of the unpleasant food causes illnesses.
3. Any community with many happy families is less violent.
4. Most lovers love entertainment but hate tedious jobs.
5. I see no honour in the behaviour of dignified people these days.
6. God created the heaven and earth for all mankind.
7. Football has become the major game in the world.

Abstract Nouns

Abstract nouns refer to ideas, feelings, or qualities that we cannot see or touch. Examples include *sorrow, relief, love, patriotism, language, air, God, Tobaski Day.*

EXERCISE 9

Underline all the concrete nouns and circle the abstract nouns in the passage below.

My grandfather, Kennie Fodei Lahai, then the paramount chief of Luawa chiefdom in Kailahhun district, was a philosopher. One afternoon, he expressed to me the confusion and concerned about creation. "God Almighty, together with His angels, created this universe and everything in it. He did the creation through words in His own language. It is only we the humans God used his hand to create. That makes us very special from all the other creatures. That is even the reason why He gave us dominion over everything He created. This also shows that He loves us more than any other creature. Love, loyalty, honesty and perfection are among the things Almighty God demands from us in return for His love for us. Love and perfection are the greatest of all. Allah wants us to love one another and be perfect like Him. But how can this be possible? Will the life be normal if it happens as He wants? For instance, all of us are made in His own image, but no one is perfect like Him. Again, if we are all perfect like Him, and we love one another like ourselves, how can the lawyers, judges, police, criminals, doctors and clergy men get their daily bread? There will be no crimes, so those who live on crime will have no source of income; no case will go to court for lawyers and judges. There will be no sickness for doctors to treat and get money. There will be no need for religion since everyone will be perfect and commits no sin. This is the great wonder about Him that no one can understand." "Anyway, let us pray for His mercy to reign on us on the Judgment day." I told him slowly when he finished speaking.

EXERCISE 10

1. *State the differences between a proper noun and a common noun.*
2. *What is the difference between a compound noun and a collective noun?*
3. *State the differences between a concrete noun and an abstract noun.*

Please carefully read and understand this fact about the kinds of nouns discussed above: All nouns are either proper or common; they are either concrete or abstract. Collective or compound nouns can also be a proper noun, common noun, concrete noun or abstract noun. Observe the examples.

Eg: 'Foundation Day' and 'Almighty God' are examples of proper noun, compound noun and abstract noun. 'Love', 'truth' and 'sadness' are examples of common noun and abstract noun. 'Banjul', 'Africa' and 'John' are examples of proper noun and concrete nouns. 'Table', 'book', 'dog' and 'boy' are examples of common noun and concrete noun.

EXERCISE 11

Place the nouns below in the appropriate categories they belong. Note that a noun can fit into more than one category.

For example the noun 'Tobaski Day' can be appropriate in the categories of proper noun, abstract noun and compound noun.

Now do the rest.

bread, butter scot, family, Peter, Banjul, Easter Sunday, mob, beauty, water, marriage, grandmother, honesty, Serrekunda, committee, ignorance, laptop, crowd, doctor, God, sister-in-law, freedom, New York, angel, happiness, Tom, teaspoon, football, patriotism, peace, Tuesday, Head of State, congregation, toothbrush, Kailahun, community, secretary general, sweet heart, boy, air, stone, prayer, holiday, John, table, sin, children, audience, authority, opinion, money etc.

Proper noun	Common noun	Collective noun	Compound noun	Abstract noun	Concrete noun

Unique Features of Nouns

Nouns have some characteristics that distinguishes them from other parts of speech. There are four distinctive features of nouns. If these features are properly understood, one can easily distinguish nouns from the other parts of speech in sentences. The four features include the following:

a) Nouns are either singular or plural, countable or uncountable.
b) Nouns indicate or show possession or ownership (possessive case)

c) Nouns could be derived from other word classes (parts of speech) by taking suffix.

d) Articles such as 'a', 'an' and 'the' come before nouns. (determiners).

Countable and Uncountable Nouns

Nouns can be either countable or uncountable. Countable nouns are nouns that we can count. Humans, animals, stones, books, houses etc. are examples of countable nouns. Nouns that we cannot count are known as uncountable or mass nouns. Gas, liquid, water, milk, sugar, rice, sand, flour, oil, kerosene, etc. are examples of uncountable nouns. Most mass nouns could be counted by their containers. For example, a gallon of paint, three bags of rice, two gallons of petrol, four cups of water.

a) **Singular and plural Nouns**: In grammar, only two numbers exist; they are one (singular) and more than one (plural). Most nouns change form to show number. A singular noun names one person, place, animal, thing or idea; while a plural noun names more than one person, place, animal, thing or idea. Plural of most nouns is formed by adding the suffix '-s' or '-es' to the singular form. Formation of plural of most nouns involves spelling change. In studying the ways nouns form their plurals, we study about regular and irregular nouns.

Regular nouns: Regular nouns are those nouns that form their plural by adding '-s' or '-es' to the singular form. Some grammarians say, no spelling change occurs in regular nouns. Instead, the suffix ('-s' or '-es') is added. Here are some examples: table-tables, chair-chairs, pen-pens, bench-benches, box – boxes, mango - mangoes etc. Below are some common rules to form the plural of nouns.

i) Add '-s' to form the plural of nouns that end with 'o' if the 'o' is preceded by a vowel sound:

Eg video-videos, radio-radios, stereo-stereos etc.

ii) Add '-es' to form the plural of some nouns ending in 'o' if the 'o' is preceded by consonant sound.

Eg: hero-heroes, zero-zeroes, echo-echoes etc.

iii) Also add '-s' to form the plural of most nouns naming musical instruments with their spellings ending in 'o', even if the 'o' is preceded by a consonant sound.

eg piano-pianos, solo-solos, banjo-banjos.

iv) Add '-s' to form the plural of nouns that end with 'y', if the 'y' is preceded by a vowel sound.

Eg: boy-boys, key-keys, tray-trays, etc.

Form the plural of a noun that ends in 'y' by changing the 'y' to '"' and add 'es', if the 'y' is preceded by consonant sound. Eg: lady-ladies, lorry-lorries, body-bodies etc. (irregular noun)

v) Add 's' to form the plural of any proper noun ending in 'y'; it doesn't matter which letter precedes the 'y'. Eg Brady - Bradys, Mansaray - Mansarays, Tarawally - Tarawallys, Touray - Tourays etc.

vi) Add 's' to form the plural of some nouns ending in 'f' or 'fe' if the 'f' or 'fe' is preceded by vowel sound. Eg: hoof-, hoofs, proof-proofs safe-safes etc.

Note that some nouns are exceptions to this rule. Eg: wife-wives, knife-knives, leaf-leaves, loaf - loaves.

vii) Form the plural of most nouns ending in f or fe by changing the f or fe to v and add es. eg half-halves, self-selves etc

viii) Add '-es' to form the plural of nouns ending in 'ch', 'sh','s', 'x,' 'z'. Eg: church-churches, clash-clashes, class-classes, glass-glasses, box-boxes, buzz-buzzes etc

Irregular nouns: These are nouns that do not follow any specific rule in forming their plurals. In some cases, the spelling change affects the vowel sounds. Eg: tooth-teeth, foot-feet, man-men, woman-women, goose-geese.

Some nouns have the same singular and plural forms. Eg: sheep-sheep, deer-deer, furniture-furniture, news-news, information-information etc.

Very few nouns such as scissors, trousers, pliers etc, have no singular form. They are always used in plural form. To form the singular form, add 'a pair of' to the plural form.

Eg: a pair of trousers, a pair of scissors, a pair of pliers etc.

Some nouns are plural in form but singular in meaning. In other words, the spelling ends with 's' but have a singular meaning. Most of these nouns name the branches of knowledge offered in learning institutions. Eg: Economics, Physics, Mathematics, Politics, Linguistics, etc.

The following are other examples of irregular plural. Most of these words are borrowed words from other languages.

Eg: radius ... radii, focus ... foci, alumnus ... alumni, syllabus ... syllabi

Form the plural of a word that its spelling ends with 'is' by changing the 'is' to 'es'.

Eg: crisis ... crises, emphasis ... emphases

Form the plural of a word that its spelling ends with 'um' by changing the 'um' to 'a'.

Eg: medium ... media, datum ... data, curriculum ... curricula,

To form the plural of a compound noun, first identify the most important word in the compound noun and then follow the rule it takes. Eg:

Singular	Plural
grandfather	grandfathers
grandchild	grandchildren
head of state	heads of state,
passer-by	passers-by
brother-in-law	brothers-in-law
secretary general	secretaries general

EXERCISE 12

Fill the spaces in the table with the singular or plural of the noun against each.

Singular	Plural	Singular
leaf		Sunday
piano		
box		
reverend father		head of state
	pliers	man
church		
a pair of trousers		secretary general
plateau		
	oxen	lorry
	thieves	
bibliography		testimony
	ladies	chief
	deer	
	data	July
hero		syllabus
	in-laws	Friday
tomato		

	mice	hoof
phenomenon		
toy		noise
evidence		
	politics	breakfast
man		
	foxes	roof
self		crisis
lorry		Fatou
part of speech		man of war

Plural	*Singular*	*Plural*
		synopses
Furniture		Tourays
children	linguistics	
		passers-by
		news
crises	Tomato	
	toothbrush	
noises		bases
	donkey	
feet	Glass	
	Battery	
	Wife	
beaches		radii
	Mansaray	
	Radio	
		criterion
stadia	Knife	
		bodies
halves	Pygmy	
	Foot	

proofs	Key	
	medium	
women	Focus	
	Ass	
	Fish	
		bodies
	figure of speech	

EXERCISE 13

Rewrite the following sentences in the plural form

Singular: This man has one child.   **Plural:** These men have children.

Singular	**Plural**
1. A cat is a small animal.	_____
2. There is a bird up the tree.	_____
3. The boy has a book in his bag.	_____
4. There is one pupil in class.	_____
5. That girl has a bicycle.	_____
6. His tooth is aching.	_____
7. A man is coming with a dog.	_____
8. I heard a story about him.	_____
9. Here is a mouse in a box.	_____
10. She is washing her foot in a bowl.	_____

b) *Possessive Case*

Nouns change form to show possession or indicate ownership. When they do so, they usually take apostrophe (') and sometimes **s**.

Eg: Paul's chair [the chair that belongs to Paul], the goat's tail [the tail of a goat], the writer's request [request made by the writer], Mendy's black pen [the black pen Mendy owns].

Most singular nouns, add an apostrophe (') and s to form the possession or relationship. Eg: boy's room, devil's hole.

A singular or a plural noun that ends with '**s**' will take only an apostrophe without '**s**' to show relationship or possession. Eg: girls' society, players' demands, teachers' reply, class' contribution, Moses' pen etc. Other plural nouns that do not end with '**s**' take apostrophe and '*s*'. to indicate possession. Eg: men's society, children's outing, women's club etc.

If two or more people own a single item, place the apostrophe '**s**' after the name of the last person. Eg. Paul, Fodei and Lahai's bag is in my room. Amie, Fatou and Mujeh's room is empty.

If each of the persons separately owns an item, make each person [noun] possessive. Eg. Amie's, Saata's and Mansaray's mangoes are on the table. Father's, mum's and sister's bags are in the store.

EXERCISE 14

Write the possessive form of the phrases below

Eg: legs of the dogs, … the dogs' legs,
plate for my father, … … my father's plate
a car of the president, … . the president's car
union of students, … . students' union

1. room for the boys
2. association for men
3. money for the class
4. tail of the monkey
5. book for Thomas
6. a pen for Peter and Paul
7. pens for Tom and Med each
8. mother of Fodei
9. brother of Tom and Fatu
10. property of the family

11. bag for Moses
12. club for girls
13. day for African children
14. meeting for teachers
15. office of the principal
16. house of Mr. Peter
17. food for the dogs
18. games for the children
19. photos of my mother
20. words of God
21. car for the principal
22. bus for the teams
23. blessing from father
24. beliefs of Christians

c) **Formation of Nouns**

Most nouns are derivative words. This means that they are formed from other parts of speech by taking or dropping an affix.

{An affix is a letter or letters that are added to a root word which will change either the word class, number, tense or meaning}.

When letter(s) come at the beginning of the word, they are called prefix. Eg. unhappy, disapprove, impossible, irregular etc. If the letter(s) come at the end of the word, they are referred to as suffix. Eg: happiness, lawlessness, friendship etc. Common affixes include able, ish, ness, less, ion, ment, ism, ism, d, ed, un, dis, mis, etc.

Other parts of speech	Noun form
develop (verb)	development
foolish (adj)	foolishness
treat (verb)	treatment
sad (adj)	sadness
investigate (verb)	investigation
fit (adj)	fitness

EXERCISE 15

The words in the table below are verbs, adjectives or adverbs. Write the noun form of each of them in the space provided against them. Some have more than one noun form. Note that this exercise will also help to overcome spelling problems.

	Word		*Noun form*
Eg	laugh	verb	laughter
1	develop	verb	
2	peaceful	adj	
3	honest	adj	
4	happy	adj	
5	friendly	adj	
6	pray	verb	
7	capable	adj	
8	quiet	adj	
9	treat	verb	
10	foolish	adj	
11	patriotic	adj	
12	free	Adj/verb	
13	hopeless	adj	
14	faithful	adj	
15	timely	adj	
16	enslave	verb	
17	bravely	adv	
18	intelligent	adj	
19	gentle	adj	
20	ungodly	adj	
21	breathe	verb	
22	honour	verb	
23	capable	adj	
24	create	verb	
25	popular	adj	

	Word		Noun form
eg	inform	verb	Information, Informant
26	true	adj	
27	sinful	adj	
28	communicate	verb	
29	entertain	verb	
30	lead	verb	
31	participate	verb	
32	beautifully	adv	
33	advise	verb	
34	die	verb	
35	responsible	adj	
36	do	verb	
37	difficult	adj	
38	mad	adj	
39	effective	adj	
40	understand	verb	
41	appreciate	verb	
42	environmental	adj	
43	depend	verb	
44	explain	verb	
45	difficult	adj	
46	totally	adv	
47	happily	adv	
48	necessary	adj	
49	prepare	verb	
50	advocate	verb	

d) **Nouns immediately follow determiners.** Determiners are words that qualify nouns. In other words, they make the meaning of a noun clear and specific. Determiner could be an article: *a, an* or *the*. Only modifiers come between article and noun; they all function as modifiers. Determiners immediately follow nouns for easy clarification of their meaning. Eg a table, <u>an</u> apple, the world etc

Grammatical Functions of Nouns in a Sentence

Noun is one of the parts of speech that is frequently used in communication. It plays six different grammatical roles in sentences: *(subject, direct object, indirect object, object of preposition, predicate nominative and appositive)*

a) **Subject of a sentence**: As subject of a sentence, a noun performs the action expressed by an action verb in a sentence, or the sentence gives information about it. Eg Ebrima dances skilfully. Banjul is a small city. Ebrima and Banjul are subjects in the respective sentences.

EXERCISE 16

Underline the noun that functions as subjects in each sentence below.

1. Kailahun is my home town.
2. My uncle usually brushes his cocoa and coffee farms.
3. Fandu, a village in Kailahun district, is a nice place to live.
4. The indigenes are very peaceful, brave, wise and educated.
5. That region is the backbone of Sierra Leone.
6. In the past, Kailahun enjoyed very attractive culture.
7. Several people from that area appear prayerful and hardworking.
8. The information about the village was provided by the chief.
9. The teams performed excellently in the last game.
10. The pupils came late to school this morning.
11. Do you know the boys that fought for me?
12. Here are the boys I told you about yesterday.
13. There is a boy in this school that can fight me.
14. Do your family eat Benachi and Nyebeh?
15. The youth nowadays hardly consult their elders.

b) **Direct object**: Nouns also function as direct objects in sentences. When it does so, it receives the action expressed by the transitive verb in the sentence. If you want to identify direct object in a sentence, ask *what* or *who* after the verb in the sentence. The *noun or pronoun* that serves as an answer to the question is a direct object.

I killed the **bird**. Killed what? *the bird*. So ***the bird*** is the direct object.
You stopped the **car**. Stopped what? *the car*.
The police shut an **armed robber**. Shut who? an armed rubber.
I love my **parents**. love who? *my parents*.
Hermata hit the **door**. Hit what? *the door*
The policeman stopped the **car**. Stopped what? *the car*
The bird, the car, an armed robber, my parents and *the door* received the actions of killed, stopped, shut and love respectively; so they are direct objects of their respective sentences.

EXERCISE 17

Underline the nouns that function as direct objects in the sentences below.

1. The Smiling Coast has admirable leadership.
2. The clever gentleman has made plenty achievements.
3. This small semi-desert nation receives many visitors every year.
4. Some of these visitors perform wonders in this peaceful nation.
5. Some citizens hate the visitors for the wonders they perform.
6. When I knocked the door of the desert house, it opened.
7. One must take his time to deal with some desert dwellers.
8. They love the way-farers from far away homes.
9. I love The Gambia and the Gambians.
10. We speak both French and English.

c) **Indirect object**: This is a noun to whom or what, or for whom or what something is done in a sentence. It often comes between the verb and the direct object in a sentence. Eg He wrote <u>Joe</u> a letter. She bought <u>the girl</u> a pen. *Joe* and *the girl* are indirect objects in the respective sentences. In some cases the indirect object can be preceded by a preposition showing the person or thing something is done. For example, He wrote a letter <u>to Joe</u>. She bought a pen <u>for the girl</u>. **Note:** *A prepositional phrase cannot function as direct or indirect object.*

EXERCISE 18

Underline the direct objects and circle the indirect objects in the sentences below

1. In my school, one old man tells the pupils stories every day.
2. He will ask them to tell their parents the stories.
3. This man sometimes buys his children some bread to eat.
4. Some children send him gifts from their parents.
5. When they come, he opens them his gate to enter.
6. My grandfather wrote my dad many fork tales.
7. When I was young, my grandmother bought me many toys.
8. He sent us invitation cards for his birthday party.
9. When I was in Kailahun, I wrote them this letter.
10. The government awards honest citizens contracts.

d) **Object of preposition**: A noun or pronoun is referred to as object of preposition when it follows a preposition in a sentence. When it does so, the noun will not work alone. It works together with the preposition as *a prepositional phrase*; wherein the phrase functions as single part of speech (i.e., as an adjective or an adverb). Eg: to the **school**, behind the **house**, after the **exam**, for my **mother,** for **him**, against **her**, to **them** etc.

EXERCISE 19

In the short paragraph below, underline the prepositional phrases and circle the nouns or pronouns that function as object of preposition.

I went to town this morning to buy some food for my family. In the supermarket, I spoke to my old friends briefly. I returned to my car and quickly jumped into it as time was not in my favour. By the car there was an old woman. She talked to me in a low tone and pointed to her empty belly. With me, was very little amount. I took One hundred Dalasi from the wallet in my bag and gave her. She prayed for abundant blessing from God in Heaven to rain on me. I put her in my car and drove her to her residence. At home, her family received her happily and thanked me a lot for my generosity.

It is interesting to note that a noun phrase or a noun clause can perform any one or more of the functions stated above.

v Predicate Nominative/Appositive: As either a predicate nominative or appositive, a noun renames another noun in a sentence. As **a predicate nominative**, the renaming noun is separated from the subject by a linking verb and it appears in the predicate section of the sentence. Eg. Jarju is <u>our prefect</u>. That man is <u>a pastor</u>. (*our prefect* and *a pastor* are predicate nominative in the respective sentences.)

vi As **an appositive**, it is separated from the noun it renames by a comma.

Tom, <u>my brother</u>, is here. Pa Kebbie, <u>the chairman</u>, has come. (*my brother* and *the chairman* are appositives in the respective sentences. They rename the subjects, Tom and Pa Kebbie respectively.)

EXERCISE 20

In the sentences below, underline the appositives and circle the predicate nominatives.

1. That tall man, the noble prize winner, is our new manager.
2. Mr Juana, <u>Paul's brother</u>, is the former Managing Director of SALWACO.
3. Bob Marley, legend of reggae, was admired by many people.
4. John Peter Mendy is my best friend.
5. My best friend is John Peter Mendy.
6. Ensah, the winner of the competition, is my brother.
7. My brother, the dancer, is Mambu.
8. He is our English teacher.
9. The world biggest reggae star, Bob Marley, died but left message for his fans.
10. Mr Jusu Koroma, the new chief, is that smartly dressed gentleman.

EXERCISE 21

State the grammatical name and function of the underlined nouns or noun phrases in the sentences below.

1. I kicked the <u>ball</u> up the tree.
2. T.M. loves Mary, his <u>wife</u>.
3. <u>Amie</u> speaks <u>French</u> very well.
4. <u>Gaima</u> did not like to see Jane.
5. <u>Tom</u> narrated the <u>story</u> of <u>devil</u>.
6. <u>Paul</u> was protected by the <u>police</u>.
7. I sent <u>Musa</u> a <u>box</u> of books.
8. I love the <u>story</u> about the devil.
9. The <u>football</u> broke the window <u>glass</u>.
10. <u>Mr Mendy</u> teaches <u>History</u> in grade ten.
11. <u>God</u> creates <u>man</u> and <u>woman</u>.
12. I wrote my <u>mother</u> a <u>letter</u>.
13. <u>Music</u> is a root of <u>happiness</u>.
14. <u>Paul</u> is the <u>boy</u> who killed the <u>bird</u>.
15. Narrate your <u>story</u> to <u>Fatu</u>.
16. The <u>earth</u> is the <u>home</u> for all.
17. Teach <u>Elizabeth</u> the song.
18. Yesterday, <u>Mr. Joepi</u> was hit by a <u>car</u>.
19. Mrs Lahai bought <u>Joseph</u> new <u>football</u>.
20. <u>Joseph</u> bought Mr. Peter <u>a car</u>.
21. This <u>girl</u> loves to eat in <u>plate</u>.
22. Jainaba, my <u>friend</u>, has gone home.
23. Behind <u>Fodei</u>, there are followers.
24. We will ask <u>Amie</u> when you call.
25. I wrote <u>Peter</u> an <u>essay</u> about the <u>school</u>.
26. <u>Timy</u> will play the <u>game</u> in the evening.
27. <u>Yekujar</u>, my <u>friend</u>, was a <u>criminal</u>.
28. Tell the <u>boy</u> to call me tomorrow.
29. <u>Pat K</u> was the <u>head</u> of our <u>team</u>.
30. <u>Ted</u> bought his <u>daughter</u> a <u>pen</u>.
31. The <u>students</u> participated in <u>class</u>.

32. Our class prefect, Jattou, is rich.
33. Many people are happy for John.
34. Mrs Jarju, my friend, sold her car to Jeku.
35. The huge buffalo damaged the bridge on the river.
36. The man, Paul, is loved by God.
37. I don't like the pot you bought.
38. These guys are my bosses.
39. Narrate the event that your father taught Tommy.
40. Joe reads my blind mother the Bible always.
41. In the kitchen, there is a pot.
42. The snake was killed by the dog.
43. Papa hopes to see Mama healthy.
44. Tom, our chief, is not around.
45. Pa Buba, our father has come.
46. Brima is my younger brother.
47. The boy was seen at home.
48. Foolish pupils love idleness.
49. The girls were called by mum.
50. Massa Sama in my heart-to-heart.

Pronouns

A pronoun is a word that is used to replace a noun. In other words, pronouns are words used in the place of nouns. Pronouns can also replace other pronouns. A noun or a pronoun that is replaced (or referred to) by another pronoun is called an ***antecedent.*** The antecedents in the following examples are in boldface and the pronoun is underlined.

Joseph, have you eaten your food?
Peter puts his book on the table.
The **dog** wags its tail happily when it sees me.
They passed their examinations.
Amie and her **parents** are in their home.

In some cases, a pronoun can be used without an antecedent. When this happens, it means that the pronoun is already understood. The pronouns used in the following examples have no antecedents, but the context makes it clear for us know the referent. It is very cold outside. They were playing the game. He is happy to see me.

EXERCISE 22

Circle the antecedents of the underlined pronouns in the sentences below. Some antecedents have more than one pronoun. Make an arrow from each antecedent to its pronoun (s).

1. We told John about our party and about his uniform.
2. Peter, your bag is in our room and we are stepping out.
3. They were called in our party for their presentation.
4. We did not listen to our teacher.
5. Binta is our club president who has worked remarkably for us.
6. We need to praise her for the effort.
7. They told us not to sleep in their room, but we did not listen.
8. I narrated the story, but my audience was sleeping.
9. Though it was interesting, yet she didn't hear it.
10. The children play good football, but they don't score goals.
11. They are not popular among their fans.
12. Mother told us where she and Fatu were going and where our key was.

Types of Pronouns

Several kinds of pronouns are dealt with in this work. They include personal pronoun, possessive pronoun, reflexive pronoun, intensive pronoun, interrogative pronoun, relative pronoun, demonstrative pronoun and indefinite pronoun.

Personal Pronouns: These pronouns that are used to refer to the speaker or speakers, the person or persons spoken to and the person or persons spoken about.There are general three persons: First person, that's the person speaking. Eg: I, we, me and us. The second person is the person spoken to. Eg: you; and the third person is the person spoken about. Eg: he, she, it, him, her, they and them.

Table of Personal Pronouns

Persons	Subjective Case		Objective Case	
	singular	**plural**	**singular**	**plural**
1st person	I	we	me	us
2nd person	you	you	you	you
3rd person	he, she, it	they	him, her, it	them

Pronouns in subjective/nominative case perform action, while those in objective case receive action.

EXERCISE 23

Select the pronoun in each bracket that can best complete the sentence.

1. Amie greeted (they, them) first, and later (me, I).
2. First, she spoke to (he, him) and later to (us, we.)
3. (She, Her) and (them, they) are not at peace.
4. You, (they, them) and (us, we) have to meet on the matter.
5. (Him, He) told (we, us) (she, her) secret.
6. You told Tom and (me, I) what happened to (they, them).
7. (His, He) is the man who gave (we, us) the news.
8. (She, her) came to (we, us).
9. (Me, We) received information about (them, they)
10. (Them, They) sent (we, us) to (they, them).
11. All (her, she) wanted was for (him, he) to say the truth.
12. (I, Me) bought (them, they) the book.

Possessive Pronouns: These types of pronouns indicate or show ownership or relationship. There are two sets of possessive pronouns. The first set includes: mine, his, hers, its, ours, yours and theirs. All of them, except the first one, end with **s**. *They are used to replace possessive nouns;* that is both the possessor and the possessed item.

This is Peter's bicycle. ... ... This is **his**.
Mary's pen has lost. ... ... **Hers** has lost.

Joe and Tom's bed is small. ... ... **Theirs** is small.
I played your ball. ... ... I played **yours**.
They broke my plate. ... ... They broke **mine**.
Peter destroyed our house. ... ... Peter destroyed **ours**

The underlined words in the sentences are possessive nouns (possessor & possessed item). They are replaced by the pronouns in boldface.

The other set of possessive pronouns are:(its), (his), my, her, our, your and their. These pronouns replace only the possessor (s), but not the possessed items. They can also function as possessive adjective because they modify nouns by indicating their ownership.

Mary's book is on the table. ... ... **Her** book is on the table
Thomas' room is dirty. ... ... **His** room is dirty.
Put the cat's food in the plate. ... ... Put **its** food in the plate
Peter and John's food is on the table. **... ...** **Their** food is on the table.

In the examples above, *her, his, its and their* function as both pronouns and adjectives. They are pronouns because they have antecedents, and they are also adjectives because they modify nouns. Note that both *his* and *its* are in the two sets.

EXERCISE 24

Select the pronoun in the brackets that best completes the sentence.

1. Is this your book? Yes, it is (me, my, mine)
2. That is Ebrima's pen. Are sure it is (he?, hers?, his?)
3. Amie owns the bag. I'm sure it is (his, hers, her)
4. My daughter and I own the bus; it is (we, ours, our)
5. My children keep (theirs, their) room neat and tidy.
6. The dog ate (his, her, its) food.
7. That one is mine; and this is (your, yours.)
8. Our sister bought this bag. It is (her, hers.)
9. My little dog wags (it's, it, its) tail anytime it sees me.
10. (It, it's, its) food has got finished.

Reflexive and Intensive Pronouns: These two kinds of pronouns have very close link. They end in self or selves. They are also called compound pronouns. As **reflexive pronoun**, it refers to a noun and directs the action back to it. It has the subject of the sentence as its antecedent. It carries information as such when it is omitted from the sentence; the meaning of the sentence will change or not be completed.

Eg: John bought a pen for *himself.* You have to praise *yourself.* She abused *herself.*

As **intensive pronoun**, it just lays emphasis on the doer of an action. It carries no information, so even if it is omitted, the meaning of the sentence will still remain the same. In most cases, intensive pronoun comes immediately after the noun or pronoun it emphasises. For example, They *themselves* have to do the work. We *ourselves* have to copy this note or we have to copy this note *ourselves.*

Persons	Reflexive and Intensive Pronouns	
First Person	**singular**	**plural**
	myself	ourselves
Second person	yourself	yourselves
Third Person	himself, herself, itself	themselves

Here are more examples of reflexive and intensive pronouns.

As reflexive pronoun	As *intensive* pronoun
I cut myself with the sharp knife.	You wrote the story yourself.
He won himself a nobel prize.	The pastor himself preached.
They called themselves heroes.	It broke the stick itself.
She sewed herself a nice dress.	She did the painting herself,

Note: Do not use either the reflexive or the intensive pronoun in the place of a personal pronoun. It is wrong to say: Myself was not around. Say: I was not around.

EXERCISE 25

Read the following passage below and differentiate the reflexive pronouns from the intensive pronouns according to the way they are used. (Please don't consider the exactness of the sound.)

In the assembly today, the principal (**1**) <u>himself</u> addressed the pupils. He advised us to be hardworking and depend on (**2**) <u>ourselves</u> in future. He said we should be doing the assignments for (**3**) <u>ourselves</u> instead of depending on others. One little girl, who had confidence in (**4**) <u>herself</u> and dressed (**5**) <u>herself</u> in red costumes, stood up by (**6**) <u>herself</u> and clapped for the principal. Our teachers (**7**) <u>themselves</u> clapped after the girl. The girl told her friends to sing the song they (**8**) <u>themselves</u> wrote for the principal. I admired the girl (**9**) <u>myself</u>, so I walked to her by (**10**) <u>myself</u>. My little dog (**11**) <u>itself</u> followed me waggling its tail. By (**12**) <u>himself</u>, Ebrima got up, pointed his hand towards me and shouted 'You (**13**) <u>yourself</u> told me that you can do the same for (**14**) <u>yourself</u>!'

Interrogative Pronoun: An interrogative pronoun introduces questions. Who, whom, whose, what and which can act as interrogative pronoun?

Eg: **Who** killed the rat? **What** did you do? **Which** is yours?

Relative Pronoun: These pronouns introduce relative subordinate clause. Most often, the clause introduced by relative pronoun functions as adjectival clause. The relative pronoun also acts as subordinating conjunction as it connects related ideas in a complex sentence by making one to depend on the other. The words that function as relative pronoun include who, whom, that, whose and which.

Eg: The boy **who** killed the rat is here.
I narrated the story **that** you wrote.
She sent the book **which** you bought.
The writer **whom** you criticized has replied.
The girl **whose** mother sent us the bag has come.

Demonstrative Pronoun: This pronoun points out persons, things, places, animals or ideas. Four words function as demonstrative pronoun. They include *this, these, that* and *those*. Use *this* and *that* to point out singular nouns. *These* and *those* are used when we refer to plural nouns. Use *this* and *these* to point out noun(s) that are closer to the speaker; and *that* and *those* to refer to noun(s) that are far away from the speaker.

This is my bag.	**These** are our books.
That was our cap.	**Those** are her dresses.
This is our house.	**These** were your friends.
That was our hiding place.	**Those** were their mistakes.

Like *which* and *what*, the four demonstrative pronouns will also function as adjective. When they stand directly before a noun, they are referred to as demonstrative adjectives.

Eg: *This* ball is his. *These* caps are yours. *That* desk is short. *Those* plates are new. **That** ball was not there. **Those** cups were full. **This** map was clear. **These** men were brave.

Indefinite Pronouns: This kind of pronoun refers to an unidentified person or thing. Some indefinite pronouns, though their antecedents are always plural, yet they are singular in nature, so they agree with a singular verb. Those that are plural in nature, agree with plural verbs. Others can agree with both singular and plural verbs. Below are commonly used indefinite pronouns.

Singular Plural Either
another, everybody, nothing, both, all
anybody, everyone, anyone, few, any
everything, anything, neither, many. most
something, somebody, one, others, none
nobody, someone, either, several, some
other, no one, each

Note that most of the singular indefinite pronouns are plural in meaning; this means that they are used for plural nouns which will serve as their antecedents, yet they agree with singular verbs.

Study the pronouns and their antecedents in the paragraph below. The pronouns are underlined while their antecedents are in boldface.

Sixteen **leaders** attended the meeting, <u>everyone</u> was dressed in max. **They** agreed to disagree, yet, <u>everybody</u> was against the act. **Few** of them hate corruption but <u>everyone</u> corrupts. **They** talk a lot, eat a lot and waste a lot of public funds on meetings, yet **no one** implements the outcome. We call **them** Excellency, but <u>none</u> provides excellent leadership for the people.

Everybody loves comfort. (*singular*)
He bought mangoes but *all* were rotten. (*plural*)
I had only a bucket of water, but *all* has wasted. (*singular*)
Amie has drunk the milk, but *some* is still in the cup. (*singular*)
Many were present but *some* were asked to return. (*plural*)
Fifteen matches were scheduled, but *several* were postponed. (*plural*)
He brought four books and *all* are interested. (*plural*)

It is important to note that some indefinite pronouns can also function as indefinite adjectives. When they do so, they are immediately followed by the nouns they modify.

Indefinite Adjective: *Each* team is determined to win the trophy.
　　　　　　　　　　　Several people were present at the ceremony.
　　　　　　　　　　　All religions preach peace and love.
Indefinite pronoun: *Each* of the teams is ready to play the game.
　　　　　　　　　　　Several of the girls are beautiful.
　　　　　　　　　　　All of them are not serious in class.

31

CHAPTER 2

VERBS AND VERB TENSES

Verbs are words that express action or state of being. Verbs are used to indicate the time an action, event, or activity takes place, will take place or took place.

Every sentence contains at least a verb. Verbs have distinct grammatical roles and features, which include the following:

- Verbs express action or state of being.
- They indicate time of action or state of being.
- They agree with their subjects in person and in number.
- Unlike other phrases, verb phrase contains verbs only.
- Verbs physically change form to enable them to allocate time to action or state of being.

Kinds of Verbs

Action and *Be* form of Verbs

Action verb tells what the subject of the sentence does or possesses. An action verb can express both mental and physical actions.

Mental state verbs express actions that take place in the mind or brain and stay there. The activity is abstract as it cannot be seen or heard.

Examples: I always **think** about my daughter. She **dreams** of me often. We **fear** that the rain may disturb us. They **hope** to God and **believe** in Him.

Action verbs: These kinds of verbs express actions that are physically displayed. We can see or hear the activity when it is in progress. The verbs in the following examples express physical actions. The children **dance** and **play** the game very skilfully. She **writes** and **calls** every month. You **drive** us to school every morning.

EXERCISE 1

In the short passage below, underline the action verbs and circle the non-action verbs.

This morning, I did not get up from bed early. The reason was that I went to bed very late last night, because supporters from Kailahun were celebrating SLPP victory. I woke up mearly in the morning to fetch water so that I will take my bath and prepare for the day's activities. The only tap in our area, Kebawana, was parked full of people who were all very anxious to get water and make haste to schools and working places. Few lazy children were reluctantly playing, singing and running about. While I stood in confusion thinking what to do next, I quickly remembered the burst pipe at Gbanyawalu around the house of my friend. I last passed by the area three days ago, and it was at night. I decided to run to the place and collect my water there. I ran as fast as my legs could allow me. When I reached there, the damaged pipe was fixed. I returned to where I was but from a far distance, I saw nobody there. I was happy and confused. I was happy because I thought I could easily get the water and go home soon; but again I wondered as how the large crowd I left few minutes ago could have all filled their containers and left so soon. To my greatest dismay, the tap was not running any longer when I reached there.

Be Form of Verbs

The '*be*' forms of verbs are verbs that only describe the condition or the state of being of nouns. They are also called ***non-action verbs*** because they do not express action, and they do not take direct object. This means they are intransitive verbs. They function as linking verbs and auxiliary verbs. Some function as action verbs. Below are forms of *be* verbs: *am, is, are, was, were, be, been, (**has, have, had, do, does, did**)* It is interesting to learn that the verbs in the bracket can also function as both action verbs and helping verbs. When they appear with a main verb, it is referred to as helping verb. When they appear alone without a main verb, they are referred to as main verbs. Observe the examples below:

As action verb	As helping verb
Peter **has** a pen.	Peter **has** gone home.
We **have** some books.	We **have** done the assignment.
I **had** Le 5,000 yesterday.	I **had** heard about him before I saw him.
I **do** some work every morning.	I **do** not know you.
He **does** the work at night.	She **does** not speak English.
They **did** the work yesterday.	We **did** not see them

Linking Verbs: These be-verbs: *am, is, are, was* and *were* can also function as helping verbs and linking verbs. When they function as helping verbs, they appear with a main verb; but when they function as linking verbs, they appear alone without a main verb. They appear between the subject and its complement, thus linking the two together. Linking verbs express the state of being of a subject by renaming, identifying or describing it. They do not take a direct object because they do not express action.

As linking verb	As helping verb
I am healthy.	I am reading.
The boy is a dancer.	The boy is dancing.
We are the winners.	We are winning the game.
She was very clever.	She was working hard.
The boys were happy.	The boys were laughing.

It is interesting to note that few action verbs also function as linking verbs. Action verbs such as *grow, feel, look, smell, appear, become, remain, seem, sound, taste* etc, can also function as linking verbs. When each one of them is used as linking verb, it can be substituted by one of these *be-verbs: am, is, are, was* or *were* depending on tense it is used in.

as linking verbs as action verbs

Eg: The boys **grew** old.	The boys **grew** some vegetables.
(The boys **were** old.)	
I **felt** cold and tired.	I **felt** pain in my joints.
(I **was** cold and tired)	
Paul **looks** healthy.	Paul **looks** for good health.
(Paul **is** healthy.)	
The perfume **smells** pleasant.	She **smells** the perfume often.
(The perfume **is** pleasant.)	
The ghost **appears** fearful.	The ghost **appears** to him often.
The ghost **is** fearful.	
The food **tasted** delicious.	He **tasted** the food.
The food **was** delicious.	

EXERCISE 2

The verbs in boldface are used as both linking verbs and action verbs in the short passage. Circle the action verbs and underline the linking verbs.

My friend prepared some food for me this afternoon. When I **(1) tasted** it, the food **(2) tasted** very delicious. In fact, its aroma wetted my appetite. It **(3) smelt** like good food. Although my brother did not eat it, but when he **(4) smelt** it, he confirmed that it was actually a mouth-watering food. "I have **(5) looked** at it, and it **(6) looked** nice." He laughingly said. "You **(7) grow** too much love for my brother these days!" My brother said to my fiancée. "Yes, it is because he too **(8) grows** mature these days." She smilingly responded. Though she **(9) felt** the pain she sustained from fire burn, yet she **(10) felt** happy when she was praised for the nice food she prepared. My fiancée and my brother **(11) sounded** happy. Their voices **(12) sounded** in a way that made me happier. Suddenly, a passer-by **(13) appeared**, and told us that we **(14) appeared** like a happy family. We all laughed and told him good-bye.

Modal Auxiliary Verbs: These are other forms of be-verbs. They function as helping verbs; they are used with *'main verbs'* to express possibility, permission, wish, certainty, obligation, suggestion, politeness etc. They include: *can, could; will, would; shall, should; may, might; must, ought to etc.* Other verbs such as *dare, need, have to* and *used to,* share the same features with modal verbs. The features include the following:

i) Modal verbs cannot take any affix such as "ing", "d", "ed" to form other tenses; or add "s" to agree with the third person singular subject.

ii) They are not followed by an infinitive except **ought to** and **used to**

Uses of Modal Auxiliary Verbs:

a) **Can, could:** *Could* is the past tense form of *can.* They are most often used to express ability, permission, doubt, suggestion, possibility or politeness. Eg:

He <u>can</u> speak Mende and Fula.	*(ability)*
We <u>can</u> play football if you want.	*(suggestion)*
You <u>could</u> drink too much water when you were a child.	*(ability)*
They <u>could</u> speak only two languages at early age.	*(ability)*
What <u>can</u> they have been doing up to now?	*(doubt)*
<u>Could</u> we meet next tomorrow?	*(polite request)*
<u>Could</u> you give your book?	*(polite request)*

b) **Will, would:** *Would* is the past tense form of *will.* They are used to express prediction, willingness/commitment, certainty, polite request etc.

I <u>will</u> give you fifty thousand dalasi.	*(willingness/commitment)*
I <u>will</u> do my assignment at night.	*(willingness/commitment)*
We <u>will</u> be adults in future.	*(prediction/certainty)*
I <u>will</u> be in trouble if he comes here now.	*(certainty/possibility*

<u>Would</u> you mind leavng us alone for few minutes?	*(gentle request)*
<u>Would</u> you pay my school fees?	*(gentle request)*

c) **Shall, should:** *Should* is the past tense form of *shall.* We use them to express instruction, suggestion or advice, prediction, hope/wish, polite request etc.

We <u>shall</u> be in Banjul next week.	*(prediction)*
<u>Shall</u> we meet under the big tree in the valley?	*(polite request)*
All candidates <u>should</u> stay in class after paper one.	*(instruction)*
You <u>should</u> not drink and drive.	*(instruction/advice)*
If you <u>should</u> change your position, do let me know.	*(wish/hope)*
My daughters <u>should</u> start school very soon.	*(suggestion/advice)*
I <u>shall</u> like to invite my family.	*(suggestion)*

d) **May, might:** *Might* is the past tense form of *may.* They are used to express uncertainty, request, wish/hope, suggestion etc. Eg:

It may rain this afternoon.	*(uncertainty)*
They might have lost the case.	*(uncertainty)*
May I bring my books for correction?	*(request)*
May his gentle soul rests in peace.	*(wish/hope)*
We may visit them if they come.	*(suggestion)*

e) **Must, have to:** These two express the same meanings. They indicate obligation, possibility, a very strong commitment, command or certainty. Eg:

All workers must report to work on time.	*(command)*
I have to do my assignment now.	*(obligation/strong commitment)*
You must go home now.	*(command)*
He has to come tomorrow.	*(certainty)*

Auxiliary/Helping Verbs: The linking verbs and the modal verbs are all be form of verbs. So when any one of these verbs appear with a main verb in a sentence, it is referred to as *auxiliary/helping* verb. In such case, it helps the main verb to complete its meaning.

Eg: The boys **are** playing. He *is* writing a story. He **will have** finished his assignment by next week. They **do** not like you in the room. It **has been** raining all day. I **am** writing a story. He **is** dancing to the music. Joe **was** looking for a pen. They **were** eating. We **are** running. Note that two or more helping verbs will appear with only one main verb in a verb phrase. Commonly used helping verbs include: **am, is, are, was, were, be, been, being, do, did, does, has, have, had, will, would, can, could, shall, should, may, must, might** etc.

The main verb plus the helping verb (s) make up the verb phrase.

EXERCISE 3

In the sentences below, underline the helping verbs once, linking verbs twice and circle the action verbs.

1. I will talk to you about my best friend's favourite fruits.
2. He is a man that is loved by many people in the community.
3. He is in the good books of all the main authorities.
4. He can help anyone that could be in need of his service.
5. His mother was a very good singer in this society.
6. They are all tall and popular in their family.
7. They are the owners of the tallest building in the city.
8. John Mendy works for the family in the city.
9. He has diligently worked for them for many years.
10. They considered him now as a member of the family.

EXERCISE 4

Use each of the verbs listed below in two sentences; in one sentence as linking verb, in another as helping verb. (open)

Eg: We <u>are</u> friends.   *We <u>are</u> eating fried plantain.*

	as linking verb	as helping verb
are		
is		
am		
were		
was		

Verb Phrase: This is made up of one or more helping verbs and a main verb, all working together as single part of speech (verb). The main verbs always come last in the phrase. In the examples below, the verb phrases are underlined, helping verbs are italicised and the main verbs are in boldface.

Eg. We *<u>have been</u>* **<u>eating</u>** all day.
Very soon, they *<u>will have been</u>* **<u>running</u>** for two hours.
They *<u>have</u>* **<u>gone</u>** home.

Sometimes other words interrupt the verb phrase. These are words that sometimes come between the helping verb and the main verb. Eg I <u>did</u> not **eat** the food. You <u>have</u> not <u>been</u> ***paying*** attention.

EXERCISE 5

Identify the verb phrases in the sentences below; underline the helping verbs and circle the main verbs.

1. I will go home and tell them about the meeting tomorrow.
2. Tee-man has told everyone to inform the people about the meeting.
3. I believe everyone has to do so when we all return home after school.

4. They will be monitoring the boys who will be cleaning around.
5. The meeting will have been completed before the bell rings for lunch.
6. Some students were eating their lunch when the teacher was calling them.
7. The boys will be playing the game while the girls will be cleaning around.
8. Those who have been playing the game will not attend the meeting.
9. Mr. David, who has taught for five years, was ringing the bell.
10. They had finished the work three days before my father came.

EXERCISE 6

Use the verb phrases below in sentences correctly. (open)

Eg. John <u>was sleeping</u> when I came in.

1. was eating
2. had gone,
3. have come,
4. will be sleeping
5. were punished
6. shall have been talking,
7. am waiting,
8. shall have written,
9. cannot do
10. had taught,
11. has cried
12. will have been dancing
13. are fighting
14. would have stopped

Transitive and Intransitive Verbs

Transitive verb: Verbs can either be transitive or intransitive. A transitive verb takes a direct object. A noun or a pronoun that receives or suffers from the action expressed by a transitive verb is called **direct object**. A verb is transitive if you can answer the question *what?* or *whom?* after it.

Eg: The boy killed the snake. (killed what?) My sister knocked the door. (knocked what?) The teacher slapped the boy. (slapped whom?) She loves me. (loves who?)

Intransitive verb: An intransitive verb does not take a direct object; instead, it is often followed by an adverb or adverbial phrase which modifies the verb by answering one of the following questions: *how? when? where? or to what extend?*, about the verb. Eg:

a) The baby cries at night.
b) They run to the school.
c) We slept soundly.
d) He drove away.
e) The car stopped immediately.
f) The tourists walked down the road.
g) He knocked at the door.
h) We spoke after the game.
i) You sing for everyone.
j) They cooked for the workers.

It is important to note that some verbs can be used transitively and intransitively.

Eg He *grows* vegetables.	(transitive)
The vegetables *grow* well.	(intransitive)
The police *stopped* the car.	(transitive)
The car *stopped* immediately.	(intransitive)
He **knocked** the door.	(transitive)
He **knocked** heavily.	(intransitive)
She **speaks** French.	(transitive)
She **speaks** fluently.	(intransitive)

EXERCISE 7

In the short passage below, all the verbs are in boldface, circle the verbs used as transitive and underline the intransitive verbs.

We **(1) travelled** by bus yesterday. On the way, the police officers **(2) stopped** our bus and the driver **(3) stopped** immediately. Their boss **(4) walked** to the bus and **(5) pulled** the door. It **(6) opened** widely. He **(7) asked** all of us to **(8) come** down from the bus. We **(9) obeyed** his command. They **(10) checked** the vehicle first, and then our luggage. When they were satisfied, they **(11) asked** us to **(12) climb** in the bus and **(13) move**. When we **(14) did** so, one of the officers **(15) pushed** the door and the door **(16) moved** slowly and **(17) closed**. We **(18) continued** the journey. We **(19) spent** long time on our way and **(20) arrived** very late. When we **(21) reached** home, we **(22) were welcomed** by our family members. Everyone was very happy to **(23) see** us. Though **(24) tired** by the long journey, yet we were all healthy.

The Principal Parts of Verbs

The principal parts of verbs are the different physical forms verbs take to indicate tenses. There are four principal parts or forms of any verb. It is one of these forms that is used to show or allocate time to action. Their grammatical names are **base form, past tense form, present participle form** and **past participle form** respectively. Let us observe the four physical forms the verb **'go'** takes to indicate tenses. The base form is **go**, past tense form is **went,** the present participle form is **going** and the past participle form is **gone. Eat** is the base form, **ate** is the past tense form, **eating** is the present participle form and **eaten** is the past participle form.

a) **Base form**: The first principal part of any verb is the base form, which refers to the bare verb itself, without affix such as *d, ed, s,* or *ing*. It is the form of the verb that is represented as a lexical entry in the dictionary. It is sometimes referred to the infinitive form and it may be preceded by 'to'. Some common examples include the following: (to) write, (to) play, (to) sing, (to) sleep etc.

b) **Present form**: This is the form of the verb that is used to refer to **simple present** When a verb is used in the *simple present tense* form, the bare form of the verb is used except for the third person singular where it takes the suffix 's' or '-es'.

Eg: They **move** often from one city to another.

We **jump** up when we are happy.
I **eat** every day.
You **sleep** at night.
He **goes** to school everyday.

c) **Past tense form:** This is another principal part of the verb which is used to indicate an action or event that has taken place in the past. Regular verbs follow the same pattern to form their past tense form. The pattern is that *d* or *ed* is added to the base form. Eg: jump**ed**, look**ed**, danc**ed**, lik**ed**, lov**ed**, mov**ed** etc. Irregular verbs follow different patterns to form their past form. Eg: went, slept, drove, wrote, drew, swept etc. When a verb is used in the past tense form, it doesn't appear with helping verb.

Eg. I **went** early home after school.

They **spent** the holiday in Freetown. He **finished** the work very late. My dad **drove** me to school. They **ate** all the food in the village.

d) **Present Participle form:** This is the part of verb that takes the '-ing' suffix. When this suffix is used with the verb, it indicates the progressive or the continuous tense. The present participle form of all verbs end with the suffix '*-ing*' and they always appear with helping verb (s). The helping verbs that appear with verbs in progressive form are: *am, is, are, was, were, will/shall been, have/has/had been, will/ shall have been.*

There are three helping verbs that appear in the **present continuous tense**. They are *am, is* and *are. Am* appears with **I**; *is* appears with *he, she* or *it. Are* appears with *they, you* or *we.* Observe the examples below.

I *am* studying. He *is* reading. She *is* sleeping. It *is* rainning. We *are* ridding. You *are* walking. They *are* praying.

There are two helping verbs that appear in the **past continuous tense**. They include *was* and we*re*. *Was* appears with *I, he, she* or *it*. *Were* appears with *they, you* or *we*. Look at the examples below.

I *was* driving. He *was* sweeping. She *was* laughing. It *was* moving. They *were* working. You *were* fighting. We *were* dancing.

e) **Past Participle form:** The Past Participle form of a verb is often used with one of these helping verbs (*has, have* or *had*) to indicate an action that has been completed. '*Have*' and '*has*' are used with the past participle form of the verb to express the present perfect tense. Use **has** if the subject of the sentence is **third person** singular (*he, she* or *it*). Use **have** with any other subject. '*Had*' appears in the past perfect tense; it does not matter the number or person of the subject.

Eg: They **have moved** to another city this year.
We **have jumped** up this morning.
I **have eaten** my lunch.
You **have driven** us roughly.
She **has slept** soundly.
He **has given** it to us.
She **has spoken** to them.
The boy **has gone** home.
He **had kicked** the bucket.
I **had slept** before you came.
They **had written** the letter to the chief before.
You **had gone** before it rained.

Regular and Irregular Verbs

Verbs are usually categorised as either regular or irregular. This depends on how their past tense are formed. Regular verbs are those verbs that take the suffix '-**d**' or '-**ed**' to form their past and past participle; while irregular verbs take different forms. They do not have any specific rule to form the past and past participle There are examples of irregular verbs in the table. Please learn them by heart. The **present participle** form is not included in the table. The **present participle** form of any verbs is formed by adding '*ing*' to the base. This happens in three ways. Some basic verbs just take the 'ing' without adding or subtracting any letter, some verbs double the last letter while others omit the last letter before adding the ***ing***. Observe the examples below.

last letter is doubled before 'ing'	last letter is omitted before 'ing'	no addition or omission of letter before 'ing'
sit – sitting	dance – dancing	eat – eating
plan – planning	love – loving	look – looking
put – putting	move – moving	jump – jumping
begin – beginning	give – giving	wait – waiting
set – setting	like – liking	sleep – sleeping

The past participle forms end with 'en'			
	Base	**Past**	**Past Participle**
1	choose	chose	chosen
2	arise	arose	arisen
3	give	gave	given
4	rise	rose	risen
5	see	saw	seen
6	shake	shook	shaken
7	speak	spoke	spoken
8	steal	stole	stolen
9	eat	ate	eaten
10	break	broke	broken
11	be	was, were	been
12	fall	fell	fallen
13	beat	beat	beaten
14	awake	awoke	awaken
15	befall	befell	befallen

16	foresee	foresaw	foreseen
17	interweave	interwove	interwoven
18	overeat	overate	overeaten
19	mistake	mistook	mistaken
20	override	overrode	overridden
21	unfreeze	unfroze	unfrozen
22	shave	shaved	shaven
23	take	took	taken
24	wake	woke	waken
25	write	wrote	written
26	weave	wove	woven
27	repay	repaid	repaid
28	forbid	forbade	forbidden
29	forget	forgot	forgotten
30	forgive	forgave	forgiven
31	freeze	froze	frozen
32	forsake	forsook	forsaken
33	hide	hid	hidden
34	mistake	mistook	mistaken
35	ride	rode	ridden
36	smite	smote	smitten
37	swell	swelled	swollen
38	thrive	throve	thriven
39	drive	drove	driven
40	bite	bit	bitten
41	retake	retook	retaken

The base, past and the past participle forms are all the same.

	Base	Past	Past Participle
42	put	put	put
43	read	read	read
44	rid	rid	rid

45	cut	cut	cut
46	hit	hit	hit
47	set	set	set
48	shed	shed	shed
49	slit	slit	slit
50	upset	upset	upset
51	thrust	thrust	thrust
52	sublet	sublet	sublet
53	undercut	undercut	undercut
54	underbid	underbid	underbid
55	burst	burst	burst
56	cast	cast	cast
57	hurt	hurt	hurt
58	inset	inset	inset
59	bet	bet	bet
60	let	let	let
61	proofread	proofread	proofread
62	shut	shut	shut
63	simulcast	simulcast	simulcast
64	telecast	telecast	telecast
65	mishit	mishit	mishit
66	misread	misread	misread
67	miscast	miscast	miscast
68	split	split	split
69	spread	spread	spread
70	pre-set	pre-set	pre-set
71	typecast	typecast	typecast
72	bid	bid	bid
73	broadcast	broadcast	broadcast
74	born	born	borne

The base and the past participle are the same		
	Base	**Past**	**Past Participle**
75	become	became	become
76	run	ran	run
77	outrun	outran	outrun
78	overcome	overcame	overcome
79	come	came	come
80	overrun	overran	overrun

The past and the past participle are the same		
	Base	**Past**	**Past Participle**
81	bind	bound	bound
82	creep	crept	crept
83	have	had	had
84	ling	flung	flung
85	spoil	spoilt	spoilt
86	stand	stood	stood
87	grind	ground	ground
88	hang	hung	hung
89	spin	spun	spun
90	bleed	bled	bled
91	breastfeed	breastfed	breastfed
92	light	lit, lighted	lit, lighted
93	deal	dealt	dealt
94	spit	spat	spat
95	spill	spilt	spilt
96	spend	spent	spent
97	speed	sped	sped
98	slink	slunk	slunk
99	slide	slid	slid
100	smell	smelt	smelt
101	dig	dug	dug
102	buy	bought	bought

103	build	built	built
104	bring	brought	brought
105	fight	fought	fought
106	find	found	found
107	sit	sat	sat
108	overhang	overhung	overhung
109	stave	stove	stove
110	stick	stuck	stuck
111	sting	stung	stung
112	string	strung	strung
113	sweep	swept	swept
114	swing	swung	swung
115	burn	burnt	burnt
116	teach	taught	taught
117	tell	told	told
118	think	thought	thought
119	understand	understood	understood
120	win	won	won
121	wind	wound	wound
122	keep	kept	kept
123	feel	felt	felt
124	kneel	knelt	knelt
125	lend	lent	lent
126	lay	laid	laid
127	catch	caught	caught
128	sling	slung	slung
129	hold	held	held
130	lead	led	led
131	strike	struck	struck
132	learn	learnt	learnt
133	leap	leapt	leapt
134	hear	heard	heard
135	leave	left	left

136	lose	lost	lost
137	make	made	made
138	meet	met	met
139	mean	meant	meant
140	overhear	overheard	overheard
141	pay	paid	paid
142	catch	caught	caught
143	say	said	said
144	seek	sought	sought
145	send	sent	sent
146	shine	shone	shone
147	sell	sold	sold
148	shoot	shot	shot
149	weep	wept	wept
150	lie (not true)	lied	lied
151	shed	shed	shed

These verbs follow no specific pattern

	Base	Past	Past Participle
152	blow	blew	blown
153	go	went	gone
154	forgo	forwent	forgone
155	draw	drew	drawn
156	fly	flew	flown
157	grow	grew	grown
158	outgrow	outgrew	overgrown
159	bear	bore	borne
160	throw	threw	thrown
161	know	knew	known
162	swear	swore	sworn
163	wear	wore	worn
164	sew	sewed	sewn
165	lie (to lie down)	lay	Lain
166	tear	tore	torn

167	underlie	underlay	underlain
168	undo	undid	undone
169	withdraw	withdrew	withdrawn
170	sow	sowed	sown, sowed
171	overthrow	overthrew	overthrown
172	redraw	redrew	redrawn
173	do	did	done
174	forbear	forbore	forborne
175	forswear	forswore	forsworn
176	overdo	overdid	overdone

In these verbs, letter 'I' in the base changes to 'a' in the past form and into 'u; in the past participle form

	Base	Past	Past Participle
177	spring	sprang	sprung
178	shrink	shrank	shrunk
179	sink	sank	sunk
180	sting	stung	stung
181	begin	began	begun
182	swim	swam	swum
183	stink	stank	stunk
184	ring	rang	rung
185	drink	drank	drunk
185	slay	slew	slain
186	sing	sang	sung

These are regular verbs. Their past and past participle forms end with d or ed.

	Base	Past	Past Participle
187	look	looked	looked
188	jump	jumped	jumped
189	love	loved	loved
190	move	moved	moved
191	talk	talked	talked

192	listen	listened	listened
193	cry	cried	cried
194	call	called	called
195	carry	carried	carried
196	dance	danced	danced
197	walk	walked	walked
198	work	worked	worked
199	laugh	laughed	laughed
200	shout	shouted	shouted
201	clean	cleaned	cleaned
202	watch	watched	watched
203	wash	washed	washed
204	fetch	fetched	fetched
205	cook	cooked	cooked
206	play	played	played
207	pray	prayed	prayed
208	wait	waited	waited
209	waste	wasted	wasted
210	kill	killed	killed
211	kick	kicked	kicked
212	observe	observed	observed
213	visit	visited	visited
214	study	studied	studied
215	fix	fixed	fixed
216	fill	filled	filled
217	pain	pained	pained
218	pick	picked	picked
219	inform	informed	informed
220	search	searched	searched
221	employ	employed	employed
222	gain	gained	gained
223	greet	greeted	greeted
224	gather	gathered	gathered

225	develop	developed	developed
226	start	started	started
227	stop	stopped	stopped
228	report	reported	reported
229	travel	travelled	travelled
230	prepare	prepared	prepared
231	like	liked	liked
232	live	lived	lived
233	want	wanted	wanted
234	tire	tired	tired
235	care	cared	cared
236	open	opened	opened
237	replace	replaced	replaced
238	close	closed	closed
239	represent	represented	represented
240	ask	asked	asked
241	copy	copied	copied
242	destroy	destroyed	destroyed
243	imitate	imitated	imitated
244	discuss	discussed	discussed
245	receive	received	received
246	deceive	deceived	deceived
247	refuse	refused	refused
248	defend	defended	defended
249	clap	clapped	clapped
250	climb	climbed	climbed
251	descend	descended	descended
252	ascend	ascended	ascended
253	expect	expected	expected
254	accept	accepted	accepted
255	excuse	excused	excused
256	confirm	confirmed	confirmed
257	change	changed	changed

258	charge	charged	charged
259	explain	explained	explained
260	promote	promoted	promoted
261	demote	demoted	demoted
262	vote	voted	voted
263	elect	elected	elected
264	narrate	narrated	narrated
265	appoint	appointed	appointed
266	connect	connected	connected
267	contact	contacted	contacted
268	push	pushed	pushed
269	count	counted	counted
270	confess	confessed	confessed

Please note that the division of these irregular verbs is done purposely to make it easier for learners to study the words and spellings by heart. There are more irregular verbs; please search for them and learn them.

EXERCISE 8

Construct short sentences on each line in the tense written against the line. The subjects and verbs are given for every set of lines. Observe the two examples below and follow the format. (Note: Revisit and practice these exercises after reading the next verb tenses (open)

He/eat	
He **eats** some food daily.	*simple present tense*
He **ate** some food yesterday.	*simple past tense*
He **will eat** some food tomorrow.	*future tense*
He **is eating** some food now.	*present continuous tense*
He **was eating** some food when I came.	*past continuous tense*
He **has eaten** some food.	*present perfect tense*
He **had eaten** the food before we came.	*past perfect tense*

They/go	
They **go** to school always.	*simple present tense*
They **went** to school.	*simple past tense*
They **will go** to school.	*future tense*
They **are going** to school.	*present continuous tense*
They **were going** to school.	*past continuous tense*
They **have gone** to school.	*present perfect tense*
They **had gone** to school.	*past perfect tense*

Now do the rest.

a) **I/give**

_____ simple present tense
_____ simple past tense
_____ future tense
_____ present continuous tense
_____ past continuous tense
_____ present perfect tense
_____ past perfect tense

b) **She/do**

_____ simple present tense
_____ simple past tense future tense
_____ present continuous tense
_____ past continuous tense
_____ present perfect tense
_____ past perfect tense

c) **We/set**

_____ simple present tense
_____ present continuous tense
_____ future tense
_____ simple past tense
_____ past continuous tense
_____ present perfect tense
_____ past perfect tense

    d) **It/ring**

    _____ present continuous tense

    _____ simple past tense

    _____ future tense

    _____ simple present tense

    _____ past continuous tense

    _____ present perfect tense

    _____ past perfect tense

    e) **He/choose**

    _____ simple present tense

    _____ future tense

    _____ present perfect tense

    _____ simple past tense

    _____ past continues tense

    _____ present continuous tense

    _____ past perfect tense

    f) **You/fly**

    _____ simple present tense

    _____ simple past tense

    _____ future tense

    _____ present continuous tense

    _____ past continuous tense

    _____ present perfect tense

    _____ past perfect tense

    g) **They/fight**

    _____ simple present tense

    _____ simple past tense

    _____ future tense

    _____ present continuous tense

    _____ past continuous tense

    _____ present perfect tense

h) **We/sing**

_____	simple present tense
_____	past continuous tense
_____	present perfect tense
_____	simple past tense
_____	future tense
_____	present continuous tense
_____	past perfect tense

i) **I/spread**

_____	past perfect tense
_____	present continuous tense
_____	simple past tense
_____	past continuous tense
_____	present perfect tense
_____	future tense
_____	simple present tense
_____	future perfect tense

j) **It/sit**

_____	past perfect tense
_____	present continuous tense
_____	past continuous tense
_____	future continuous tense
_____	simple past tense
_____	future tense
_____	simple present tense

k) **She/eat**

_____	past perfect tense
_____	past continuous tense
_____	present perfect tense
_____	future tense
_____	present continuous tense
_____	simple present tense
_____	simple past tense

l) **He/draw**

_____	past perfect tense
_____	present perfect tense
_____	past continuous tense
_____	simple present tense
_____	simple past tense
_____	future tense
_____	present continuous tense

m) **We/speak**

_____	past perfect tense
_____	past continuous tense
_____	present perfect tense
_____	future tense
_____	present continuous tense
_____	simple present tense
_____	simple past tense

n) **They/teach**

_____	past perfect tense
_____	past continuous tense
_____	present perfect tense
_____	future tense
_____	present continuous tense
_____	simple present tense
_____	simple past tense

o) **You/sweep**

_____	past perfect tense
_____	past continuous tense
_____	present perfect tense
_____	future tense
_____	present continuous tense
_____	simple present tense
_____	simple past tense

p) **She/break**

_____ past perfect tense

_____ past continuous tense

_____ present perfect tense

_____ future tense

_____ present continuous tense

_____ simple present tense

_____ simple past tense

q) **I/run**

_____ past perfect tense

_____ present continuous tense

_____ simple present tense

_____ past continuous tense

_____ present perfect tense

_____ future tense

EXERCISE 9

Write the base, the past or the past participle of the verbs in the blank spaces below.

	Base	**Past**	**Past Participle**
1		slid	
2		made	
3			slunk
4	smell		
5	dig		
6		dreamt	
7			spent
8	feed		
9		flew	
10	find		

11			dwelt
12	fling		
13		got	
14	grind		
15			run
16	sleep		
17			jumped
18		rang	
19			fixed
20			hung
21		burnt	
22			held
23	bid		
24		bit	
25			broken
26		caught	
27			cut
28		hurt	
29	hit		
30	clothe		
31	leap		
32	feed		
33			sat
34			spelt
35			sprung
36	blow		
37			proofread
38			broadcast
39	keep		
40			lost
41			knelt
42	lend		
43	lie		

44			lain
45		laid	
46	overhear		
47		paid	
48			said
49		sought	
50	sell		
51			shone
52			sent
53	know		
54		cried	
55		put	
56	fight		
57		gave	
58	drink		
59		drew	
60			burst
61		cast	
62	let		
63			written
64	fall		
65			spread
66		meant	
67	deal		
68	withstand		
69	go		
70			shot
71			met
72	sing		
73		set	
74		shod	
75			Borne
76	breathe		

Verb Tenses

Tense is a distinctive aspect of verb that indicates time of action or state of being expressed by the verb. The time expressed by tenses helps the language users to allocate time to activity. There are three **basic tenses**: present, past future. Each of them has the simple, *perfect, progressive* and *perfect progressive.* The <u>perfect</u> indicates *completed action*; the <u>progressive</u> shows *ongoing actions* and the <u>perfect progressive</u> shows *ongoing action that will be completed at a specified time.* Observe the verb or the verb phrase in each of the tenses in the table below.

Verb Tense	Simple	Progressive	Perfect	Perfect Progressive
Present	play/s	am/ is/are playing	has/have played	has/have been playing
Past	played	was/were playing	had played	had been playing
Future	will/shall play	will/shall be playing	will have played	will have been playing
Present	write/s	am/is/are writing	has/have written	has/have been writing
Past	wrote	was/were writing	had written	had been writing
Future	will/shall write	will/shall be writing	will have written	will have been writing
Present	go/es	am/is/are going	has/have gone	has/have been going
Past	went	was/were going	had gone	had been going
Future	will/shall go	will/shall be going	will have gone	will have been going

Simple Present Tense: This tense expresses three different actions which include, and it is formed by the <u>basic form</u> of verb.

a) Unchanging situation or an action or event that is permanent or true at all times. Eg: God *is* great. Africa *is* one of the continents on earth. Both men and women *are* images of God.

b) Recurring or habitual actions. Eg: Christians *celebrate* Christmas every year. He *works* in Freetown. Sierra Leone *elects* new parliamentarians after every five years.

c) Universal truth or the truth at the moment. Eg: Retired Brigadier Maada Bio *is* the president of Sierra Leone. I *am* twenty-five years old. Real Madrid *is* the champion of football clubs in Europe.

Simple Past Tense: This tense expresses situation/condition or action that started and completed in the past. The tense is formed by past form of verb. Remember that the regular and irregular verbs form their past tense form differently as it is stated earlier. Eg: John *chose* to live with us. We *drove* around. She *jumped* over the fence. Peter *moved* to the city.

There is one interesting thing we should learn about the first two tenses stated above, that is there is no verb phrase in the simple predicates in the examples. This means the verbs do not appear with helping verbs.

Simple Future Tense: This tense describes situation or action that will take place in the future. There are three different ways this tense can be expressed.

a) *Will/shall* appears with the basic form of verb to indicate the future tense. Eg: They *will buy* the food for the family. We *shall overcome* all problems in death.

b) by using *am, is* or *are* together with *going to* plus the *simple form of verb:* I *am going to report* him to the principal. She *is going to prepare* food for the family. We *are going to win* the match.

c) by using the *present tense* form of verb and *time adverb*. Eg: We *close* school **next week.** His leave *begins* **tomorrow**. They *resume* work **next month.**

Present Progressive Tense: This tense expresses action or condition that is happening or going on as the speaker is speaking or at the same time the statement is written. The tense is formed with an appropriate form of the verb 'be' (am, is, are)) plus present participle form. Eg: I *am writing* a story. President Bio *is fighting* corruption in the country. We *are studying* our notes.

Past Progressive Tense: This describes a past action; that is an action that was in progress or going on in the past when another action occurred. The past progressive tense is formed by using *was* or *were* with the <u>present participle form</u> of verb. Eg: He *was playing* football when I saw him. We *were reading* when the light went off. The baby *was crying* when her mother came in. They *were working* when we arrived.

Future Progressive Tense: The future progressive tense expresses continuous or ongoing action that will take place in the future. *Will be* or *shall be* plus <u>present participle form of verb</u> will make this tense. Eg: Schools *will be closing* for holidays tomorrow. We *shall be electing* our new leaders next week. He *will be celebrating* his birthday next tomorrow. I *shall be moving* to my new building next month.

Present Perfect Tense: This tense describes an action that started in the past and has just ended or continues in the present. It is formed by using **has** or **have** with the <u>past participle form</u> of a verb. Eg: I *have taught* for ten years. He *has won* three trophies for the club. We **have worked together** for fifteen years. They *have eaten* the food.

Past Perfect Tense: It is used to express an action that occurred in the past before another past action, or at a particular time in the past. This tense is formed by using **had** and the <u>past participle form</u> of a verb. Eg: He *had heard* about the man before he saw his picture. She *had finished* writing the exam before twelve o'clock noon. We *had eaten* all the food by the time he arrived. My parents *had married* before they gave birth to me.

Future Perfect Tense: This describes an action that shall have happened or occurred in future before another action, or before a specific time. It is formed by using **will/shall have** and the <u>past participle form</u> of a verb. Eg: The old man *will have driven* for five hours before we meet them. They *will have fought* twice before ten o'clock tomorrow. I *shall have graduated* from university before I work. We *shall have built* strong relationship by the time we marry.

Present Perfect Progressive Tense: This tense expresses an action or event that began in the past, continues into the present, and may even extend to the future. The tense is formed by using **has/have been** and the <u>present participle form of verb.</u> Eg: He *has been writing* books to earn income. *They have been planning* to marry and stay together. We *have been praying* for peace to prevail in our community. She *has been working* hard to get a very good result.

Past Perfect Progressive Tense: It describes action or event that started in the past and was still in progress before it was interrupted by another event. *Had been* and the *present participle* form of the verb make this tense. Eg: I had been expecting my father when I slept. Before she married, she *had been moving* about like a pendulum without partner. Before humans were created, Satan *had been living* with God as friend. The previous government *had been mismanaging* the resources of the nation before President Bio took over governance. He *had been running* from office to office before last month.

Future Perfect Progressive Tense: This describes an ongoing action or event in the future that will happen before a specified time in future. The tense is `formed by using *will have been* with *present participle* form of verb. Eg: By two o'clock tomorrow, they *will have been walking* for six hours. We *shall have been living* in the Gambia for eight years by August 2018. By December, I *will have been teaching* for twelve years.

This short passage is about a football match between Chelsea and Manchester United. It is written in three different tenses; past, present and future tenses. Please observe the verbs or the verb phrases.

Simple Past Tense

When they **started** the match, <u>Mata</u> **passed** the ball to his own defence. Fellani **kicked** it to Rooney in Chelsea's midfield. <u>John Terry</u> **ran** quickly, **collected** the ball and **crossed** it to <u>Williams</u>, who **tapped** it over <u>Smalling</u>; he **jumped** and **headed** it to Oscar. The skilful Brazilian midfielder **placed** and **played** the ball on the ground. He **struggled** and **passed** <u>Martial,</u> who **pulled** him down. The referee **blew** his whistle for foul. Fabregas quickly **kicked** the ball to Matic who **ran** faster and **possessed** it. The three giant defenders **blocked** his way, but he **dribbled** the ball among them, **lifted** it up and **pushed** it towards Hazard. The skilful Belgian back-striker **managed** to jump high up and **sent** the ball to Diego Costa who **bent** down low and **headed** it into the net.

Simple Present Tense

When they **start** the match, Mata **passes** the ball to his own defence. Fellani **kicks** it to Rooney in Chelsea's midfield. John Terry **runs** quickly, **collects** the ball and **crosses** it to Williams, who **taps** it over Smalling, and **jumps** and **heads** it to Oscar. The skilful Brazilian midfielder **places** and **plays** the ball on the ground. He **struggles** and **passes** Martial, who **pulls** him down. The referee **blows** his whistle for foul. Fabregas quickly **kicks** the ball to Matic who **runs** faster and **possesses** it. The three giant defenders **block** his way, but he **dribbles** the ball among them, **lifts** it up and **pushes** it towards Hazard. The skilful Belgian back-striker **manages** to jump high up and **sends** the ball to Diego Costa who **bends** down low and **heads** it into the net.

Simple Future Tense

When they **will start** the match, Mata **will pass** the ball to his own defence. Fellani **will kick** it to Rooney in Chelsea's midfield. John Terry **will run** quickly, **collect** the ball and **cross** it to Williams, who **will tap** it over Smalling, and he **will jump** and **head** it to Oscar. The skilful Brazilian midfielder **will place** and **play** the ball on the ground. He **will struggle** and **pass** Martial, who **will pull** him down. The referee **will blow** his whistle for foul. Fabregas **will** quickly **kick** the ball to Matic who **will run** faster and **possess** it. The three giant defenders **will block** his way, but he **will dribble** the ball among them, **lift** it up and **push** it towards Hazard. The skilful Belgian back-striker **will manage** to jump high up and **send** the ball to Diego Costa who **will bend** down low and **head** it into the net.

Most important information about verb tenses is that when any verb tense is used in a passive voice, it moves a step ahead into tense. So to understand the true verb tense in a passive voice, change the sentence into active voice. Observe the examples below.

Passive Voice Active Voice Tense

Bread is often eaten by Paul. Paul eats the bread often. simple present tense
The bread was eaten by him. He ate the bread simple past tense
The book will be written by Amie. Amie will write the book. simple future tense
The bell has been rung by John. John has rung the bell. present perfect tense
The house is being built by us. We are building the house. present continuous
The trophy will be won by her. She will be winning the trophy. future continuous

Observe the positive and negative sentences in all tenses in the tables below.

Negative Sentences				
Tense	**Subject**	**Helping Verbs + not**	**Main Verb**	**Direct Object**
Simple Present	He	does not	speak	our language.
Simple Past	We	did not	call	them.
Simple Future with Will	You	will not	win	the game.
Future with going to	she	is not going to	lead	you.
Present Continuous	I	am not	speaking	French.
Past Continuous	Paul	was not	writing	the letter
Future Continuous	They	will not be	taking	the examination.
Present Prefect	He	has not	paid	his fees.
Past Perfect	It	had not	worked	well. *
Future Perfect	We	won't have	eaten	lunch before 1 pm tomorrow.
Present Perfect Continuous	She	hasn't been	discussing	the matter.

| Past Perfect Continuous | You | hadn't been | obeying | the laws. |
| Future Perfect Continuous | I | won't have been | listening | by now next week. * |

Positive Sentences				
Tense	**Subject**	**Helping Verb**	**Main Verb**	**Direct Object**
Simple Present	He	. . . .	Plays	football.
Simple Past	She	. . . .	Killed	the rats.
Simple Future with will	It	Will	Eat	some food.
Future with going to	You	are going to	Pay	my money.
Present Continuous	We	Are	speaking	English.
Past Continuous	They	Were	driving	the car.
Future Continuous	You	will be	watching	the match.
Present Perfect	The boys	Have	done	the assignment.
Past Perfect	you	Had	written	a book.
Future Perfect	Paul	will have	sung	the songs.
Present Perfect Continuous	She	has been	dancing	for an hour.
Past Perfect Continuous	I	had been	teaching	for years.
Future Perfect Continuous	We	will have been	reading	for two hours by 8 o'clock.

Note: After studying this table, you are advised to revisit exercise 8 of this chapter to test your understanding.

EXERCISE 10

Select the appropriate verb in the bracket that correctly completes each sentence.

1. I would have (call/called) you yesterday if I (had/have/has) a phone.
2. Tom (explain/explained) to us the problem you have in school.
3. Peter, (explain/explained) to Mr Bassie the story about his home.
4. We (eats/ate/eat) breakfast before going to school every morning.
5. We (sing/sang) three songs before the game (play/played).
6. Our chief (have/has) just been elected by the simple majority.
7. It (was/has/had) rained for an hour before Massa (arrived/arrives) home.
8. They were (danced/dancing) when the call (comes/came) in.
9. She can fluently (speak/speaks) Mende and English.
10. Who (narrates/narrated) the story of black magic often?

Phrasal Verbs

This is a group of words that always function as verb. Phrasal verbs contain two or more words. The first word is always a verb which is followed by either an adverb or a preposition, or both. The adverb or the preposition that follows the verb is called a ***particle***. Most phrasal verbs express idiomatic meanings that we need to learn. In most cases, the separate meanings of the verb and the particle(s) cannot be sum-up to in knowing the meaning of the phrasal verb. Here are few examples of phrasal verbs: *hang around, laid around, wait around, play around, turn on, turn round, turn down, turn up, switch on, switch off, break out, break through, break in, break into, break down, put up with, put on, put up, put in, arrived on, arrived at, arrived by, sit down, sit next to, stand up, give out, give up, give in, etc*

Eg. Please try to <u>put up with</u> him.

Put up with is the phrasal verb meaning ***tolerate***. But the separate meanings of ***put, up*** or ***with*** cannot sum up to ***tolerate***. However, there are other phrasal verbs whose meaning can match with the separate meaning of the verb and the particle(s). This normally happens when the verb and the particle(s) keep their usual meanings. <u>stand up</u>! The separate meanings of **stand** and **up** are sum-up to the phrasal verb '*stand up'* Ok <u>sit down</u>!

Some particles have a particular meaning that is the same even when they are used with different verbs.

Eg. The carpenter left his tools <u>lain around</u> in his workshop. In this sentence, the particle *around* adds the meaning '*with no particular purpose, use or aim'*. So *around* can be used in similar way with different verbs like play around, sit around, walk around, hang around, wait around etc.

Meaning and use of phrasal verbs

The meaning expressed by phrasal verb can be equivalent to one-word verb.

Eg: I will <u>put on</u> my new shirt. Don't <u>stick out</u> the building beyond the mark. In these sentences, **wear** and **project** can be equivalent to **put on** and **stick out** respectively. So in formal writing, you are advised to use one-word verb because it is more formal. Phrasal verbs are more appropriate in informal writing or speech though they are accepted in formal writing or speech too.

Uses of Phrasal Verbs: Phrasal verbs function either transitively or intransitively. Some can function both ways. Those that function transitively are also called **separable verbs**. This means that the particle(s) can be separated from the verb to allow the direct object to either go before or go after the particle.

Please <u>switch off</u> the light. Please <u>switch</u> the light <u>off</u>.
Don't <u>put on</u> that television. Don't <u>put</u> that television <u>on</u>.

In these sentences, the phrasal verbs function transitively; this means that they take the direct objects, **light** and **television**. **Light** receives the action expressed by the phrase verb; *switch off*, while **television** receives the action expresses by the phrasal verb, **put on. Note that it is advisable to place pronousn between the verb and the particle; but always place the direct object that is too long, after the particle**

Eg: Please <u>turn</u> it <u>down</u>. ***Correct***
Please <u>turn down</u> it. ***Incorrect***
Please <u>switch off</u> the bright bulb that is in my room. ***Correct***
Please <u>switch</u> the bright bulb that is in my room <u>off.</u> ***Incorrect***

In the sentences above, the phrasal verbs function transitively; this means they take on object.

Please <u>shut up</u> your month.
I asked her to <u>shut up.</u>
Shut up functions transitively in the first sentence, and intransitively in the second sentence.

CHAPTER 3

ADJECTIVES AND ADVERBS

Adjectives modify nouns or pronouns. They make the language clear and colourful. They give different kinds of details about the word (s) they describe, so that the meanings of the words will become more definite and specific. They provide information that answer one of these questions (*which one?, whose ...?, what kind?* or *how many?*) about the words they modify. Study the sentences below carefully; you will notice that all the adjectives are underlined. The underlined word in each sentence gives additional information about the nouns it modifies.

1. Njala University is a <u>reputable</u> institution.
2. The <u>green</u> van is very slow.
3. The <u>outdated</u> truck has an <u>oversized</u> trailer.
4. Jainaba is so <u>dull</u> in class.
5. The bicycles we bought were all <u>new.</u>
6. Tuesday was <u>cloudy</u> and <u>humid</u>.
7. The <u>old</u> man is wearing a <u>blue</u> suit.
8. The workers are very <u>displeased</u> with their salary.
9. He is a <u>good</u> player of basketball.
10. The work was <u>hard</u> but <u>manageable</u>.
11. The campus has <u>excellent</u> water supply.
12. The <u>stupid</u> boy laughed uncontrollably.
13. The boy said he was <u>sad</u>.
14. The <u>mad</u> dog chased people at night.

Types of Adjectives: The kinds of adjectives include descriptive adjective, articles and derivative adjectives (*adjective of noun, adjective of pronoun and adjective of number.*)

Descriptive Adjectives: This kind of adjective tells the way a noun or a pronoun looks like or appears. It makes nouns more distinctive than, for instance, articles or determiners do. Most descriptive adjectives give information about the size, shape, colour, age, use and texture of the word they describe. Examples of descriptive adjective includes 'beautiful', 'tall', 'black', 'old', 'intelligent', 'clever' etc.

Group A	**Group B**
I have **the** pens.	You have **big** pens
They have **British** pens.	We have **blunt** pens.
She has **John's** pens.	She has **short** pens.
I have **two** pens.	I have **new** pens.
He has **his** pen.	He has a **red** pen.

All the words in boldface in the sentences above are modifying pens, but only those in Group B give concrete descriptive information about the pens, so they are descriptive adjectives. All those in Group A, except *the,* are derivative adjectives.

Articles: These include *a, an* and *the*. They are considered as the most commonly used adjectives. *A* and *an* are called ***indefinite articles*** because they modify no specific noun (person, animal, place or thing). In other words, they refer to any person; any place, any animal or anything. Use *a* with a singular noun that begins with a consonant sound (letter). Eg: a pen, a chair, a table, a boy, a house.

Use *an* with a singular noun that begins with a vowel sound (letter). Eg: an eye, an inch, an onion, an axe, an orange.

The is called ***definite article*** because it describes a specific noun. In other words, when *the* precedes any noun, it implies that the noun has been mentioned earlier and it is understood already; or it means it is the only kind that exists within. It can precede both singular and plural nouns beginning with either consonant or vowel sound (letter).

Eg: The eggs are rotten. The Lord is my protector. The teacher is in class. The president was on television last night.

Derivative Adjectives: The name, ***derivative,*** suggests that these kinds of adjectives are derived from other parts of speech. It is interesting to learn that other parts of speech can function as adjectives. Nouns, pronouns and verbs are among other parts of speech that can function as adjective in sentences. One by one we are going to study them in detail.

Proper Adjective: These are proper nouns but they function as adjectives. When a proper noun displays or demonstrates an adjectival quality, it is referred to as proper adjective. In other words, they are adjectives formed from proper nouns and they are used to make the meaning of nouns specific or distinctive and clear. The spellings of proper adjectives always begin with a capital letter.

Proper Noun Proper Adjective

Proper Noun	Proper Adjective
Africa	African politics
Islam	Islamic country
Sierra Leone	Sierra Leonean writer
America	American jet
Jola	Jola dance
Mende	Mende chief

EXERCISE 1

Underline the proper adjectives in the sentences below.

1. Nowadays, the Chinese goods dominate the African markets.
2. Most European football clubs buy African players.
3. Many English teachers in the Gambian schools are foreigners.
4. A Sierra Leonean writer from the Mende ethnic group has won a prize.
5. Christmas celebration will start on Tuesday evening next week.
6. United Nations secretary general is Paul Lahai.
7. The current American president is controversial and unreliable.
8. One Nigerian movie was launched in the Bakau stadium yesterday.
9. The Gomez families within the Majango ethnic group are religious.
10. I was born in Islamic faith but I grew up and I'm living in Catholic faith.

Adjectives derived from Pronouns:

Some pronouns can play double role. They can replace and describe nouns. When they describe noun, they immediately follow it, and in some cases they don't have antecedent. Possessive pronouns, demonstrative pronouns and indefinite pronouns can function as adjectives.

Eg: <u>My</u> food finished this afternoon.	*possessive pronoun as adjective*
<u>Her</u> food in the kitchen is delicious.	*possessive pronoun as adjective*
<u>That</u> hat belongs to this gentleman.	*demonstrative pronoun as adjective*
<u>These</u> books in the box are interesting.	*demonstrative pronoun as adjective*
<u>Each</u> student was asked to stay in school.	*indefinite pronoun as adjective*
<u>Several</u> boys were here for the party.	*indefinite pronoun as adjective*

EXERCISE 2

In the sentences below, underline the pronouns that function as adjective.

1. That moment I saw them, her kid, Paulina, was in their car with her doll.
2. My little dog will chase their car and your cat away from our compound.
3. Her father had gone to collect another wife from her family in our village.
4. This morning, I saw Mr. Lans and his children in their car.
5. We have finished our work for this academic year.

Adjectives derived from other nouns:

Sometimes, words that are usually nouns can function as adjectives to describe other nouns. They provide information that answer questions like *what kind?* or *which one?* about the nouns. Theseadjectives describe and name persons, animals, places and things.

Eg *noun adjective*	*noun adjective*
book book cover	city city mayor
mango mango tree	street street boy
steel steel door	stone stone wall
iron iron bar	brick brick wall

Compound Adjective

Compound adjectives also exist. Sometimes a compound word can describe a noun or a pronoun. Most compound adjectives are derived from compound nouns. The entities of compound adjectives are sometimes written as closed, hyphenated or separate words. Most often, a compound proper adjective is written as separate words. Observe the examples below:

long-term effect	*warm-blooded* animal	*(hyphenated word)*
battle-front commander	bi-lingual school	*(hyphenated word)*
desktop computer	*landlord* decision	*(single word)*
classroom discussion	breakfast table	*(single word)*
South American bird,	*West African* organizations	*(separated words)*

EXERCISE 3

Read the short passage below and underline the nouns that function as adjective.

There are many street children in the car park. They sit under the big mango tree near the iron pole in Bakau park. These children spend the whole day discussing football news. Some of them have skin diseases and eye infections. There is only one boys' room for all of them where they pass Monday and Friday nights. Two days ago, I spoke to Talk-in-Blues, their leader. He told me that most of the garage children have parents that care for them but they only love independent lives. 'They want to feel the reality of life of this wicked world.' He concluded.

EXERCISE 4

In the sentences below, underline all the nouns that function as adjective.

1. The bush people who live near Mamba mountain are peaceful.
2. My school bag was among the things the forest fire destroyed.
3. The mango leaves and the banana leaves are common in the forest region.
4. Hers is a street boy; they meet behind Jokor Night Club.
5. The forest animals living in Luawa chiefdom are different from the sea animals.

EXERCISE 5

Circle the adjectives in the short passage below and underline the word (s) each modifies. Articles and pronouns are not included.

During moonlight night, I sometimes decide to walk home after practice rather than traveling in the overcrowded, noisy and smelling buses. My weak and lazy friends sometimes decide to travel home in those old rotten cars. One night, I met a very tall, huge and fearful man standing in a dark corner of the road. He coughed and cleared his throat, and then called me. "You short and thin man! Come here, or you stand and wait for me!" His heavy voice frightened me. I stood to attention like that black and high statue standing at Westfield. I looked at his gigantic structure, and then, at my tiny and feeble structure. I became very timid. I looked around me but there was no one around. I put my hands and head up and called my dead father. I prayed to the great saviour to come to my rescue. Just when I put my shivery head down, I saw a white effigy of the legend president with his long sword in his hand, about to redeem me. Then a very bright light from a latest brown-new black American hummer car flashed on me. My poor ghost went in deep trance. It was Mambu B. Sheriff, one of my long-time intimate friends that approached. With a wide smile plastered on his shiny forehead, he opened the huge door of the car and waved me in. My fear was gone.

EXERCISE 6

Fill in the blank spaces in the passage below with the appropriate adjectives.
(open)

Mustapha went to the _____ room to search for his _____
book. Since the light in the room was too _____, he found it
difficult to see the _____ book which was right under the _____
table. His _____ daughter was also sleeping on the _____ bed in
the corner. His _____ wife was not around. She came later with her
_____ sister. The husband was very _____ at the time they came
in. His wife's sister too was very _____ All of them searched for the
_____ book, but in vain. When it was day, they saw the _____
book rapped in a _____ bundle placed under the _____ table.
Mustapha was very _____ when his wife showed him the book. There
was a very _____ story in the book. It was about _____ devil, but
the writing was very _____ to read. _____ people were eager to
read this _____ book of Mustapha.

Degrees of Comparison of Adjectives

In grammar, degree means the forms modifiers (*adjective and adverb*)
take to indicate comparison. There are two forms of degree of comparison.
They are comparative degree and superlative degree. Modifiers have to
change their morphology to enable them to indicate judgment. Regular
adjectives take two different forms for the comparative and superlative
forms:

a) The suffix *'er'* or *'est'* may be added to the end of the adjective.
b) The word *'more'* or *'most'* will precede the modifier.

For the irregular adjectives, they assume entirely different forms.

Regular Modifiers: The comparative and superlative degrees of most
modifiers are regular. There are two rules governing the formation of
regular modifiers. The first rule concerns the modifiers of one or two
syllables. The second rule concerns three or more syllable modifiers. Add

er to form the comparative degree of most one or two syllable adjectives, and *est* to form the superlative degree.

It is important to note that the most common way to form the comparative and superlative degrees of most one or two syllable modifiers is to add er and est rather than more or most. Some examples are given below.

Adjective	Comparative degree	Superlative degrees
big	bigger	biggest
tall	taller	tallest
small	smaller	smallest
short	shorter	shortest
fast	faster	fastest
clever	cleverer	cleverest
poor	poorer	poorest
rich	richer	richest

Where *er* and *est* sound awkward in your ears, you can use *more* and *most*. Very few one and two syllable modifiers take *more* and *most* to form their comparative and superlative degrees.

Eg:	adjective	comparative	superlative
	Honest	more honest	most honest
	just	more just	most just
	pleasant	more pleasant	most pleasant

Use **more** and **most** to form the comparative and superlative degrees of all three or more syllable modifiers. Eg:

Adjective	Comparative	Superlative
fortunate	more fortunate	most fortunate
beautiful	more beautiful	most beautiful
diligent	more diligent	most diligent
dependable	more dependable	most dependable
ambitious	more ambitious	most ambitious

Irregular Modifiers: Irregular modifiers are not many, but to understand and use them correctly; one has to take a mental note of them.

Adjective	Comparative	Superlative
bad	worse	worst
badly	worse	worst
good	better	best
well	better	best
many	more	most
much	more	most
little	less	least (exception)

The three pairs of the above modifiers differ only in the positive, but have similar forms in both the comparative and superlative degrees.

Notice that *bad* and *good* are adjectives, so use them only to modifier a noun or a pronoun. In most sentences, they come after linking verb as predicate adjectives. *Badly* and *well* are adverbs and they must be used to describe an action or state of being. They must be placed as close as possible to the word they modify.

Positive	comparative	superlative
far (*distance*)	farther	farthest
far (*extent*)	further	furthest

Here, the forms of the positive degrees are similar, but the forms of both the comparative and superlative degrees are different.

EXERCISE 7

Fill in the spaces with the appropriate comparative adjective.

1. The light shines as _____ as the moon.
   (a). dull, b). white, c). bright)

2. The competitors ran as_____ as the wind.
   (a). quick, b). fast, c). faster)

3. The orange is as _____ as a ball.
   (a). biggest, b). round, c). red)

4. The girl is as _____ as a palm tree.
   (a). tall, b). taller, c). tallest)

5. That lamp is as _____ as my grandmother.
   (a). old, b). older, c). big)

6. Their voices were as _____ as the roar of lions.
   (a). louder, b). loud, c). loudest)

7. The truck was as _____ as a horse.
   (a). weakest, b). poorer, c). weak)

8. Your school bag is as _____ as a big rock.
   (a). heavy, b). heavier, c) light)

9. His family is as _____ as a corrupt president.
   (a). reach, b). rich, c). poor)

10. We are as _____ as newly married couples.
    (a). happy, b). sad, c). happiest)

Unequal Comparisons:

Use the comparative degree of any modifier plus ***than*** to make unequal comparison of two objects.

Eg: Kailahun is bigger **than** Nyandehun.

Old people are <u>more</u> satisfied **than** the youths.
The president is richer **than** the beggar.
Massa is <u>more</u> beautiful **than** Tudia.

Godly people are <u>more</u> honest **than** religious people.
We are happier **than** our neighbours.
They are weaker **than** us.
Unity is stronger **than** division.

EXERCISE 8

Fill in the spaces with the appropriate comparative adjective. (open)

1. My elder brother is_____ than me.
2. My teacher is _____ than yours.
3. Our school is _____ than theirs.
4. Africa is _____ than Europe.
5. The boys are _____ than the girls.
6. Stone is _____ than cotton.
7. Water is _____ than oil.
8. Education is _____ than money.
9. Heaven is _____ than Hell.
10. Heroes are _____ that the cowards.

Less and **least** are the opposite of **more** and **most** respectively. They too can be used to form the comparative and superlative degrees of most modifiers.

Eg: **adjective comparative degree superlative degree**

acceptable less acceptable	least acceptable
explicit less explicit	least explicit
expensive less expensive	least expensive

EXERCISE 9

Write the comparative and superlative degrees of the adjectives below.

Adjective	Comparative	Superlative
1. weak		
2. difficult		
3. fine		
4. easy		
5. tall		
6. precious		
7. sweet		
8. lazy		
9. strong		
10. new		
11. dull		
12. fat		
13. heavy		
14. brilliant		
15. fast		
16. effective		
17. rich		
18. quick		
19. happy		
20. moderate		
21. wicked		
22. bad		
23. far		
24. old		
25. educative		
26. foolish		
27. light		
28. rude		
29. famous		
30. serious		
31. beautiful		
32. little		

33. ugly _____ _____

34. active _____ _____

35. poor _____ _____

36. playful _____ _____

37. honest _____ _____

38. funny _____ _____

39. religious _____ _____

40. deadly _____ _____

41) stubborn _____ _____

42. decent _____ _____

43. short _____ _____

44. good _____ _____

45. long _____ _____

46. small _____ _____

47. cruel _____ _____

49. notorious _____ _____

50. slim _____ _____

Order of Adjectives in Sentences

It is important to learn the ways adjectives distinguish or describe nouns or pronoun. A noun can be described by specifying its number, name, ownership, size, age, shape, color, origin, material or purpose. Nouns can also be described by opinion or qualifying adjectives. So when you want to modify a noun with more than one specification, you must know the sequence they follow. The sequence in which adjectives appear in series to modify noun or pronoun is stated below. The formula is **NOpiSASCOMP.** This formula will help you to understand the proper order adjectives take in sentence.

Number Opinion, Size, Age, Shape, Colour, Origin, Material, Purpose, NOUN

Two beautiful big new short black Nigerian plastic shopping bags

Five popular large old round red Gambian rubber drinking cups

EXERCISE 10

Choose the correct option that best completes the following sentences.

1. The man is wearing a _____ shirt.
   a) yellow, new, long
   b) long, new, yellow
   c) new, long, yellow

2. She is a _____ woman.
   a) tall, thin, young
   b) thin, young, tall
   c) tall, young, thin

3. The blacksmith makes _____ tools.
   a) excellent, farming, rice
   b) farming, rice, excellent
   c) excellent, rice, farming

4. Last night, Paulina arrived from a _____ trip.
   a) camping, long, two-day
   b) long, two-day, camping
   c) two-day, long, camping

5. I love to play with _____ ball.
   a) red, big, new
   b) big, new, red
   c) big, red, new

6. The _____ girl did well in the test.
   a) intelligent, young, Sierra Leonean
   b) young, Sierra Leonean, intelligent
   c) Sierra Leonean, intelligent, young

7. We offered _____ cows for their rescue.
   a) ten, big, black
   b) ten, black, big
   c) big, black, ten

8. The herbalists have discovered a _____ treatment for Ebola virus.
    a) native, new, great
    b) great, new, native
    c) great, native, new

9. I am going to wear my _____ tie in the party.
    a) big, cotton, blue
    b) blue, big, cotton
    c) big, blue, cotton

10. Please clean those _____ bottles.
    a) three, water, empty
    b) three, empty, water
    c) water, empty, three

11. They placed the mad boy's property on the _____ stone.
    a) green, round, big
    b) round, green, big
    c) big, round, green

12. Her brother's pet is a _____ horse.
    a) brown, big, Gambian
    b) big, brown, Gambian
    c) Gambian, big, brown

13. He is eating from a _____ plate.
    a) small, old, wooden
    b) wooden, old, small
    c) small, wooden, old

14. Our _____ teacher talks for hours!
    a) brilliant, philosophy, young
    b) young, philosophy, brilliant
    c) brilliant, young, philosophy

Adverbs

Adverbs are words that modify verbs, adjectives or other adverbs. When an adverb is used to modify a word, it answers one of the following questions: (**Where? When? Why? How? To what extend? or In what way?**) about the word.

Traditionally, there are four kinds of adverbs. They include the following; adverb of place, adverb of time, adverb of reason and adverb of manner. An adverb of place indicates the place where an action occurs. It answers the question *where?* about the verb. An adverb of time shows the time an action occurs, and it answers the question *when?* about the verb. An adverb of manner tells the way an action occurs, and it answers the question *to what extend or how? about the verb.* (It is interesting to note that it is only **adverbs of manner** that can modify an adjective or another adverb.) An adverb of reason indicates purpose or reason for an action, and it answers the question *why?* about the verb. Most often, an adverb of reason appears in the form of **a prepositional phrase** or infinitive.

Types of Adverbs: It is interesting to learn that most adverbs are derived from other parts of speech: adjectives, nouns or prepositions plus their objects.

Adverbs derived from adjectives: Reasonable numbers of adverbs are derived from adjectives. Most adjectives add the suffix *ly* to play the role of an adverb. Some grammarians call them descriptive adverbs. They qualify or describe verbs by telling how or to what extend their actions are expressed. Eg: slow-ly, *quick-ly*, rude+ly, sudden-ly, calm-ly, serious-ly etc.

Adverbs derived from nouns: Some words that usually function as nouns, naming (**place** or **time**), can also function as adverbs. When they do so, they state the time or place of an action or event. They answer the questions such as **where** or **when** about the verb they qualify. Some of the words include: home, today, yesterday, tomorrow, morning, afternoon, evening, last week etc.

Eg: We went *home* to see our parents. *(Adv of place)*

My father arrived *yesterday*. *(Adv of time)*
The president spoke *last night*. *(Adv of time)*

Adverbs derived from prepositions: Prepositions normally appear with a noun or a pronoun, which serves as *object of the preposition*. When a preposition appears alone without a noun or a pronoun, it is referred to as an adverb. A preposition with its object can also function as adverb. When it does so, it is called adverbial phrase. Eg:

He moved **behind** <u>the door</u>.   *(preposition)*
He moved **behind**   *(adverb)*
They kicked the ball **up** the tree.   *(preposition)*
They kicked the ball **up**.   *(adverb)*
She went **near** the book.   *(preposition)*

Adverb modifies verb

Eg: The boy **kicked** the ball <u>up</u>.   *(**Preposition as adverb**) Where?*
Tom **kicked** the ball <u>up the tree</u>.   *(**adverbial phrase**) Where?*
The young players **went** <u>home</u>.   (**noun as adverb**) *Where?*
I am **walking** <u>slowly</u>.   (***adverb***) *How?*
People **sit** <u>on their bottoms</u>.   (**adverbial phrase**) *How?*
They also **sit** <u>on their benches</u>.   (adverbial **phrase**) *Where?*
My father **arrived** <u>yesterday</u>.   (**noun as adverb**) *When?*
The villagers **pray** <u>at night</u>.   (adverbial **phrase**) *When?*
The old man **sleeps** <u>soundly.</u>   *(descriptive adverb)*
                         To what extent? Or how?

The girl **hit** the door <u>hard.</u>   *(descriptive adverb)*
                         To what extend? Or how?

The thieves **went** <u>to steal</u>.   *(**Infinitive**) Why? or where?*
The thieves **went** <u>for money.</u>   *(**adverb phrase**) Why?*

In the examples above, the words in boldface are verbs and the underlined words are adverbs or adverbial phrases qualifying the verbs. In the brackets are the grammatical names of the modifiers. At the end of every sentence is the question they answer about their respective actions they qualify.

Adverb modifies adjective	*Adverb modifies another adverb*
These girls are **very** beautiful.	The old woman walks **very** slowly.
Those boys are **too** clever.	The young boy runs **too** quickly.
They are **extremely** generous.	She writes her exams **rather** carefully.

Negative adverb

Negative adverbs change the meaning of a sentence from positive to negative. *Not* is the only word that functions as negative adverb.

Eg: I will go to school tomorrow. I will **not** go to school tomorrow.
He passed the end of year exam. He did **not** pass the exam.

EXERCISE 12

In the paragraph below, underline the adverbs and circle the words each adverb qualifies.

I saw many people in our school compound yesterday. All of them were smartly dressed, and they walked quietly to the principal's office. The secretary, who appeared too busy, quickly came out and smilingly showed them seats. They patiently waited. Suddenly, the principal's car drove up and slowly stopped in front of the office. She worriedly came down from the car. She stood to attention and quickly glanced at the strangers. 'Why are you here and how long have you being here?' She surprisingly asked them. 'Our children invited us here to sign documents on their behalf.' One of the men timidly got up and responded to the principal's question. 'I was expecting you yesterday to sign those documents, not today. I don't believe if I have anything like that on my agenda today.' She angrily told them and boastfully walked into her office and slowly and proudly sat in her comfortable chair.

EXERCISE 13

Use the adverbs listed below to fill the blank spaces provided in the short passage below: (firmly, slowly, suddenly, immediately, quietly, aloud, quickly, too, heavily, seriously, late)

I reached home very … … 1 … … last night. There was no light. I … 2.. … and … .3 … … walked into the house. I was … .4 … … afraid. I called but I received no answer. I thought of my dead father and I … … 5 … … imagined his ghost standing near me. I … … 6 … . … returned towards the veranda. I figured the thick black darkness behind me like a real object chasing me. I felt its cold and gigantic hands … … 7 … … placed on my shoulder. I shouted … … 8 … . … and … … 9 … … … ran outside. It was at this moment I saw my weakened grandmother … … 10 … … … struggling with her paralyzed legs to come to my rescue. Understanding her voice, I jumped on her and we … … 11 … … hugged each other.

EXERCISE 14

Underline the adverbs in the following sentences.

1. The forest fire spread rapidly.
2. September mornings are really cool.
3. She did rather well in the exams.
4. He told us to talk quietly in the darkness.
5. The huge supporters of the president matched across.
6. The young woman drank the juice slowly.
7. It is exactly 3:00 in the morning.
8. The dog quickly pounced on the snake.
9. They marched happily through the garden.
10. Jinnah is always late for school.
11. Could you please leave her alone?
12. The green car is extremely magnificent.
13. She seldom did well on tests.
14. Green, white and blue are definitely my favourite colours.
15. He carried the bucket of water very carefully.

CHAPTER 4

PREPOSITIONS, CONJUNCTIONS AND INTERJECTIONS

A preposition is a word that shows relationship between words, most often nouns and or pronouns, in a sentence. Prepositions are most often followed by a noun or pronoun in a sentence. The noun or pronoun that follows a preposition in a sentence is called **object of the preposition.** The preposition plus its object(s) form a **prepositional phrase**. Prepositions show relationship in three ways: association, location and direction. Prepositions can be made up of more than one word. Notice how changing the preposition in the sentences below will change the relationship between *bag* and the *table*.

The bag is *on* the table.
The bag is *under* the table.
The bag is *behind* the table.
The bag is *near* the table.

Commonly used prepositions include the following:

at	into	about	around	between
in	from	aside	before	against
on	over	after	front	outside
of	near	within	towards	
by	side	along	without	
to	down	among	during	despite
up	upon	below	across	besides
for	with	since	behind	beneath
off	next	above	inside	according to
out	until	under	beside	through

It is very interesting to learn that most prepositions always go with certain words for special meanings. This means that it will be ungrammatical to use these prepositions without the appropriate word it goes with. Here are some prepositions and the words they attach to. Observe and learn them by heart.

abide by

abstain from

absorbed in

adhere to

addicted to

admit to/into

accustomed to

accused (sb) of (sth)

advantage of (sth)

affection for

affected with

afraid of

agree to (proposal)

agree with (sb)

agree (sth)

aim at

aloof of

assure of

disassociate from

associate with

approve of

assent to

aspire to/for

ashamed of

apply for (sth)

apply to (sb)

akin to

approach to

appetite for

apologize to (sb)

apologize for (sth)

appeal to (sb) for (sth)

anxious for (sb)

anxious about (sth)

angry about, at (sth)

angry with, at (sb)

alternative to

contend with

contemporary with

consist of

connected (sth), to (sb)

careful about

caution about/against

charge with

claim to, on (sth)

clash with (sb), over (sth)

collide with

collude with (sb) in (sth)

concern for/ about

capable of

conducive to

comply with

compliment on

compassion for

compensation for

compatible with

compare to/with

comment on

confidence in

conform to

conformity with
campaign against/ for
ban on
ban (sb) from (sth)
bad at (not good at)
bad for (harmful)
believe in
beneficial to
benefit from/by
blame (sb/sth) for (sth)
boast of
burden (n) on
busy with
march on
married to
marvel at
concentrate on
meditate on
nag at
mourn for
negligent in
nervous about
notorious for
obedient to
listen to
longing for
lust for
look/stare at
liable to
leave for
lead to
laugh at
lament over
lack of
kind/cruel to
interfere with

invest in
involved in
irrelevant to
meddle in (sth) with (sb)
keen on
lacking in
irrespective of
infected with
insisted on
interact with
interaction between
interfere with (to prevent)
interfere in (get involve)
dispose of
die of
disgruntled with/at
different from
deviate from
devoid of
desist from
detrimental to
delight in
depend on/upon
deal with
doubtful about
decline in/of
eager for
eligible for
engaged (sb) to (sb),
engaged in/on (sth)
enthusiastic about/for
entrust (sb) with (sth)
entrust (sth) to (sb)
envious of
envy at
entitle to

equal to

escape from

essential to

excel at/in

excuse (sb) for (sth)

fail in

faith in

faithful to

famous for

fearful for

feed on

fight with (sb)

fight about/for (sth)

fill (sth) with (sth)

fill in (sth)

fit/unfit for

fed up with

free from/of

glad about (happy for)

glad of (grateful)

glance at

good at (able to do sth well)

good for (suitable)

grateful to (sb) for (sth)

grief at/over

grieve for/ over

guilty of/about

harmful to

heir to/of

hint at

hope for/to/of

hopeful about

hostile to

habit of

identical with

ignorant of/about

impart on (sb/sth)

imposed on

impress (sb) with (sth)

infected with

objected to

obsession with

opportunity for (sb/sth)

opportunity of doing (sth)

open to

partial to

partially for (sth)

passion for (sth)

persist in (doing sth)

pleased with

pleasing to

popular with

pray to god

pray for (sb/sth)

prefer (sb/sth)

preferable to

pretext for

prevail on (to persuade)

prevail over (to defeat)

prevent from

pride in

prior to

prohibit from

prone to

proud of

provided (sb) with (sth)

provided (sth) for (sb)

pessimistic about

positive about

quarrel about (sth)

quarrel with (sb)

ready for

reconcile (sth) with (sth)

recover (n) from

recovery (v) from

refer to

reference to

rejoice at/over

related to

rely on

remind of

remorse for

request for

resemblance to

responsible for (sth)

responsible to (sb)

restricted to

rid of

rob of

resign from

search for

seek for

senior/junior ... to

resign from

sensitive to/about

short of

similar to

giggle/laugh at (to provoke)

smile/giggle/laugh to (genuine)

sorry about/for

spend on

stick to

subjected to

succeed in

succumb to

suffer from

supply (sb) with (sth)

supply (sth) to (sb)

surprise at

suspect of

suspect (sb/ sth) of (sth)

suspicious of

sympathize with

thankful for (sth)

thankful to (sb)

desire/hungry for

threaten (sb) with (sth)

tired of

tremble with

true to

use to

venue for

wait for

withdraw from

wonder about (think about)

wonder at (be surprised)

worthy of

yearn for

EXERCISE 15

Fill in the blank spaces with the correct preposition

1. Please put the stone _____ the table. (on, inside, up)
2. He has built a bus park _____ the hospital. (across, in front of, to)

3. A re you going _____ the school? (at, between, to)
4. They put their pens _____ my bag. (after, out, in)
5. She put the letter _____ the two books. (between, in, over)
6. The river is flowing _____ the bridge. (up, of, under)
7. May I hang my coat _____ the door? (between, on, to)
8. The children are running _____ us. (away, from, through)
9. Whois that man walking _____ the house? (at, towards, under)
10. Would you like to walk _____ the park? (on, through, over)
11. You can read books _____ the library. (in, on, over)
12. I was standing _____ the door when you called. (behind, across, out)
13. _____ the mountain, there is a river. (at, below, in)
14. They ran _____ the hill. (in, up, with)
15. The picture is _____ the sofa. (of, above, among)
16. The bank is _____ the street. (across, through, at)
17. They walked _____ the road. (on, out, with)
18. We came here _____ the doctor's office. (at, from, of)
19. Get the dog _____ the kitchen table! (off, in, at)
20. There is a lamp hanging _____ the table. (over, under, of)
21. We ran _____ the house. (into, up, above)
22. The table is _____ the bed. (beside, over, through)
23. Your letter is _____ the things on my desk. (among, between, at)
24. There's a mouse _____ the refrigerator. (across, with, behind)
25. My shoes are _____ the closet. (at, off, on)
26. The market is _____ the centre of the town. (at, beneath, below)
27. The necklace is _____ my neck. (around, over, at)
28. There's a man sitting _____ the bus. (in, across, on)

EXERCISE 16

In the paragraph below, underline the preposition and circle its object. Note that some prepositions have more than one object.

My father sent a letter to the chief about the complaint the community people made to him. The people complained about the criminal behaviour of the youths in the area. The youths together with the young adults in the area have adopted the habit of taking drugs, armed robbery and prostitution. After reading the letter, the chief called the community elders and put the matter across to them. In the elders' meeting, my father sat next to the chief. I was called to serve as secretary for them. Behind me was the chief's elder son, Kaliru. He was the head of a ChristMus Prayer group that used both the Bible and the Quran. They claimed to be very prayerful and religiously holy, yet they were truly ungodly. Their meeting place was called ChurMosq Centre; a place that was widely believed to be the breeding and meeting ground for the criminals and the prostitutes. In fact, it was believed that he, Kaliru, was the head of one of the notorious group in the community. He remained silent throughout the meeting, and from time to time, the embarrassment plastered on his father's face, showed up. Towards the end of the meeting, Kaliru made very little contribution that was not even necessary. He told the people that he believed that God is greater than any criminal and that the people should put their problems to God to fight for them. At the end of the meeting, we all decided to summon all the members of community into a general meeting to further deliberate on the matter.

EXERCISE 17

The words in boldface in the short paragraph below function as either a preposition or an adverb. Underline the preposition and circle the adverb.

This morning, we went **(1) to** Kailahun Community Stadium **(2) for** a football match. **(3) Before** the match started, I stood **(4) up** and prayed **(5) to** God to give me the zeal to play the game **(6) with** full strength. When the game started, the first ball they kicked passed **(7) by**; I chased it (8) **with** speed and jumped (9) **over**. My opponent that was standing (10) **nearby** ran (11) **forward** and kicked it (12) **inside**. Two players ran (13) **after** the ball and stood (14) **before** facing each other. (15) **Next to** me was our skilful player, known as '*Play Maker*'. He was fast to trap the ball (16) **up** and bring it (17) **down**. He dribbled it passed and found his way (18) **towards** the goal where he kicked the ball (19) **through**. When I turned (20) **round**, the goalkeeper was (21) **on** the ground while the ball was already (22) **in** the net. The exciting spectators cheered and shouted (23) **above** their voices. The game ended shortly (24) **after;** and the score line was two-one (25) **against** the opponent team. When the game ended, the fans went (26) **to** their various homes and our own team went (27) **to** the hotel where the coach thanked us (28) **for** our wonderful performance.

Conjunctions

A conjunction is a word that joins or connects words or groups of words together. The types of conjunctions include coordinating conjunction, correlative conjunction and subordinating conjunction.

Coordinating Conjunction: It joins words or word groups that have the same function in a sentence. Coordinating conjunction includes 'and', 'but', 'so', 'or', etc. Eg:

a) Eliz <u>and</u> Fatou are eating. (*It joins compound subject*)
b) Paul will come <u>but</u> will not eat. (*It joins compound predicate*)
c) She is clever <u>but</u> unserious. (*It joins compound predicate adjective*)
d) Amie cannot sing, <u>nor</u> does she dance. *(It joins simple sentence)*

Correlative Conjunction: This also connects words or groups of words; but usually, it appears in pair and is more forceful and precise than the coordinating conjunction.

Eg: either ... or, neither ... nor, both ... and, not only ... but (also), whether ... or, just as ... so etc.

a) <u>Neither</u> Elizabeth <u>nor</u> Jarju is in class.
b) <u>Both</u> Paul <u>and</u> Amie are here.

c) <u>Either</u> you <u>or</u> your brother will be given the prize.

d) <u>Not only</u> the boys <u>but even</u> the girls wear trousers these days.

EXERCISE 18

Fill in the blanks with the appropriate correlative conjunction. Use commas where necessary.

1. _____ my brother _____ my sister lives in Sierra Leone.
2. _____ my dog, _____ my cats can chase rats at night.
3. _____ my mother _____ my father was born in this country.
4. _____ I _____ you will go to the store.
5. _____ soccer _____ tennis is a nice sport.
6. _____ my car _____ my truck need to be repaired.
7. _____ I come over, _____ you come around.
8. _____ you _____ your friends are old enough to enter
9. _____ I love you, _____ I can't ignore my family.
10. _____ the students _____ their parents are invited.

Subordinating Conjunction: This conjunction always introduces subordinate clause. It is used to join two complete ideas together, and by doing so, it will make one of the ideas subordinate (dependent) to the other. Subordinating conjunctions could be grouped according to their grammatical roles which include indicating *time, place, cause, condition, concession* and *comparison.*

a) **Subordinating Conjunctions used to indicate time** include: *after, when, as soon as, as long as, before, once, still, since, till, until, whenever, while* etc.

Eg, We went home **when** the match was over.
Everyone went away **as soon as** they arrived.
The boys suffered **until** their parents came and rescued them.

b) **Subordinating Conjunctions used to indicate place** include *where and wherever.*

   Eg. They met us **where** the meeting was going on.
   She follows us **wherever** we go.

c) **Subordinating Conjunctions used to indicate cause** include: *as, because, in order that, since, so that* etc.

   Eg. We went home **because** it was raining.
   The work was not properly done **since** the workers were not monitored.

d) **Subordinating Conjunctions used to indicate condition** include: even if, if, in case, provided that, unless, etc.

   Eg. We will not leave **unless** you pay for our labour.
   They will come **if** you call them.

e) **Subordinating Conjunctions used to indicate concession and comparison** include: although, as though, even though, though, whereas, while etc.

   Eg. He passed the exam **even though** he did not study.
   She respects everyone **though** she is old and very rich.

It is important to note that subordinating conjunctions most often introduce adverbial clauses in a complex or compound complex sentences; they may even appear at the beginning of a sentence.

EXERCISE 19

Use the appropriate conjunction to fill in the spaces. (open)

1. We will run _____we did not tie our shoes lace.
2. We can eat lunch _____ you like.
3. _____ I am happy, I will smile.

4. She behaves _____ she rules the world.
5. We lost control _____ he took his leg off the crutch.
6. He is going to eat _____ his friends say he can't.
7. _____ you finish eating your vegetables, you may eat cake.
8. _____ our parents were dead _____ we educated ourselves.
9. _____ it is cold out, I'm not going to wear my jacket.
10. We will start work _____ the sun rises.
11. I am a vegetarian _____ I don't eat animal flesh.
12. I waited _____ my father bought the bags.
13. We ran _____ we were scared.
14. I want to go _____ money grows on trees.
15. We got to the scene of the crime _____ the robbers ran away.
16. I'm not leaving _____ you say you're sorry.
17. We cannot go to school _____ we have not paid the fees.
18. I have to wait _____ she has promised to come.
19. ____ we do not find him there, we'll move to the city _____ he lives.

Interjections

An interjection is a word that is used to express feelings or emotions and it functions independently. In other words, interjections have no grammatical connection with other words in a sentence. They are always separated from the sentence by either a comma or exclamation mark. Interjections express variety of feelings such as joy, fear, anger, surprise, exhaustion, dismay or sorrow. Some common interjections include ah, dear, hey, ouch, goodness, hurrah, whew, alas, gracious, oh, wow etc.

Hurrah! My team has won.
Wow! Here comes my sweet heart.
Hey! Leave that place!

EXERCISE 20

Underline the interjections in the following sentences.

1. Whew! That was close.
2. Careful! The tiger is hungry!
3. Yes! I think I will have more tea please.
4. Thanks! I needed that.
5. Wow! That was easy!

PART 2

SENTENCE STRUCTURE

CHAPTER 5

PHRASES AND CLAUSES

Introduction: Most often, a group of words function or play the same grammatical role as a single word does in a sentence. In other words, the various grammatical functions of different phrases are always equivalent to single words. They refer to names like nouns, they modify and qualify adjectives and adverbs and they express actions as verbs do. Subordinating-word-groups are named by the function they perform in a given sentence. Phrases are one of the two categories of subordinating-word-groups. Other subordinating-word-groups are the subordinate clauses.

As a noun, a phrase or a subordinate clause can function as subject, direct object, object of preposition, appositive or as predicate nominative in a sentence.

- As an adjective, a phrase or a subordinate clause can modify a noun or a pronoun as adjectives do in sentences.
- As an adverb, a phrase or a subordinate clause can qualify/describe a verb or an adjective.
- A verb phrase it can express action just like a verb does in a sentence.

Eg: Thomas has a **red** book.

The tall black boy has a book **with a red cover**.
Anyone I consult will buy a book **that has a red cover**.

In the set of sentences above, the underlined words '*Thomas*' is a noun, '*The tall black boy*' is a noun phrase *and* '*Anyone I consult*' is a noun clause. They all function as subject in their respective sentences. The words in boldface '*red*' is an adjective, '***with a red cover***' is an adjectival phrase; and '***that has a red cover***' is an adjectival clause. All of them modify the noun '*book*' in their respective sentences.

The truth is <u>what he told us</u> **cleverly**.
This is the hole in <u>which snakes enter</u> **at night**.
Where we went, we got <u>what we wanted</u>. Or
We got <u>what we wanted</u> **where we went.**

In the other set of sentences above, the underlined words <u>what he told us</u>, <u>which snakes enter</u> *and* <u>what we wanted</u> are all noun clauses. They function as **predicate nominative, object of preposition** and as **direct object** respectively.

The words in boldface, *cleverly,* is an adverb and it describes the manner of the action *told*. *At night* is an adverbial phrase; it indicates the time of the action *entered*. **Where we went** is an adverbial clause; shows the place of the action took place. Now one after the other, let's delve into them.

A phrase is a group of related words without a subject and a finite verb and it functions as single part of speech. Phrases play three linguistic roles in sentences:

a) They add more information to a sentence.
b) They make the ideas in the sentence clear or distinct.
c) They make language colourful and flamboyant.

The frequently used phrases include noun phrase, prepositional phrase (**adjectival** and **adverbial phrases**), verb phrase, verbal and verbal phrases (**participial, gerund** and **infinitive phrases**) and appositive phrase.

Noun Phrase

A Noun phrase is a group of related words containing noun and others words that can modify it. A noun is always the main word in a noun phrase. The modifiers may be determiners (articles, noun, pronouns, numbers, adjectives etc.). Eg: the man, Musa's book, my pen, ten tables, the fat black woman, tall old man, small village boy, wicked young lady etc. A noun phrase may have more than one modifier as in the following examples:

<u>Two tall black boys</u> are coming.
<u>My short red pencil</u> is missing.
<u>This man</u> is <u>our new chief.</u>
He washed <u>four small green cups</u>.
<u>The car</u> you bought was owned by <u>the head</u> of <u>our club</u>.
<u>We</u> sang the <u>old song</u> yesterday.
They talked to <u>the fact old lady</u>.

All the underlined words in the sentences above are noun phrases.

EXERCISE 1

In the short passage below, underline all the twenty-seven noun phrases and state the function of each as it is used in the sentence.

Our team won the match that was played yesterday in our village. Every fan from the surrounding villages was present and they were extremely happy for the players. When the final whistle was blown, the jubilant fans jumped into the field to embrace the players. Even my grandmother, the oldest person in the village celebrated the victory. A week to the match, everyone fervently prayed for our young team to carry the day. Traditional worshippers too called on our ancestors to support the team. If we would have lost the match, many heads in the village sport committee would have rolled. Now that the team has qualified to play the district league next season, we must encourage our young players; and we will try to get few experienced players too. We hope to bring trophies home in time to come.

EXERCISE 2

Use the noun phrases below in sentences. If anyone starts a sentence, please capitalize the first letter. (open)

1. the tall girl
2. the red book
3. this laughing cat

4. happy Christmas
5. worst enemy
6. sweet mangoes
7. the principal
8. public opinion
9. two beautiful girls
10. huge black car
11. hard-to-satisfy man
12. the dull man
13. public transport
14. the tall palm tree
15. idiot sycophant
16. natural mystic
17. that fat woman
18. my small brother
19. yellow leaves
20. biggest occasion
21. the high chair
22. deep river
23. heavy stone
24. gentle lady

Prepositional Phrase

A prepositional phrase is a group of words that is introduced by a preposition and ends with a noun or a pronoun. The noun or the pronoun that precedes preposition is called an *object of preposition*. The object of preposition may have modifiers or determiners. A prepositional phrase may have a compound object of preposition. Few examples of prepositional phrase are: to them, across the wide street, above the high mountain, with him, for her, under the table, in front of ours, outside the house, to my father etc.

EXERCISE 3

In the short paragraph below, underline all the prepositional phrases and circle the objects of the preposition of each phrase.

In my class, there are fifteen boys and twelve girls. Each seat is occupied by two pupils. Fatou Gibba, the girl with the most admirable character, sits near Abass, the prefect of the class. Behind them are Jarju and Kamara, the two best friends. The seat adjacent the latter's seat is occupied by the two admirable and brilliant twins. Towards the left hand corner, there the noise causing group is. Above them is the ceiling fan. The crin-cran sound from it and the offensive noise from this notorious group make the class unpleasant whenever there is no teacher. On the wall in front of the class is our wide blackboard. Whenever the English teacher comes into our class, the pupils sit on their bottoms and listen without writing. He will clearly explain the concepts for us to understand; after which he writes the summary of the note on the board for us to copy. At the end of any lesson, he will urge us to either ask questions or to make contributions. Whether we ask questions or not, he will continually fire us questions until the entire topic he taught within the time scheduled for each period.

Adjectival Phrase

When a prepositional phrase modifies a noun or a pronoun, it is called an adjective phrase, because it does the work of an adjective. When it does so, it answers one of the questions *(what kind? or which one?)* about the noun or pronoun it describes. Eg:

The **man** under the bridge is sleeping.
The pair of **trousers** on the bed has been ironed.
The **pen** in my bag doesnot work.
The **flowers** behind the house are beautiful.
The **lady** with the bag is my sister.

Note that when a prepositional phrase modifies a noun or a pronoun, it immediately follows the noun or the pronoun. Secondly, it also answers the question, (which?), about the noun or pronoun it modifies.

EXERCISE 4

In the sentences below, underline the adjectival phrases and circle the words each phrase modifies.

1. The books in the principal's office are very new.
2. Plenty novels among the books were written by Africans.
3. Those boys under the trees sing aloud in our class.
4. There is a boy who narrates stories about the forest devil.
5. Some teachers from other countries do not speak our native languages.
6. The big apples on the table are not in good condition.
7. In the class, I sit behind the girl with the black bag.
8. There are different kinds of fish in the river below the mountain.
9. Several children above the age of ten are from low income earners.
10. Some of the boys around the mansion are strangers from the university.

Adverbial Phrase

When a prepositional phrase modifies a verb, an adjective or an adverb, it is called an adverbial phrase; it does the work of adverb.

Eg: The man is **sleeping** in the room. *(sleeping where?)*
She **was born** in January. *(born when?)*
They **spoke** with courage. *(spoke in what way?)*
The man **is sleeping** under the bridge. (sleeping where?)
A pair of trousers **is hanging** on the wall. (hanging where?)
I **put** the pen in my bag. (put where?)
He **planted** beautiful flowers behind the house. *(planted where?)*
The lady **was dancing** with the bag. *(dancing how?)*
This note **is regarded** by my readers as the best. *(regarded to what extent?)*

EXERCISE 5

In the short paragraph below, underline the adverbial phrases and circle the words each phrase modifies.

We passed by the river and entered into the forest to fetch some fire wood. In the river, we saw too many little fishes swimming around with few bigger ones. A long black snake was chasing the bigger fishes with terrific speed. I sent my machete in the water to cut the snake, but I missed it. It came out of the water and climbed up a big tree. On the top of the tree were several birds and their nests. They all flew away in the air when they saw the black cobra climbing the tree. We spent time watching the drama between the snake and the birds. When it reached on the top, the snake started searching in the nests one after the other for eggs. In one of the nests where it found eggs, it spent more time. Few birds flew on it and pecked it with their powerful beaks. It was a serious battle we witnessed.

EXERCISE 6

Use the prepositional phrases in two sentences each; in one sentence, use it as adjective phrase, and in the other sentence as adverb phrase. (open)

Prepositional Phrases	as an adjectival phrase to modify a noun or a pronoun	as adverbial phrase to modify a verb, an adjective or adverb
against us	The two goals **against us** is an advantage to them.	He scored the two goals **against us** in last week match.
in my farm	The work **in my farm** is not too difficult for them.	We worked **in my farm** yesterday for the money.
at home	Your behaviour **at home** was not acceptable at all.	**At home**, he put up unacceptable behaviour.
outside the hut	The place **outside the hut** is owned by my father.	We will build **outside the hut** on our father's land.

between them		
behind the box		
below the hill		
near you		
with President Bio		
under him		
to the school		
on the stage		
among them		
before Tobaski		
for the priest		
from God		
over the bar		
below standard		
after pray day		
within the club		
about her		
across the road		
beside me		
by the church		
during lunch		
without him		
near the sea		
above the tree		
up the sky		
into the water		
down the road		
adjacent theirs		

Verb Phrase

A verb phrase is made up of one main verb and one or more helping verbs all acting as simple predicate. A verb phrase makes an action very clear as it indicates time of action.

Eg:

The boy <u>is sleeping</u> in the room.
We <u>had been dancing</u> for a week when Dad arrived.
He <u>*has been sleeping*</u> for two hours.

Sometimes other words interrupt the verb phrase in a sentence. Eg:

I ***will*** definitely ***be taking*** my bag to school tomorrow.
May I ***ask*** my mum for the key?

Here are few examples of verb phrases: am eating, is sleeping, are reading, was running, were working, has written, have slept, had weaved, does not speak, shall have been brushing, will have been reading, can climb, could have done, should have eaten, may be etc.

Sometimes other words will appear within the verb phrase. Eg: should **not** do, do **not** laugh, would **not** give, shall **never** be etc.

Please learn about other verb phrases and practice using them in sentences.

Verbals

Verbal are verb forms that functions as noun, adjective or adverb. There are three kinds of verbals. They are participle, gerund and infinitive; each of these has its form of phrase.

Participles and Participial Phrases

Participle: This is a word formed or derived from a verb form but functions as adjectives. Participles answer adjectival questions about the noun they modify. The two types of participles are the present participle and the past participle. The present participle form ends with *ing*, while the past participle end in two different ways. The regular verbs end with ***d*** or ***ed;*** the irregular verbs follow different patterns. Here are some examples:

We are living in a <u>developing</u> **country**. ...	*Present participle*
The <u>moving</u> **car** hit the little girl. ...	*Present participle*
The <u>sitting</u> **government** is working.	*Present participle*
There are few <u>developed</u> **countries** in Africa. ...	*Past participle*
The <u>edited</u> **documents** are on the table. ...	*Past participle*
<u>Written</u> **information** will never change.	*(irregular) Past participle*
The <u>broken</u> **chair** is behind the door.	*(Irregular) Past participle*

The words underlined in the sentences above are participles and those in boldface are the nouns they modify.

Participial phrase: This is made up of the participle plus its modifiers. *Prepositional phrase*, *adverb* or *direct object* often accompanies the participle in the participial phrase. The grammatical names of the accompanying words are in the bracket Eg:

The **report** *<u>edited</u> <u>by the secretary</u>* got lost.	*(**Prepositional phrase**)*
<u>Developing</u> <u>slowly</u>, **Gambia** is becoming an economic giant in the sub region.	*(**adverb**)*
<u>Growing</u> <u>rapidly within our society</u>, **technology** is changing our ways of life.	*(**adverb &** **prepositional phrase**)*
The **pastor**, *<u>preaching</u> <u>slowly</u>*, convinced the congregation.	*(**adverb**)*
<u>Dancing</u> <u>in clubs</u>, the **group** won the competition.	*(**prepositional phrase**)*
The **committee** *<u>monitoring</u> <u>the exam</u>* is vigilant.	*(**direct object**)*
<u>Sitting</u> <u>by the river with his lover</u>, **Paul** wrote the story.	*(**double modifiers**)*

The groups of words underlined in the sentences are participial phrases; the words in italics are the participles and those in boldface are the nouns the phrases describe.

EXERCISE 7

In the sentences below, put in bracket all participle or participial phrases. Underline the present participle once and past participle twice; then circle the noun or pronoun each participle or participial phrase modifies.

1. The talking parrot is destroying my growing plants.
2. The kite flying in the air will land on the waving leaves.
3. It is the flowing water that brought down this broken statue of the king.
4. The caring parents will treat the ill-mannered behaviour of their children.
5. SLPP dancing group won the advertised position.
6. The APC party won the general elections in 2012.
7. The sailing boat found itself in an unknown destination.
8. Please bring me the broken chair that is in the dressing room.
9. The exciting fans continuously clapped for their winning team.
10. Sleeping up the ceiling, my neighbour's cat cannot catch any rat.
11. Some children, pampered and spoilt by their parents, will rudely behave in forbidden places.
12. Your singing toy scattered the documents edited and compiled by the secretary.
13. The suspended activities will resume on the first working day of this week.
14. Running like a kangaroo, the boy will take the first position in the awaiting event.
15. Sitting on the tree, my parrot plucked the easily destroyed buds on the tree.
16. Moving along the river, Paul sang a love song for his widely admired Massa.
17. The old woman, walking slowly, saw the lost and forgotten ring in the grass.
18. The fast growing economy has no effect on the less and slowly developing nations.
19. The boy feeling uneasy to speak, waved vigorously to the loud cheering spectators.
20. Developing slowly in the sub region, Sierra Leone will soon feed her rapidly growing population.

Infinitive and Infinitive Phrase

Infinitive: It is made up of the words *to* and a base form of a verb. In other words, infinitive is a basic verb that is usually preceded by *to*. It can function as *a noun*, as *an adjective* and as *an adverb* in a sentence. Be careful not to confuse the infinitives and a prepositional phrase that begins with *to*. The infinitive, *to* is followed by a verb, while in prepositional phrase *to* is followed by a noun or a pronoun.

As a noun, an infinitive functions as a ***subject***, as ***direct object*** or as a ***predicate nominative.***	**As a noun** – subject – direct object – predicate nominative	***To sleep*** is good. He loves ***to eat***. His hobby is ***to read***.
As an adverb, it modifies *verb* or *adjective*	**As an adverb** – modifies a verb – modifies an adjective	<u>Use</u> the library **to read**. I'm <u>ready</u> **to read**. It is too <u>dark</u> **to read**.
As an adjective, it modifies noun or pronoun.	**As an adjective** – modifies a noun – modifies pronoun	Bo is a <u>city</u> **to admire**. This is <u>time</u> **to pray**. He is <u>somebody</u> **to copy**.

Here are some more examples:

He is **a boy** <u>to admire</u>. *(as adjective)* It is ***good*** <u>to learn</u>. *(as adverb)*
Mujeh is **a girl** <u>to copy</u>. *(as adjective)* We ***use*** money <u>to buy</u>. *(as adverb)*
We ***want*** them <u>to work</u>. *(as adverb* To read is an advantage. *(as noun)*
They are **afraid** <u>to speak</u>. *(as adverb)* They are ***men*** <u>to fear</u>. *(as adjective)*
<u>To smoke</u> is not good. *(as noun)* He loves <u>to pray</u>. *(as noun)*

Infinitive Phrase: An infinitive phrase is made up of an infinitive and the words that modify it. The modifiers of infinitive could be a noun, an adverb or a prepositional phrase. This phrase performs the same functions in a sentence as the infinitive. As a noun, an infinitive phrase functions as a subject, a direct object and a predicate nominative in a sentence. As an adjective, it modifies a noun or a pronoun; and it modifies a verb when it functions as adverb. Here are some examples:

As a noun, an infinitive phrase functions as subject, direct object or predicate nominative.	**As a noun** – subject – direct object – predicate nominative	**To read** aloud is hard for him. He loves **to read** in the library. Part of my duty is ***to read*** Bible.
As an adjective, it modifies noun or pronoun.	**As an adjective** – modifies a noun – modifies a pronoun	Bo is a city **to admire** in Sierra Leone. This is *time* **to read** your Bible. He is *somebody* **to copy** slowly.
As an adverb, it modifies verb or adjective.	**As an adverb** – modifies a verb – modifies an adjective	**Use** the room **to read** your note. I am ready **to read** my stories. He is fit **to read** *clear and aloud*.

EXERCISE 8

In the sentences below, underline the infinitive once and infinitive phrase twice; then state the function of each infinitive or infinitive phrase.

1. To eat with kings is considered as special blessing.
2. He loves to move about at night.
3. To find a life-changing job is also a difficult job.
4. They are wealthy enough to live on few dollars per day.
5. Ms Massa is a lady to admire and copy for her neatness.
6. Humans are creatures to study carefully.
7. Are you ready to pay for it now?
8. He laughed to satisfy everyone in the party.
9. I will pay to eat and dance for the rest of the day.
10. Now is the time to pray.
11. We have come to mourn our grandparents.
12. The tradition demands us to do so.
13. We bring them to entertain us.
14. To do hard work may be dangerous to your health.
15. They deserve to win the scholarship.
16. To talk like a parrot is what I admire.

17. He has come to disturb us today.
18. Tell them to move backward.
19. Mohamed has come to see us for his arrangement.
20. To be a man is not a day job.

Gerunds and Gerund Phrases

Gerund: This is a verb with '*ing*' ending that functions as a noun. It can function in most of the ways as noun does in a sentence.

Eg: **Dancing** is his hobby. ... ...   *(as subject)*

He loves **dancing**. ... ...   *(direct object)*

Saturdays are his best day for **dancing**.   *(object of preposition)*

His favourite activity is **dancing**.   *(predicate nominative)*

'Dancing' is used in all the sentences above as a gerund.

Gerund Phrase: This is made up of gerund accompanied by a direct object, a noun, an adverb, or a prepositional phrase.

Eg: ***Eating*** complete diet develops the body.   *(gerund + direct object)*

Stage ***dancing*** promotes them. ... ...   *(noun + gerund)*

Story **telling** is his favourite hobby. ... ...   *(noun + gerund)*

Cleaning the compound is part of his duty.   *(gerund + direct object)*

Reading lonely is her best hobby. ... ...   *(gerund + adverb)*

He loves **dancing** on the stage. ... ...   *(gerund + prepositional phrase)*

The groups of words underlined in the sentences are gerund phrases. In each phrase, the word in boldface is a gerund, the others are its modifiers.

Like gerund alone, a gerund phrase functions as subject, direct object, object of preposition or predicate nominative in sentence.

Eg: *Studying for an examination* is not easy. (***subject***)

Paul has started *reading for the exam*. (***direct object***)

<u>*Reading many books*</u> *helped him to do better* in the exams. (**subject of the sentence**)

His biggest problem is *reading aloud.* (**as predicate nominative**)

Note that any word that ends with (ing) may function as a verb, a participle or a gerund.

Eg: He is running. (*Running* **is part of the verb phrase.**)

The running water overflowed the compound. (*Running* **is a participle modifying water.**)

Running saves him. (*Running* **is a gerund naming what saves him**)

EXERCISE 9

In the sentences below, underline the gerund once and gerund phrase twice; then state the function of each gerund or gerund phrase.

1. Questioning is part of policing.
2. Asking too many questions helps to fish out the truth.
3. Ansumana loves reading romantic novels.
4. Keen listening and careful writing make a journalist effective.
5. What all coaches want is winning matches.
6. I stopped writing my examination on Friday.
7. They started smoking when I was not born.
8. Dancing will make people famous in the society.
9. He is paid for teaching in two schools.
10. Gossiping is killing.
11. Laughing to people is equal to healing their wounds.
12. Lying to people is similar to stealing their belongings.
13. Watching and peeping are part of his crime.
14. Drinking and smoking are not part of fasting.
15. She loves singing for God and dancing in the club.
16. Diving and swimming are his best hobbies.
17. Her best events are running and jumping.
18. Laughing the old man put them into trouble.
19. Finishing the race was everyone's target.
20. Bringing people together is our aim.

Appositive and Appositive Phrase

Appositive is a Latin word meaning 'to put near or next to'. In grammar, it is a noun or a noun-equivalent that is placed next to another noun or pronoun to identify, rename or explain it. Although the appositive and appositives phrases are not modifiers, yet they function as adjective; in that they add detail information that makes the noun or a pronoun specific or distinct.

Eg: Dr. Jammeh, *the president,* was on TV last night.
Ai-Gbahan's first drama, *Cutting the Chains*, is on the table.
Mr. Tamba, *our class teacher*, was not in school yesterday.
My beautiful wife, *Massa Sama*, is very hard working.

Please note that appositive and predicate nominative perform similar grammatical function in some respect, but they are not the same. Their major difference lies in the way they separate from the noun they specify. An appositive is separated from the word it specifies by comma (,), while the predicate nominative is separated from the word it specifies by a linking verb. Observe the examples below.

Tee Boy, the tailor, will come tomorrow.   **(appositive)**
Tee Boy **is** the tailor; he will come tomorrow.   **(predicate nominative)**
Mrs. Aruna, our teacher, has bought a car.   **(appositive)**
Mrs. Aruna **is** our teacher; she has bought a car.   **(predicate nominative)**

Appositive phrase: This is made up of appositive plus the words that modify it; and makes its meaning more specific and clear. The modifiers in the appositive phrase could be an adjective or an adjective-equivalent that is placed next to the appositive to add information or details.

Eg: **Mr. Bassie, the principal** *of the school,* **is addressing the pupils.**
Mama Fatou, the mother *of the young girl,* **is laughing.**
J. B. Jammeh, the former president *of this nation,* **will come back one day.**
Adam and Eve, the first people *God made,* **were pure and holy.**

EXERCISE 10

In the sentences below, underline the appositive once and appositive phrase twice; then circle the word (s) each renames or identifies.

1. We met him, the prize winner, on our way to the school.
2. The boy you told us about, Jusu, is in town.
3. The subject matter, condemnation of drug abuse, is in place.
4. The two hills, Maamba and Turgboo, are in Sierra Leone.
5. We met him, the principal, on our way to the school.
6. His autobiography, At Last, won him award in the 80s.
7. I want to spend the holiday with parents in my village, Fandou.
8. 1975, the year I was born, was graceful year for my family.
9. Paulina, our prefect, will be with our English teacher, Mr. V. Bangali.
10. The president visited two schools, Methodist and National.
11. The highest mountain, Maamba, is very close to my village.
12. They informed the chief, man of the people, about our party.
13. In the book, Simplify English Grammar, grammar is simplified.
14. Cutting the Chain, a drama written by Paul, is very interesting.
15. We saw cobra, the worst tropical snake on earth, in the forest.
16. Mohamed Kallon, Sierra Leonean international footballer, is generous.
17. Baba Alpha, a very faithful Muslim, has become a born-again pastor.
18. Massa Sama, the wife of the writer, is very beautiful.
19. Foday Sankoh, the leader of RUF rebels, died at the end of the war.
20. He obtained a degree, BA Education, from the prestigious Njala University.

Clauses

A clause is a group of related words that contain a subject and a predicate. There are two types of clauses. They are independent and subordinate clauses.

Independent Clause: This is also known as a main clause. It is a group of words with subject and predicate that can express a complete thought. A main clause can stand by itself as a simple sentence. Eg:

He is my brother.	She has your books.
We shall go home.	They will eat some food.
They are dancing.	We fought them like rebels.

An independent clause may be joined with a coordinating conjunction and a comma, as in the following examples:

The distance is long, so we'd better leave earlier.
The referee called the player, and gave him a yellow card.

Dependent Clause: This is also known as a subordinate clause. This type of clause is a group of related words with subject and predicate that cannot stand on its own and express a complete thought. Subordinate clauses are equivalent to one word. This means that they can function as a single part of speech in a sentence. To understand the meaning of a subordinate clause, and it must be linked with the main clause. Subordinate clauses are most often introduced by subordinating conjunctions,.

Common Characteristics or Features of Subordinate Clauses

a) All subordinate clauses are made up of a group of related words
b) The group of words must contain subject and predicate (finite verb).
c) Every subordinate clause is equivalent to a single word; in other words, it functions as single part of speech.
d) They cannot express a complete sense.
e) Adverbial, adjectival or relative clause always appear in complex and compound complex sentences only.
f) These three clauses will never be part of the simple sentence; instead, they modify a word in the simple sentence.
g) Noun clause is always part of the sentence, and if it is omitted, the meaning of the sentence will not be complete.

Few examples of subordinate or dependent clauses include the following:

1. *who came from Freetown last week*
2. *that you bought yesterday*
3. *when they ring the bell*
4. *if they want my friend*
5. *whoever comes around*
6. *whatever you want*

These groups of words above cannot express a complete idea and therefore do not make meaning when used in this form. We can only understand the meaning of dependent clause when we join it with an independent clause.

1. He is my <u>brother</u> ***who came from Freetown last week***.
2. She has the <u>book</u> ***that you bought yesterday***.
3. ***When they ring the bell***, we <u>shall go</u> home.
4. ***If they want my friend,*** they will call him.
5. Give the card to ***whoever comes around.***
6. ***Where his mother was working*** is very far from here.
7. I know the place ***where his mother was working***
8. I will do ***whatever you want.***

Types of Clauses

The types of clauses are noun clause, adjective clause, relative clause and adverb clause. Note that subordinate clauses are named by their functions in sentences. A clause is referred to as a noun clause when it plays the role of a noun in a sentence. It is called adjectival clause when it describes a noun or a pronoun in a sentence. It is an adverbial clause if it modifies a verb, adjective or other adverb. A relative clause is a subordinate clause that is introduced by a relative pronoun. It can function as a noun, an adjective or an adverb.

Noun Clause

When any subordinate clause functions as a noun, it is called a noun clause. It serves as part of sentence, so when it is cut off from it, part of the information the sentence conveys will be lost.

What we experienced was terrible.

I will tell you ***what you have never heard.***

Noun clause functions in the sentences as:	Examples
Subject	*Whatever you do* is not your business.
direct object	You must bring <u>whoever you choose</u> to *the meeting.*
object of the preposition	The waiter talked to *who was waiting around*.
predicate nominative	The final is *whatever you say*.
direct object	My father decided *which university I was to attend*.
Subject	*Where he placed the pen* was a mystery to everyone.
object of the preposition	Pass on the information to *whomever you meet*.
predicate nominative	What you wanted to hear was *what he said*

EXERCISE 11

In the sentences below, underline the noun clauses and state their grammatical function as they are used in the sentence.

1. My parents have to decide who should be my wife.
2. I was asked to choose where we should visit.
3. We saw the hole in which he dropped the pen.
4. You decide how you want to spend your money.
5. The truth is what you told me in the meeting.
6. Where she spent the night was unknown to all of us.
7. Every Muslim must have faith in whatever the Quran says.
8. What you told me about him is fact.
9. Children will believe whatever their teachers say.
10. The madman remembered where he lived and worked.
11. What I do with my money is not your business.
12. The final is what they agreed on in the meeting.
13. The way Jesus cured the blind man was a mystery to everyone.
14. Tom told us what the problem in the village was.
15. They showed us the hole in which the rat entered.
16. Even if she fails should not border you.

17. The way the case was judged beat everyone's imagination.
18. Whatever you may need should be taken along.
19. People will talk about whatever you do or say.
20. Pass on the news to whomever you meet on the way.

Adjectival Clause

An adjectival clause is a subordinate clause that modifies a noun or a pronoun. An adjective clause does the work of adjective, and unlike any other subordinate clauses, adjectival clauses are introduced either by a pronoun or by an adverb only.

Eg: The man _we met at the gate_ has gone home.
The man you sent me to was attending a meeting.
We saw the place _where the animal was killed_.
They voted out the prefect _they elected last year_.

Relative Clause

Relative clause is another type of adjectival clause. Both perform the same function as they modify a noun or a pronoun. A relative clause also functions as an adverbial clause. They are introduced by one of the relative pronouns: (**who, whom, that, which,** or **whose.)** A relative clause immediately follows the word it modifies just as an adjective does. It does not often appear in the simple sentence, except when it functions as a noun clause. It modifies word (s) in the simple sentence.

Relative clause function as adjective

Eg: I talked to our teacher that we met yesterday.
I brought the pen which you sent for me.
The man who came here this morning is my friend.
Did you talk to the man whom you were told about?
The girl, whose bicycle was stolen, reported to the police station.

Relative clause functions as noun

(It functions as direct object)
It is difficult to decide <u>who my best friend should be</u>.

It functions as direct object
We are told <u>that Pa Boakai has bought a new car</u>.

It functions as object of preposition
We saw the hole through <u>which the snake entered</u>.

Relative clause as adverb

I pray <u>that Chelsea wins the Premier League trophy</u>.
We hope <u>that God will save this world from terrorism</u>.

The underlined group of words qualify the verbs **hope** and **pray** in the respective sentences. Both answer the question **how,** about the words **hope** and **pray.**

EXERCISE 12

In the sentences below, both adjectival and relative clauses are underlined. Identify them and state their function.

1. We walked through the farm <u>where they were working</u>.
2. They told us about the man <u>we met in the farm today</u>.
3. The new phone <u>which you bought for me</u> cannot function properly.
4. He said students <u>who failed the exams</u> have been sent off.
5. The woman <u>whom you were sent to</u> passed here this afternoon.
6. The boy <u>whose pen you borrowed</u> will call you tomorrow.
7. This is the trader <u>that gave us the stolen phone</u>.
8. We showed them the street <u>where he lives</u>.
9. I got the phone <u>which you send for me</u>.
10. No one wants to see the murderer <u>who slaughtered the baby</u>.

EXERCISE 13

In the sentences below, identify adjectival or relative clause and state its function.

1. The boy who told me about you has come.
2. Paul who wrote this book is my friend.
3. We saw the hero that saved the nation.
4. The Lord that lives for all is great.
5. I saw the boy we met in the library.
6. I've been to Fandu where the hero was born.
7. We talked to the man he told us about.
8. He showed us the house where the writer grew up.
9. The girl who attends WAIS has won prize.
10. The book you bought is very interesting.
11. The greatest law God made is love for one another.
12. I read the book which was written by Paulina.
13. The man, whose death was announced, was very brave.
14. What we saw was beyond everyone's expectation.
15. We showed them the road that was safer.

Adverbial Clause

This is a subordinate clause that functions as an adverb, and it answers one of the following questions *(How? When? Where? Why? To what extent? How much? or Under which condition?)* about the word it qualifies. In other words, it specifies or throws more light on the meaning of the word it qualifies by stating time, place, reason, in which manner or to what extend it occurs. Note that adverb clause can be introduced by subordinating conjunctions, and can take various positions in sentences. When it comes at the beginning of a sentence, it must be separated from the main sentence by a comma.

I feel <u>as if I am the best</u>.	*(It answers the question **how?**)*
I will call you <u>after Juma prayer</u>.	*(It answers the question **when?**)*
We will eat <u>where we find food.</u>	*(It answers the question **where?**)*

I have more to do since <u>I didn't work last</u>. (*It answers the question **why?***)

If <u>you pay attention</u>, you will understand me. (*It answers the question **under which condition?***)

The game *played* <u>where we went yesterday</u>.

We *went* <u>where we were not expected</u>.

He *danced* <u>because he was tipsy</u>.

She *would have sung* <u>if she was happy</u>.

Here are few subordinating conjunctions that often introduce adverbial clause: *after, although, as, as if, as long as, as much as, as soon as, as though, because, before, even if, even though, how, if, inasmuch as, in order that, lest, now that, provided, since, so that, that, though, till, unless, until, when, whenever, where, wherever, while* etc.

EXERCISE 14

Underline the adverbial clauses and circle the word or words each clause modifies in the sentence.

1. When the game ended, we slowly walked back home.
2. I have contributed though you did not inform me.
3. We worked as if we were slaves from North Africa.
4. You must respect her since she is your mother.
5. As soon as you finish the exam, you will be given the ticket.
6. They came around as if they were invited.
7. She can't do it because there is no money to pay her.
8. Before you and mother came, they had fought twice.
9. She must read her book even if I am not around.
10. We can go where they were working last week.
11. I am implementing it as it was planned.
12. If the people want you to come, they will call you.
13. We will vote him out when we meet next week.
14. Let's eat the apple of wisdom since we are alone here.
15. Spread the mat if you want the fruit of knowledge.
16. He did the work while I was sleeping.

17. Unless you show me the man, I will not give you the message.
18. Whenever they arrive, the classes will start.
19. While we are waiting, let us prepare the agenda for the meeting.
20. He is a good coach inasmuch as he can take a team from zero to hero.

Where

The word *where* can introduce all subordinate clauses. When it introduces a noun clause, the clause will serve as part of a sentence; meaning, the idea the sentence conveys will not be completed if it is omitted. When it introduces an adjectival clause, it modifies a noun or a pronoun; while it qualifies/specifies a verb or an adjective when it introduces an adverbial clause. Observe the sentences below.

a) <u>Where we work</u> is very far from our home.
   (*It introduces noun clause that serves as subject*)

b) I can't dictate to you <u>where you spend your money or time</u>.
   (*It introduces noun clause that serves as direct object*)

c) He showed us the **place** <u>*where* Peter went for the meeting</u>.
   (*It introduces adjectival clause that modifies noun, place*)

d) We saw the **house** <u>*where* she was born and brought up</u>.
   (*It introduces adjectival clause that modifies noun, house*)

e) We **went** <u>*where* the boy was crying</u>.
   (*It introduces adverbial clause that modifies the verb, went*)

f) They **discovered** <u>*where* the treasure was hidden</u>.
   (*It introduces adverbial clause that modifies verb, discovered.*)

NOTE: It is important to note that all phrases and clauses are made up of group of words; however, each functions as single part of speech. The only difference between the part of speech and a phrase or a clause is that a part of speech is made up of single word; while a phrase or a clause is made up of group of words. There is no phrase or clause that is made up of just a word. In other words, a noun phrase or a noun clause performs the same function as a single-word noun does. Adjectival phrase or adjectival clause performs the same function a single-word adjective does. Adverbial phrase or adverbial clause functions as one-word adverb does. The difference between a phrase and a clause is that a clause contains a subject and a verb (predicate); while a phrase contains no subject or verb.

EXERCISE15

In the short passage below, the underlined words are grammatical structures. State the name and function of each as it is used in the passage.

"Who is the man that you were talking to **(1)** <u>when I met you</u>? If you don't tell me, I will not talk to you again and I will not do your assignment." Ousma, **(2)** <u>who has dropped out of school</u>, threatened Isatou, **(3)** <u>his girlfriend</u> that he has wasted too much time and money on. "If you don't have any trust in me any longer, tell me and I will leave you in peace." Slowly and calmly, **(4)** <u>the brilliant beautiful young girl</u> responded to her **(5)** <u>admired</u> better-half's threat. The tall sling fair coloured Wolof-Jular boy with broad smile plastered on his lips, walked slowly and majestically towards Isatou; he hugged and kissed her on the jaw. **(6)** <u>In the dark corner of the street</u>, feelings were touched and awoken while mellowing in heat slippery love. Thick blanket of quietness befell the two teenagers **(7)** <u>committing matrimonial crime</u>. After about two-minute period of transgression, voices were heard in low tones. "I love you." "I will die for you." They told each other. Bright shiny light returned and quickly absorbed the thick darkness and quietness that had befallen the two greens. **(8)** <u>What benefit they enjoyed from the transgression</u> kept them warm and at ease.

"When are you going to submit this assignment?" Ousma asked. "**(9)** <u>On the day</u> I gave you this assignment, I told you that youshould submit it on Wednesday; that's tomorrow. Since then you have not done anything. You just promised me a moment ago that you are going home with me **(10)** <u>to do the assignment</u>. Just after, you are now asking me this question?" Isatou angrily responded. "Honey, don't worry. Give me the book. Which subject is it?" He carelessly asked again. "So you did not even open this book, or watch on the cover? It is an Economics book." "Hmm? Then don't worry. That Ogar man **(11)** <u>in your school</u> doesn't know anything. Go, write any rubbish and give him. He doesn't read those books. He will mark it and give you grade." "Please Ousma, don't tell me that. Give me my book! Give me my book! Give me my book!" **Clink clank, clink clank, clink clank"** Ousma's Iphone rang. The two departed.

EXERCISE 16

In the short passage below, the underlined words are grammatical structures. State the name and function of each as it is used in the passage.

There is a small village called Manyagbah. This village is located in the middle of the Garden of Eden. This small village **(1)** <u>which is under the control of female,</u> produces all the heroes and heroines **(2)** <u>in this universe</u>. Around the village, grows very thick black and white forest that never dies. Like all communities, **(3)** <u>when it is night</u>, the village becomes very dark. Within the village itself is heat, smooth, and painted pink like in the mouth of a **(4)** <u>newly born baby</u>. This village is always moist or wet. Even though one of the major troubles in this world is attached to it, yet still every man wants to go and live there because of the natural enjoyment and comfort there. It is also interesting to know that everyman in this universe always labours for their wellbeing throughout their lives.

One day, Pa Henwa, **(5)** <u>the chief of the village</u>, had a very serious quarrel with his elder son, **(6)** <u>Njombobla</u>, concerning the village. Pa Henwa marries the woman that controls Manyagbah. On that very day, Njombobla **(7)** <u>working in the farm</u>, was advised by his father to stop the perpetual entry into the village **(8)** <u>at night</u>. He advised his son to use his idea **(9)** <u>to develop himself</u> since the trouble of the village has become a universal problem. According to his father, Njombobla spends too much time and money on this **(10)** <u>troubled</u> village. The boy wants to enter into the village and eating the *fruit of knowledge* always. "Daddy, Manyagbah is a home of every man. Our people say home is home and there is no place like home.

With all the suffering attached to this village, every day you work for her and you have never failed to enter there, except when you are sick. Why are you advising me to stop the perpetual entry into the village?" Njombobla asked his father. "I will not answer that question. But you must know that **(11)** <u>to work for this village</u> needs perfect skill and experience. **(12)** <u>What you do with your time and money</u> is not my business. I won't advise you again." His father angrily concluded.

CHAPTER 6

SENTENCE STRUCTURE

A sentence is a group of related words that expresses a complete thought or sense. In other words, a sentence is a basic unit of thought or idea that conveys a complete message. Every sentence has two essential parts: They are subject and predicate. Every sentence in English must start with a capital letter and end with one of the following end marks: a period (.), a question mark (?) or an exclamation mark (!)

    a)   Peter works as a social secretary for Ndegbormei Association.
    b)   Do you know that beautiful woman, Mrs. Lahai?
    c)   Stop lying, I'm not stupid!
    d)   Could you tell Mum that I want to see her?

Types of Sentences according to their Functions

Sentences can be classified according to what they do in communication. Based on this, there are four kinds of sentences. They are declarative, interrogative, imperative and exclamatory.

Declarative Sentence: This is a sentence that makes statement or gives information about something, somebody, event etc. A declarative sentence always ends with a period.

My grandfather was the oldest man in our village.
I will go home to visit my friend after school.
The two giants of the class are not in school.

Interrogative Sentence: This is a sentence that is used to ask a question or make requests for information, and it ends with question mark. Apart from WH questions, most other interrogative sentences often begin with verb. (WH questions are questions that are introduced by **who, whom, which, what, whose** and **how.**)

Where are your parents going to spend the holiday?
Who owns the beautiful house in the village?
Are there many boys in your class?

Imperative Sentence: This type of sentence is used to make requests or to give simple instructions or commands, and it ends with a period.

Let's turn right and walk faster.
Stand over there and pay attention.
Give me some cold water to drink.

Exclamatory Sentence: An exclamatory sentence is use to convey or express strong feelings, such as joy, fear, surprise, excitement, tiredness, dismay or sorrow; and ends with an exclamation mark.

Stop talking in class!
Run faster, you are late!
Stand there and listen!
What a reckless driver he is!

Note that most often, imperative and exclamatory sentences start with verb and they contain no overt subject. The subject is often understood from the context.

EXERCISE 1

Classify the sentences below as declarative, imperative, interrogative or exclamatory.

1. Was Papa Nukwu a traditional healer?
2. Papa is so strict that he hasn't mercy on even his father.
3. What fanatic attitude displayed by Papa in the book!
4. Does Papa's behaviour resemble a true Christian?
5. Read this sentence aloud for us to hear.
6. Oh! What a gruesome road accident!
7. There are more boys on the street than girls.

8. Where are the boys that came from Kenema for the game?
9. Remember to feed the birds and the goats in the noon!
10. Tell them to wait for me when they come.

Types of Sentences Classified according to their Structures

Sentences are also classified according to the number and type of clauses they are made up of. Thus, four types of sentences can be distinguished based on their structure. These include simple, compound, complex and compound- complex sentences.

Simple Sentence: A simple sentence has only one independent clause with no subordinate clause.

A good teacher helps his pupils.
Good students work hard to pass examinations.
My friend's best hobby is hunting.

A simple sentence may have a compound subject, a compound predicate, or both.

The congregation sings and dances in the church.
Amie and Mujeh go to school together.
The man and his children are working and talking.
Paul and Massa are reading and writing.

EXERCISE 2

Underline the simple sentences in the complex sentences below.

1. When I was in university, I had many friends.
2. Summa was very kind and hardworking, but James was unserious.
3. Hassan is very handsome and he is always smartly dressed.
4. Whenever there were ladies around, Peter appeared happy.
5. Sheriff sucks the chest apple if it is available.
6. Female's apples are full of happiness and long life.

7. Whenever Bangali was allowed to play the game, he would pay money.
8. Bockarie banks his money in treasure hole.
9. Fana perpetually checks in the devil's hole if he is alright.
10. He who keeps my laws shall prosper and be safe on Judgment day.
11. Jekujar saw the hole in which the snake entered at night.
12. John is my friend but he does not visit me frequently.
13. The holy men are God's friends though some will not see heaven.
14. The man who is called Fomba is the head of the institution.
15. We went to the farm where they were working.

EXERCISE 3

Add the subjects to the groups of words below to form simple sentences. (open)

1. _____was not too happy about it.
2. _____ is always sad.
3. _____tell you to come here?
4. _____were the students.
5. _____goes to church on Sunday with him.
6. _____ fought the war and killed.
7. _____bought for the car.
8. _____ are going to USA.
9. _____ believes he is the among others.
10. _____ advise those owners of the shop.
11. _____am right to talk to them.

Exercise 4

Add the complete predicates to the groups of words below to form simple sentences. (open)

1. All the men in the village _____
2. My late father _____
3. Fodei and I _____
4. They _____

5. Binta and her sister_____

6. Even the chairman and he _____

7. They _____

8. You_____

9. Aminata with her sister _____

10. Everyone in the city _____

11. Mr Lamina, our History teacher_____

12. Mum and Dad _____

13. Our government _____

Compound Sentence: This kind of sentence has two or more independent clauses or simple sentences that are joined by a coordinating conjunction or a comma or both; and it has no subordinate clause.

The boys were in class and the girls were dancing outside.
My father went to work but my mum stayed home to prepare food.

The simple sentences in the compound sentence are sometimes joined by a comma and always a coordinating conjunction (*and, but, or etc.*)

I went to university and I studied linguistics.
I either pay the money or remain in school, or I hold onto it and return home.
We came for the training but our coach was not around.
Charles Taylor is not one of us but he was blamed for our war.

Complex Sentence: A complex sentence is made up of one independent clause and at least one subordinate clause.

My dad will soon return home *after he finishes the meeting in school.*
Any time mother is ready, we shall have our dinner.
The man *who is sitting in the blue car* is my good friend.
(The groups of words in italics in the examples are subordinate clauses)

EXERCISE 5

Identify the complex sentences in the short passage below. Underline the simple sentence and circle the subordinate clause in each complex sentence.

Paul loves Massa because she is beautiful and mannered. He was not too happy when she did not positively respond to his proposal of marriage at the beginning. When she went to Kenema on holiday, he actually confessed to Moses that Massa's love was killing him. Moses was always with him to encourage him. Massa hosts Paul's treasures of comfort, happiness, peace and satisfaction. If this angel did not love him, he may become crazy. True love is good but sometimes it kills. Please honey; love Paul because he truly loves you. I pray that God will make and bless their love because God is love. Lovers have loved and lovers still love, but no one has ever loved his lover the way Paul loves Massa. When their waters are put together, it can produce angels that will rule the universe. When the two bloods are mixed together, it will be equivalent to precious holy water that heaven dwellers drink. So God, let it be your will to bring these lovers together so that they will make Paradise on earth.

Compound-complex Sentence: A compound-complex sentence has two or more independent clauses and one or more subordinate clauses.

    a)   I will write my story and Matta will read her novel when we reach home.

    b)   Dad talks and punishes us but mum does nothing when we go home late.

    c)   When they rang the bell, the teachers went for a meeting and the pupils went home.

    d)   Nobody sustained injury, but several houses were destroyed and a large plantation burned down when the petrol tanker burst into flame.

EXERCISE 6

Underline the compound-complex sentences in the short passage below and write TEN compound-complex sentences on your own.

When you called me, I was near the baby that was sleeping. Mum was busy and dad was sleeping while I was taking care of the baby. I actually wanted to come, but there was no way. I received the letter and I understood the contents when I went through it. I know about the meeting but I will not attend it because John will be there. I will call you and explain certain things to you when I am chanced; but you have to exercise patient. I am afraid yet I need to tell you the truth any time we see. Bye.

EXERCISE 7

Add compound sentence to each subordinate clause below to form compound complex sentence. (open) Eg: when the rain stopped

*I received your call and I came around **when the rain stopped.***

1. because she is beautiful
2. if we all win the tickets
3. when he asked me
4. if you want it
5. where we went
6. since you were not around
7. because he is my friend
8. as soon as we arrived
9. where the people were working
10. yet still he is here

Parts of a Sentence

Every sentence has two main parts, the subject and the predicate. There are three kinds of subjects and three kinds of predicates. Complements are also other essential elements of sentences. They are all discussed in detail in this chapter.

Subject: This is one of the main parts of any sentence. It is defined as a noun, a pronoun or noun equivalent that performs the action that is expressed by an action verb. It can also be defined as a noun or a pronoun that the sentence is about. In any subject-verb-order sentence, subject comes before the verb or verb phrase. The three types of subjects include simple subject, complete subject and compound subject.

Simple Subject: This is the essential noun or pronoun within the subject of a sentence. It often serves as the main word within the subject that cannot be left out.

Complete Subject: This is made up of a simple subject plus all other words in the subject section (modifiers). It tells who or what the sentence is about, or who or what performs the action expressed by the verb in the predicate section.

The tall black **boy** sings every day in our class.
The best **player** in the school has won the most precious prize.
The two **boys** that came around are my best friends in town.
The **news** you heard about our school this morning is not true.

All the underlined words in each sentence constitute the complete subject, the words in boldface are the simple subjects. The underlined words modify the simple subject in each sentence.

EXERCISE 8

Underline complete subject and circle the simple subject in each sentence below. Note that each compound or complex sentence contains more than a simple subject.

Eg: The **stories** about his journey make his novel very exciting.

1. Tamba Tengbeh of 22nd July Academy is also a writer of a literature text.
2. My favourite story in that book is 'A Sound of Thunder'.
3. The main character in the story is called Mr. Michael Henchard

4. For five dalasi, Mr. Dolington danced and laughed like a mad man.
5. The only woman in the house is preparing food for the workers.
6. On the football pitch, the trouble within the team started.
7. Because of one mistake, the laws of our land were totally changed.
8. The result of the mistake affected the future generation.
9. In our school, two hardworking teachers from university resigned.
10. With his wife, Kailahun's hero for this year, travelled for sixty days.
11. In 1975, the great writer was born in Kailahun district.
12. Fodei lived on forest birds and animals in Sierra Leone.
13. At the time, this short and tiny man was a refugee in Guinea.
14. Kpana's father was also a local tailor in Fandu village.
15. Not everyone, but the tall black boy will not enter here.
16. The old teacher attended secondary school in Kailahun.
17. In Nyandehun, there is a tall mountain called Mamba.
18. His elder brother must be given a copy of the document.
19. The new green book contains Poems, essays and stories about angles.
20. John Peter Moon of The Gambia wrote about his journey.

Compound subject: This is made up of two or more simple subjects that are connected by a conjunction such as *and, but* or *or* and have the same verb. Note that modifiers of simple subject could not be considered as part of the compound subject.

The tall boy, <u>John</u> and his sister, <u>Mary</u>, sing every day in our class.
The <u>players</u> of the school and the <u>fans</u> have won the most precious prize.
(The underlined words in the examples are the compound subjects.)

EXERCISE 9

Underline the compound subjects in the sentences below

1. The national park and the museum are the tourist sites in Sierra Leone.
2. The Macarthy Square and Buffer Zone are places people visit.
3. Water and other natural forces are agents of erosion.

4. Last year, Musu and Karim were best of friends in our class.
5. This evening, the two girls and their mother were walking along the road.
6. Sinners and non-sinners are all made in the image of God.
7. Days and nights are part of God's arrangement of His creation.
8. All the boys in the village and the girls around are my fans.
9. God and Satan together started the creation of existence.
10. To watch matches and to write stories are my best hobbies.
11. Musicians, footballers and drug traffickers make much money.
12. My father and all the families are very happy about my performance.
13. Farmers and teachers are most often looked low upon in African.

Predicates

Predicate: This is the part of a sentence that contains information about the subject. The main word in a predicate is either a verb or a verb phrase. Words within the predicate play different functions to relate or state information about the subject. There are three types of predicate. They include simple, complete and compound predicates

Simple Predicate: This is the essential verb or a verb phrase within the predicate. It is the main word in the predicate that cannot be left out in any sentence.

The tall beautiful girl <u>ran</u> across the street.
The best player in the school <u>has won</u> the most precious prize.
(The underlined words in the examples are the simple predicates)

A Complete Predicate: This is made up of a verb or a verb phrase, plus any modifier, complement or both. It tells what the subject of the sentence is, feels or does. In other words, complete predicate is made up of all the words in the predicate section.

The tall black boy **sings** *every day* <u>in our class</u>.
The best player in the school **has won** <u>the most precious prize.</u>

The underlined words in the examples above are the complete predicates. In the first sentence, the complete predicate contains verb, adverb and a prepositional phrase. The phrase functions as adverbial phrase. In the second sentence, the complete predicate contains verb phrase and a noun phrase which functions as a direct object.

Compound Predicate: This is made up of two or more simple predicates (verbs or verb phrases) that are joined by a coordinating conjunction (*and* or *or*) and have the same subject.

The beautiful girl <u>claps and dances</u> always in our village.
The best player in the school <u>has visited and thanked</u> the school authorities.

(The underlined words in the examples are compound predicates)

When either the simple subject or the simple predicate is absent in any sentence, that sentence is referred to as a ***fragment***.

EXERCISE 10

In each sentence in the passage below, underline the complete predicates and circle the simple predicate (s).

(1) Papa Nnukwu, Aunty Ifoema and her daughter, Ameka, have many things in common. (2) All of them love the tradition of their ancestors. (3) The pressure from Papa does not let anyone of them to deviate from the culture. (4) Papa Nnukwu refuses to adhere to Papa's promises for the sake of his traditional worship. (5) Aunty Ifoema studies and lectures African Studies in the university because of her love for tradition. (6) Her love for the traditional music shows that Ameka loved the African tradition. (7) All the three characters are also hard hearted. (8) Ameka and her mother are the most admirable characters in the novel. (9) The writer makes the two characters complete feminist in the story. (10) Aunty Ifoema refuses to become a reverend sister as Papa had wanted her to be before buying her a car. (11) Another issue to know is the importance of grammar (12) Grammar plays important roles in English Language learning. (13) In the

1870's it was included in the syllabus of English Language. (14) During English classes in my days in school, we learnt a lot about grammar. (15) Many English teachers ignore teaching of grammar these days. (16) School like Nusrat Senior Secondary, does not test the students on it; it is never part of their examinations. (17) Many a time, pupils study grammar without much understanding. (18) In the end-of-year exams, very few pupils pass the subject. (19) The best teacher for the subject was called Mr. Grammar. (20) After his death in the 1830's, the subject was named after him.

EXERCISE 11

Underline each compound predicates in the sentences below.

Eg: The pupils in my class sing and dance every day.

Ans: sing and dance

1. Papa disowned and abandoned his father, Papa Nnukwu.
2. His father believed and worked for the traditional gods.
3. Ameka drew beautiful objects and then painted them magnificently.
4. Have you heard or learn about the football game?
5. Jaja and Kambili spent little time but learnt a lot of new ideas at Nsukka.
6. Chelsea used the best players and won the trophy in 2012.
7. Aunt Ifoema and her children will laugh and sing happily.
8. A relative called and told Aunty Ifoema about Papa Nnukwu's ill-health.
9. Papa Nnukwu was loved and cared for by his daughter.
10. Papa fervently prayed and strictly disciplined his children.

Complements

Complements are other essential parts of a sentence. A complement is defined as a word or group of words that helps to complete the ideas started by subject or verb. There are four different kinds of complements. They are subject complements, direct objects, indirect objects and object complements. Note that all complements are found in the predicate section of a sentence.

Subject Complement: This is a noun or an adjective that appears after a linking verb, and it renames, explains or describes the subject of a sentence. There are two types of subject complements. They are predicate nominative and predicate adjective.

A **predicate nominative:** This is a noun, noun equivalent or pronoun that appears after a linking verb and it renames, or explains the subject of sentence.

Eg : Amie A. Lahai is <u>our class captain</u>.

(*our class captain* is a noun phrase (**predicate nominative**) that identifies or renames the subject of the sentence, *Amie A. Lahai*)

1. Sir Dauda Jawara was the former <u>president</u> of the Gambia.
2. Mr. Peipon and Mrs. Mansaray are our English <u>teachers</u>.
3. The old men in the car were the <u>chiefs</u> in our village years ago.
4. Mrs. Njie is the vice <u>president</u> of this nation.
5. I am the <u>hero</u> for this game.
6. You are the <u>head</u> of the group that will work tomorrow.

All the underlined words in the examples above are predicate nominatives. They help to complete the ideas about their respective subjects by telling who or what they are.

EXERCISE 12

Underline the predicate nominatives of the sentences below.

1. Massa is a queen to that mad lover.
2. His happiness and satisfaction is she.
3. My mother and father are the elders and great contributors.
4. He and others are the owners of the nightclub.
5. Who told you that John was our choice for the leadership?

6. Peace and freedom is what everybody wants.
7. The secretary and the organizer is my father.
8. Charles Fowlis is the first school I taught in the Gambia.
9. I am the only true choice of the queen of the angels.
10. They were my friends from Njala University.

A **predicate adjective:** It is an adjective that appears after a linking verb and it describes the subject of the sentence.

Eg:

This man is **old**.
That girl is **beautiful.**
This boy was **foolish**.

(*old, beautiful, foolish* are adjectives that describe the subject, *man, girl and boy respectively*. Each appears after a linking verb)

That big snake is <u>dangerous.</u>
My mother was <u>famous</u> for her generosity.
These girls are <u>popular</u> among their colleagues.
I am <u>black</u>, <u>tall</u> and <u>huge.</u>
People's power is <u>mightier</u> than any constitution.
We are <u>independent</u> but not <u>free</u>.

The underlined words are predicate adjectives in the respective sentences.

EXERCISE 13

Underline the predicate adjective in the sentences below.

1. My wife is short, black and beautiful.
2. She looks quiet, polite and very brilliant.
3. Her father is highly educated and religious.
4. The rest of the family members are peaceful and admirable.
5. In school, she was clever and serious.

6. Besides her beauty, she is strong and hardworking.
7. Our wonderful God is great and kind to us.
8. My young daughters were stubborn and playful in class.
9. The Dalasi is strong but hard to get and keep.
10. The players of Kailahun United were lost but found.

Direct Object: It is a noun or pronoun that receives the action or shows the result of an action expressed by a transitive verb. It only appears with transitive verbs. It can never follow a linking verb and it will not appear in the prepositional phrase. It answers the question whom? or what? after an action verb.

The big cat killed the *snake*. Killed what? … snake
The boy hit the little *girl* with a stick. Hit whom? … little girl

(*Snake* and *girl* are the direct objects because they receive the actions: *killed* and *hit* respectively.) Each answers one of the questions: killed what? or who?, or hit what? or who?

At times, a verb may have a compound direct object.
The police stopped *the thief* and *the mob*. I killed a snake and a rat.

EXERCISE 14

Circle the direct object in the sentences below.

1. The old buffalo killed the young lamb.
2. That small boy insulted his friend.
3. We send our parents some money every month.
4. My little dog fought an elephant two weeks ago.
5. Our teacher narrated the story about Lovidovy.
6. A perfect gentleman must speak many languages.
7. Play the game let us see.
8. Did you take your books to school?
9. Do we need them for the work?
10. The world needs peace and tranquillity.

EXERCISE 15

Underline the direct object in the passage below.

The first day I saw Massa Sama, I cherished her to be my better-half in future. At the time, I knew nothing about her. As time went on and I understood her better, I grew more love for the beautiful angel. Apart from her beauty and politeness plastered on her face, God displayed His wonderful handwork in her magnificent structure which she maintains with simple but very smart attires. Besides all, she loves and fears God, and respects everyone. When she smiles, she exposes the gap between her stainless teeth which resembles the path leading to Allah's kingdom. Her generosity cannot be underestimated. She is as kind as sun or moon that gives light to both foes and friends alike. Every morning, she takes bath, dresses up, collects her bag and moves to the highway to on-board a vehicle that will take her to her office. I love no one but Miss Sama. So help me God.

Indirect Object:

It is a noun or pronoun that appears with a direct object; and it names the person or thing that something is given to or done for. It comes between the verb and direct object. In some cases it can come after a preposition as a prepositional phrase indirect object. It can only appear with transitive verb. It cannot follow a linking verb. It answers the questions for whom? or what?, or to whom? or what? something is done.

I narrated my ***daughter*** <u>a story</u>.
I wrote my ***dad*** a <u>letter</u>.
I sent ***you*** a nice <u>book</u>.
He bought his ***son*** a very nice <u>pen.</u>

(***Daughter, dad, you*** and ***son*** are the indirect objects inn sentences above. The story was narrated to 'daughter; and 'pen' was bought for son. '*Story*' and 'pen' are the direct objects because they received the action of the transitive verbs, *narrated and bought*.)

To find the indirect object, first be certain that the sentence contains a direct object, and then ask the question *to whom* or *what*, or *for whom* or *what* the action was done.

narrated a story for whom? (my daughter).
bought a nice pen for whom? (my son)

EXERCISE 16

In the sentences below, underline the direct objects and circle the indirect objects.

1. Who bought you the new bicycle you rode yesterday?
2. My elder brother sent me this bicycle from America.
3. Are you talking about the one that you sent him an email?
4. I am going to tell him the story you told me.
5. I don't have enough credit in my phone.
6. Then write him a letter of apology.
7. We can give your grandmother few words of encouragement.
8. Please give me your pen.
9. Sing us the song you learnt in school yesterday.
10. Play Mujeh-mama the latest music in town.

Object Complement:

It is a noun, an adjective, a prepositional phrase or a participial phrase that appears with direct object and it describes or renames the direct object. It helps to complete its meaning in a sentence. This means that object complement appears only in a sentence that has direct object. It appears after verbs such as 'call', 'appoint', 'consider', 'elect', 'make', 'name' etc.

The principal named **Mr. Boima** *chairman.*   (***noun***)

*They named **him** Emmanuel, and later Christ.*   (***noun***)

They elected **Paul** *president.*   (***noun***)

I wrote the **story** *about the devil*	(***prepositional phrase***)
She drew the **picture** *of her friend*.	(***prepositional phrase***)
The artist made the **statue** *magnificent*.	(***adjective***)
Power makes **people** *great and famous*	(***adjective***)
We narrated **the incident** *relating Tom*	(*present participle*)
They know the **issues** *connected to this action*.	(*past participle*)

The underlined words in the sentences are the object complements which help to complete the meanings of the direct objects (bold words) by either renaming or describing them.

EXERCISE 17

In the sentences below, underline the direct objects and circle the object complements.

1. I will tell them the incident relating Momoh.
2. They elected Mr. Fomba president of the association.
3. Please tell your father the message from your grandfather.
4. Write the story about the coat.
5. They appointed Julius Maada Bio flag bearer of the party.
6. Write your uncle the letter about change of plan.
7. He called the hero of the class.
8. Tell the driver of this car to go to the market.
9. Peter, open for the guests the door of the main gate.
10. Have you bought them the attires for the Easter?
11. Did you tell them the message from the head of state?
12. Bring them some water from the freezer.
13. They played the ball of the season.
14. He won the club the best prize of the year.
15. We wrote the chief our report of the investigation

The Five Basic Sentence Structures

A basic sentence is a form of sentence without modifier.

subject verb
a)   Paul won.

subject verb direct object
b)   Paul won prizes.

subject verb indirect object direct object
c)   Paul won his club the prizes.

subject verb subject complement
d)   Paul is great. ... ... *(adjective)*
e)   Paul is a hero. ... ... *(noun)*

subject verb direct object object complement,
f)   Paul made the club famous.

CHAPTER 7

SUBJECT-VERB AGREEMENT

We have discussed the subject and the verb as two principal parts of a sentence. With the exception of the imperative sentence, every sentence must have a subject and a verb. As a grammatical rule, a verb must agree with its subject in number (i.e. singular or plural) and in person (i.e. first, second or third). The examples below illustrate subject verb agreement.

a) The boy is eating.
b) John has a pen.
c) Fatou prays to God.
d) My father was very old.

'Boy', 'John', 'Fatou' and 'father' are singular subjects, so they agree with the singular verbs: 'is', 'has', 'prays' and 'was'.

a) Sowe and Jero were dancing.
b) The girls are crying.
c) They visit us every weekend.
d) We give each other gifts.

'Sowe and Jero', 'girls', 'they' and 'we' are plural subjects, so they agree with plural verbs: 'are', 'were', 'visit' and 'give' respectively.

Note that a phrase or a clause that comes between the subject and its predicate must not affect their agreement. Such phrase or clause is usually set off by comma.

Yusufa, *with several of his friends*, **is** not in class.
Your opinion, *as well as his ideas*, **lacks** support.
Our players, *who enjoy great support*, **have** lost the match.
My daughter, *who enjoys parental love*, **has** lost her chance.
The hero *for all the men in the surrounding villages* **has** died.

When a sentence contains a verb phrase, the helping verb must agree with the subject in number or in person. The helping verbs such as *are, were, have* and *do* must agree with plural subjects such as *we, they* and *you*. *Was, have* and *do* also agree with *I* as singular subject. *Is, was, has* and *does* agree with *he, she* and *it*. *Am* agrees with *I* alone. Modal auxiliary verbs *Will, would, can, could, shall, should, may, might, must* etc. will agree with all subjects.

Saffa and Jusu **are** playing the game.
Seibatu **has** been working for her mother since yesterday.
Daddy **was** sleeping when we reached home.
They **were** eating the mango this morning.

Agreement with Compound Subjects

There are four different rules of agreement with compound subjects that are joined by *and, or* or *nor*.

Rule 1:

The conjunction, *and,* is always equivalent to plus, therefore, when the entities in the compound subject are joined by *and* (whether the entities are all singular, plural or mixed numbers), the subject must agree with a plural verb.

A boy and a girl **are** in class.
The boys and the girls **have** gone to the principal.
One boy and three girls **were** in our class.

However, there are exceptions to this rule. That is, when the entities in the compound subject refer to the same person, animal, thing or place the singular verb is used. Also when the word *each* or *every* precedes singular entity of a compound subject the singular verb is used.

A cup of tea, bread and butter *makes* a delicious breakfast.
The secretary and the treasurer of the school **is** my uncle.
Every boy and girl **was** asked to come to school.
Each man and woman **has** waved flags to the president.

EXERCISE 1

Select a verb in the bracket agrees with the subject in each sentence.

1. Joseph and our father (is, are) happily singing in the car.
2. Fatou and the three boys (has, have) completed the assignment.
3. The men and that boy (was, were) quarrelling yesterday for a dalasi.
4. These girls sitting here and the boys (makes, make) dresses weekly.
5. The manager with some of his workers (is, are) going for a conference.
6. A cup of tea and a loaf of bread (are, is) my best breakfast.
7. BBC and CNN (are, is) the most reliable international media.
8. The chief and the secretary of Deagbormei (is, are) my father.
9. Each man and each boy (was, were) asked to come with the fees.
10. Joe, Paul and Amie (is, are) happy about me.

Rule 2

When singular entities in the compound subject are joined by *or* or *nor,* the subject must agree with singular verb.

John, Peter or Mary *is* not in school today.
Either a cat or a dog *is* a good pet.
Neither the hunter nor his gun *was* at the farmhouse.

Rule 3

Two or more plural entities joined by *or* or *nor* must agree with plural verb.

Either the teachers *or* the pupils *were* in school on Saturday.
Neither the parents *nor* the children *are* happy to attend the party.
Either the chiefs *or* the villagers *have* not noticed his presence.

Rule 4

When a compound subject with singular and plural entities is joined by *or* or *nor*, the verb must agree with the entity that is closer to it.

Either my father *or* my brothers **were** happy about my progress.
Either the workers *or* their manager **is** not in farm today.
Neither my friends *nor* my parents **are** expected in the party.
Neither the boys *nor* a girl **has** passed the examination.

Agreement with collective nouns

A Collective noun is singular in form but plural in meaning. In other words, a collective noun names a group of persons, animals or things, yet the group is referred to as one or single unit. Some examples of collective nouns include *class, audience, team, congregation, mob, club, committee, group, family, choir, jury, staff, flock, troop, swarm, band* etc.

Collective nouns can be singular or plural. This means that, as a subject, a collective noun can agree with both singular and plural verbs. It agrees with singular verb when the members of a set or a group are all referred to as single unit or entity. It agrees with plural verb when it is used to refer to more than one set or group of people or animals. It can also agree with plural verb if the entities in the set/group are individually refereed to; that's when the members act separately from different spots or with different points of view. When the entities in the set/group are individually refereed to, add 'members' to make your idea clear. Observe the examples below:

The class **has** decided to have a Language club. (singular)
The members of the class **were** unable to decide about the election. (plural)
The teams **were** unable to decide on the time for the match. (plural)
The audience **claps** for Emerson when he is on stage. (singular)
The audience **were** divided in their opinions about his performance. (plural)
The members of the audience **were** divided in their opinions about his performance. (plural)
Our senior school team **has** won the match. (singular)
The team **have** different opinions about their coach. (plural)
The team members **have** different opinions about their coach. (plural)
The congregation **has** thrown a send-off party for the outgoing chairman. (singular)

My congregations **are** coming from different churches to grace the party. (plural)

Members of the congregations **are** coming from different churches to grace the party. (plural)

EXERCISE 2

Underline the verbs that best agree with the subject in the sentences below.

1. The family (appears, appear) very generous to us.
2. The club (is, are) not united on the appointment of their leader.
3. The family members (is, are) coming from Togo and Foni for our meeting.
4. The spectators (was, were) cheering and booing at the artist.
5. The committee (was, were) to make unanimous decisions.
6. The team (has/have) taken seats in the bus before the coach arrived.
7. The mob (have/has) set fire on three government buildings.
8. The staff in school (want/wants) the principal to resign next year.
9. The couple (love/loves) and (understands/understand) each other.
10. The staff (has, have) agreed to throw party for the outgoing principal.

Agreement with confused subjects

Confused subjects are found in inverted sentences. A sentence that is not in subject-verb order is referred to as an inverted sentence. In this kind of sentence, the verb comes f before the subject. Most interrogative sentences, or sentences that start with *here* or *there* are inverted sentences. Inverted sentences contain **hard-to-find subject**. Note that even if a subject comes after its verb, the verb must still agree with it in number or in person. One can check the subject-verb agreement in an inverted sentence by mentally rephrasing the sentence in normal subject-verb order.

Among the players in the team **is** *Peter*. ... ... ***inverted sentence***
Peter **is** among the players in the team. ... ... ***subject-verb order sentence***

Beyond our imaginations **was** *his visit.* ... ... ***inverted sentence***
His visit **was** beyond our imaginations. ... ... ***subject-verb order sentence***
Which of the books **have** *you* **read**? ... ... ***inverted sentence***
You **have read** which book. ... ... ***subject-verb order sentence***

Note that when here or there begins a sentence, it signals inverted sentence. So when putting the sentence in normal subject-verb order, the here or there is sometimes not necessary; and can be left out.

There **are** *four mangoes* on the table.
Four mangoes **are** on the table ~~there~~. Or
Four mangoes **are** ~~there~~ on the table.
Here **are** *the books* for John and Mary.
The books for John and Mary **are** here. Or
The book ~~here~~ **is** for John and Mary.
Here **are** *the boys* that fought in the garden.
The boys that fought in the garden **are** here.

Agreement with words that are plural in form

There are some nouns that are plural in form but singular in meaning. Most of these nouns name branches of knowledge. For instance, words like economics, civics, politics, ethics, linguistics, mathematics, physics, acoustics, social studies, news etc. are all plural in form but singular in meaning. When any one functions as subject, it agrees with singular verb.

Linguistics **is** a very nice course. (sing)
Bad politics **destroys** nation. (sing)
Economics **was** my best subject. (sing)
Mathematics **is** very difficult to pass. (sing)

EXERCISE 3

Underline the appropriate verb in the bracket that agrees with the subject of each sentence.

1. The president with his family (are, is) coming to visit us.
2. The man and his wife (has, have) gone home for prayer
3. The owner of the school and the principal (are, is) he.
4. Each boy and girl (was, were) sent home for the school fees.
5. She or they (has, have) not being to London.
6. Either she or I (is, am) not eating a mango now.
7. That girl with her husband (go, goes) to church every Sunday.
8. Either the women or the man (sing, sings) in the church.
9. Neither the boys nor the girls (was, were) ready to accept him.
10. Either they or I (was, were) not given the ok to study in the library.
11. My sister doesn't (has, have) degree but she is happy.
12. Here (is, are) the family we saw in town.
13. You or I (was, were) not there when he came around today.
14. They or Peter (make, makes) him laugh always.
15. My father's driver and my husband (was, were) Pa Abou.
16. Here (is, are) the men that called you this morning.
17. Mr Lahai with his family (eat, eats) mangoes most time.
18. The coach and secretary of the club (are, is) Bubacarr.
19. Neither Jarju nor the students (was, were) in school last week.
20. Horoja and her brother (have, has) bicycles at home.
21. Each man and woman (has, have) to pay the contribution.
22. Every boy and girl (has, have) the right to move about.
23. Neither our father nor our brothers (has, have) come around.
24. Massa, Paul or T-man (has, have) to come for the meeting.
25. Either my mother or father (was, were) in the graduation party.
26. Neimatu, either your friends or your sister (is, are) coming today.
27. Neither the chief nor his son (has, have) the right to control me.
28. Either the girls or the boys (was, were) ready for the job.
29. Either my father or Jusu and Tom (is, are) willing to pay my fees.
30. Either you or I (are, am, is) not hoping to repeat this class.
31. Fatou, Musu or Alice (has, have) to come for training.

32. The men or the boys (has, have) to clean the church.
33. The family members (are, is) coming from Basse, Bakau and Brikama.
34. (Is, Are) he going to school tomorrow?
35. Either the students or the teacher (was, were) not in class.
36. Neither my father nor my mother (has, have) being to Banjul.
37. Either I, Peter or you (was, were) to attend the party.
38. All the men in the club with a lady (has, have) gone to see them.
39. Either the players or their coach (was, were) not around for the training.
40. Fodei, Paul or Amie (is, are) not too known to us.
41. Neither my father nor my brothers (was, were) invited to the party.
42. Both the farmers and the teachers (are, is) less important in our society.
43. Neither prostitutes nor a criminal (are, is) allowed in the party.
44. Neither Muslims, Christians or a pageant (has, have) ever been to hell.
45. The ministers with their deputies (is, are) here for the meeting.

Pronoun-Antecedent Agreement

An antecedent is a noun or a pronoun that another pronoun replaces in a sentence. Like a verb with its subject, a pronoun must always agree with its antecedent in person and number. In addition to this, the third person singular pronoun must agree with its antecedent in gender.

Gender of third person singular pronoun

Masculine	Feminine	Neuter
he, him, his, himself	she, her, herself, hers	it, itself, its

He acquired his degree from Njala University.

In the example above, the pronoun *his* agrees with its antecedent *He*, in number (both are singular), in person, (both are third person), and in gender, (both are masculine).

Agreement with Compound Antecedents

a) Use a singular personal pronoun with a compound antecedent joined by *or* or *nor* if the entities of the antecedents are of similar gender.

Either **Peter** or **Paul** will write **his** exam well.
Neither **Fatou** nor **Bintou** has eaten **her** food.

If the compound antecedents are of different genders, use the respective singular pronouns to agree with them.

Either **John** or **Mary** will bring *his* or *her* books for the studies.

b) Use plural pronoun to agree with compound antecedent whose entities are joined by *and,* irrespective of their genders.

Baldeh and **Jarju** went to the school to collect *their* results.
Musu and **Jeneba** have gone where *they* were called.

Collective noun antecedent agrees with its pronouns

When a collective noun acts as antecedent, it must agree with its pronoun in number. It agrees with singular pronoun if the group is referred to or acted as single unit.

The **team** will play *its* final match today. *(singular)*
The **congregation** will celebrate *its* feast next week. *(singular)*

On the other hand, a **collective noun antecedent** agrees with plural pronoun if the members of the group are referred to or acted individually.

The **team** exchange greetings with *their* opponents. *(plural)*
The **class** discussed *their* experience about the excursion. *(plural)*
The **committee** elected *their* leaders last week.

It is important to note that in most cases, when the pronoun does not agree with its antecedent whether in person, number or gender, it will not make the sentence only grammatically wrong, but it will also change the intended message the sentence conveys.

EXERCISE 4

Choose the appropriate pronoun in the bracket to complete each of the following sentences.

1. John plays with (him/his/her) puppies.
2. Amie demonstrates with (his/her) legs how to dance the style.
3. Joe and (him/his/ he's) sister collected (them/their) results.
4. Many people want (we/them/their) views to be recognized.
5. (We/ Our) are here for (my/our/me) book.
6. She loves (her/she) mother than (him/he).
7. Joseph carries (them/his/her) bicycle to school.
8. Mary loves (I/me) more than (her/she) loves (they/them).
9. They are happy because (them/you/their) mother is here.
10. My plant drops (her/it/its) leaves every week.
11. Everyone has (their/his or her) own problems to solve.
12. Every man and woman will make (his or her/their) own contribution.

CHAPTER 8

COMMON SENTENCE ERRORS

When we speak or write, we use sentences to convey our ideas. The more effective and efficient sentences we use, the clearer and more magnificent our communication will be. There are sets of rules that govern sentence construction which must be followed. It is important to know and be able to identify common errors that will lead to the construction of **faulty sentences**. The sentence faults are common mistakes that affect the smooth running or clear understanding of a given sentence. The seven common sentence errors are *shifting, parallelism, fused sentence, sentence fragment, misuse of modifiers, spelling mistakes and wrong use of technical tools.* Any time anyone of these grammatical crimes is committed, sentence errors is bound to occur; which will affect the smooth flow of our thought **vis-a-vis** our message.

One after the other let us discuss the sentence errors that are mentioned above:

a)   **Shifting:** This is one of the common errors in sentence construction. When writing, many people tend to deviate or shift from one verb tense to the other or from one gender, number or person in pronoun to another.

–   Observe the shift in verb tense:

     *When Dad **was** at home, I **am** sleeping.
     *The police officers **stopped** the driver and **ask** for his license.
     *I will **write** and **sings** music.
     *He **lives** and **worked** for the family throughout is life time.

– Observe the shift in genders, numbers and persons in the sentences below;

1) **She** told me that **his** mother is at home. *shift in gender*
2) **He** has done **her** assignment. *shift in gender*
3) **They** appointed him as **his** leader. *shift in number and person*
4) **Everyone** has paid **his** fees. *shift from indefinite to definite*
5) **Everybody** is asked to reflect on **our** past. *shift in number*

Note that in most cases, the shift in pronoun will not make the sentence grammatically wrong, but it makes its meaning change, or ambiguous.

The correct form of sentences above

1) **She** told me that **her** mother is at home.
2) **He** has done **his** assignment.
3) **They** appointed him as t**heir** leader.
4) **Everyone** has paid **his/her** fees.
5) **Everybody** is asked to reflect on **his/her** past.

b) **Parallelism**: This refers to the use of dissimilar grammatical structures in a sentence. Observe the example below:

* To be kind to people is better than hating them. *(unparalleled expression)*
To be kind to people is better than to hate them. *(correct)*

* Dancing, to write stories and fight are his best hobbies. *(unparalleled expression)*
Dancing, writing and fighting are his best hobbies. *(correct)*

* To dance on stage, to writing stories and to fight battles are his best hobbies. *(parallel)*
To dance, to write and to fight are his best hobbies

*   To be wealthy, music playing and journalism make people popular. *(unparalleled)*

Wealth, music and journalism make people popular. *(parallel expression)*

c) **Fused Sentence:**

A fused sentence is also known as a run-on sentence. It is made up of two or more sentences that is incorrectly punctuated as if it is one sentence. When the technical tools are wrongly used, it will result into the formation of a fused sentence. To correct such mistake, semicolon, comma or comma and conjunction must be used to separate or join the sentences. Observe the example of fused sentence.

a)   Fatou came with biscuits for us at home and she gave me one and I ate it and it was very delicious.
b)   Jarju was tired and he managed to please his mother she was an old and sick and she was a window.
c)   Foe took out two pens from his bag his uncle brought them from Togo and gave him for us.
d)   I went to take an English test but the teacher was not in school and we did not hear from him and we waited but we did not see him.

Observe the correct form of these sentences:

a)   Fatou came with some biscuits for us at home. She gave me one. I ate it and it was very delicious.
b)   Jarju was tired, but he managed to please his mother who was an old sickly window.
c)   Foe took out two pens from his bag and gave us. His uncle brought them from Togo for us.
d)   We went to take an English test, but the teacher was not in school; and we did not hear from him.

d) **Sentence Fragments:**

This is a group of related words with end mark that is without a simple subject or a simple predicate. Also, when a subordinate clause is punctuated as if it a complete thought, it is referred to as a sentence fragment. It does express a confused and incomplete thought. Most fragments are phrases, subordinate clauses or words in series. To avoid fragment, make sure that your sentences contain subjects and verbs, and must express a complete thought.

Sentence fragment Correct Sentence

The tall black in the car is a British. The tall black **man** in the car is a British.
Who that man in the black car? Who **is** that man in the black car?
In this country have more rights. In this country **women** have more rights.
The man that we saw in town. The man that we saw in town has come.
When we arrived in the village. When we arrived in the village, everyone was present.

Positioning of modifiers

Place all modifying words, phrases or clauses as close as possible to the words they modify. If a modifier is placed far away from the word it modifies, the meaning of the sentence cannot be clear. Sometimes modifying words can be mistakenly misplaced in a sentence. Observe how the meaning of this sentence changes when the position of the phrase, *from 22nd July Academy,* changes.

a) The head boy *from 22nd July Academy* represented the school.
b) *From 22nd July Academy,* the head boy represented the school.

In sentence *a*, the prepositional phrase functions as an adjective and it modifies the noun, *head boy*. In sentence *b*, the phrase functions as adverb and it modifies verb, *represented*. It tells from which point or location the head boy is while representing the school. Observe also the position of the phrases and the words they modify in the examples above. When a prepositional phrase functions as an adjective, it stands directly after the word it describes. On the other hand, when a prepositional phrase functions as an adverb, it should be placed near the word (verb/adjective) it describes. Here are more examples.

1a) *That <u>book</u> belongs to the girl **with blue colour. (misplaced modifier)**

1b) That <u>book</u> **with blue colour** belongs to the girl. (**correct sentence**)

2a) *It was <u>announced</u> that the new entertainment centre has been opened <u>in this morning broadcast</u>. (**misplaced modifier**)

2b). *In this morning broadcast,* it was <u>announced</u> that the new entertainment centre has been opened. (**correct sentence**) or

2c) It was <u>announced</u> *in this morning broadcast* that the new entertainment centre has been opened. (**correct sentence**)

In the second sentence of each set of sentences above, '*with blue colour*' and '*in this morning broadcast*' are respectively modifying book and reported. In the first sentence of each set, the modifiers are placed far away from the words they describe. They are misplaced, so they either modify the wrong word, or they modify no word at all. Here are more examples:

* *Stolen from the office*, the minister saw the documents. (**misplaced modifier**)

The minister saw the documents *stolen from the office*. (**correct sentence**)

* *Sleeping in the box*, I saw my neighbour's dog. (**misplaced modifier**)

I saw my neighbour's dog *sleeping in the box*. (**correct sentence**)

* I have been used to wake up early *living with Muslims*. (**misplaced modifier**)

Living with Muslims, I have been used to wake up early. (**correct sentence**)

Do not position your modifier to appear as if it modifies either of the two words. Always place your modifier so that it can clearly describe the word you intend to modify.

e) **Wrong use of modifiers**

Modifiers are words or group of words that are used to describe other words in a sentence, or give additional information about the word it modifies. All adjectives and adverbs are modifiers. They specify or make distinct the meaning of words they describe. When they are effectively used, they make our ideas clear and our language colourful and flamboyant. The effective use of modifiers is guided by some simple rules which need to be understood. The general rule is that a modifier should be placed as close as possible to the word it modifies. When a modifier is placed far away from the word it modifies, it is either misplaced or dangling; it will seem to modify the wrong word or no word at all. Let us look at the two common errors (**misplaced and dangling modifiers.**)

Misplaced modifier: A modifier that seems to modify the wrong word in a sentence is known as a *misplaced modifier.*

Examples of misplaced modifier are as follows:

* Edited by the girl, the chief read the **book**. *misplaced modifier*
  The chief read the **book** edited by the girl. *correctly placed modifier*

* In the blue suit, the tall boy wrote the letter. *misplaced modifier*
  The tall boy in the blue suit wrote the letter. *correctly placed modifier*

* Behind the door, the pot was used to prepare the food for the workers. *misplaced modifier*
  The pot behind the door was used to prepare the food for the workers *correctly placed modifier*

Dangling modifier: A modifier that cannot clearly modify the correct word in a sentence is called a dangling modifier.

Here are some examples of dangling modifiers:

i) Daramy told me *in the afternoon* he will call his mother.

It is not clear whether the phrase, *in the afternoon,* is modifying *told* or *will call.* In other words, it is not clear which activity took place or will take place in the afternoon. This sentence could be rewritten in two different correct ways as thus:

a) *In the afternoon,* Daramy told me he would call his mother.
b) Daramy told me he would call his mother *in the afternoon.*

Note that in both sentences, the phrases function as adverbs. In sentence *a*, the verb *told,* is modified; while in the sentence *b*, the verb phrase, *will call,* is modified.

ii) James promised him *at night* he will do his assignments.
At night, James promised to do his assignments. (correct sentence)
James promised to do his assignments *at night.* (correct sentence)

f) **Spelling mistakes**: Spelling is the act of putting letters of the alphabet together to form words that we use in communication. When we speak, we produce sounds that we cannot see or touch, but we can only hear or perceive them. We put phonemes (syllables) together to form words. When we write, we use the phonetic symbols that represent the abstract speech sounds so as to transform the abstract sounds into a concrete form that we can see and read. Those who codified English Language selected only twenty-six (26) *Alphabet Letters* from more than one hundred and fifty phonetic symbols, to represent the speech sounds that are produced in the English language. Spelling mistake occurs when the letter (s) are used in the wrong position.

Overcoming spelling problems

It is important to note that spelling and pronunciation are very closely related. It is definitely possible that a wrong pronunciation of any word will lead to misspelling of that word. Spelling mistake is one of the common errors that most people often commit. To overcome the spelling problems, one has to develop good spelling habits by allocating special time for it and follow the steps listed below. Try these ways; they may help you.

i)   To be able to spell any word correctly, one needs to learn to pronounce the word carefully and correctly. Wrong pronunciation will result into misspelling. When you come across a new word, learn to pronounce it correctly; practice saying it aloud over and again.

ii) Learn to study words. To study any word is to identify the **hotspot** of the word. A hotspot of any word is the syllable in the word that might be difficult to pronounce or remember. Within the hotspot of any word, the arrangement of letters is often difficult to remember when spelling. Try hard to memorize the hotspot of every difficult word. Write the word from memory and check it up in a dictionary if the spelling is correct.

iii) Use of dictionary. When you find out that you have misspelled a word, look it up in a dictionary. It is not advisable to guess about correct spelling.

iv) Learn to spell words by their syllables. Syllable is a particle of sounds we put together to produce or pronounce a word. In other words, it is a part of word that can be pronounced by itself. Eg **un-for-tu-nate-ly**. The word, **unfortunately,** has five syllables. Sometimes where possible, it is necessary to break words up into their syllables if you want to spell or pronounce them correctly. It is easier to learn a few letters at a time than learning all of them at once.

v)   Another way to overcome spelling problem is to list words that are very difficult to spell. Then you follow the steps below:

   a)   Look at each word carefully to notice the arrangement or pattern of the letters. Try to see the word in your mind.
   b)   Pronounce each syllable of the word to yourself over and again.
   c)   Write the word and check its spelling in a dictionary.
   d)   Repeat the list until you can spell each word correctly.

vi) We can also learn the spelling of a word by studying its morphology. Another word for morphology is structure or word-formation. There are **root words** and **derivative words**. Root word is the bare word without an affix. Most root words can change into other words when affixes are added to them. Words that are formed out of other words are known as **derivative words**.

An affix is a letter or letters that are added to a root word which will change the number, tense, the word class or the meaning of the root word. An affix includes prefixes and suffixes. Prefixes come at the beginning of a word while the suffixes come at the end. Observe the examples below.

*Un*friend**ly**, *inter*nation**al**, *un*fortunate**ly**, help**less-ly**, *un*known, *un*comfort**able,** *un*diplomat**ic.** Many nouns take affix ('s', 'es') to form their plural forms; so also a lot of verbs take suffix to form their past tense, continuous tense or participle forms. Commonly used affixes include: ***un, out, in, s, ed, n, ism, ish, able, ment, ion, less, ness, ing, er, est, ly,*** etc.

So studying the morphology of words will help you not only to overcome your spelling problems, but it will also help you to understand the meaning and origin of words.

It is also very important to learn the spelling of the plural form of irregular nouns, and the past and participle form of irregular verbs. Mastering these areas will help learners to overcome their spelling difficulties.

g) **Technical Tools**: The technical tools include the use of punctuation marks and capital letters. The correct use of these tools will be explained later in this book. Please remember to follow those instructions.

Styles and Skills of Sentences Construction

Now that we have learnt about the sentence errors, we must also learn to limit or avoid them totally in our writing exercises. Besides sentence errors, there are other skills and styles that make a piece of writing look magnificent. Learn to write an effective essay; that is using different sentence structures, different sentence beginning and different sentence lengths. You can also use of both active and passive voices to make your sentences more effective. Lastly, organize your ideas for easy comprehension using the appropriate transitional words. One after the other, let's discuss the skills in details.

A) **Use of Different Sentence Structures:** In any form of writing, one is advised to use different sentence structures. With the help of the appropriate connectives, one can join two or more ideas (simple sentences) to form a compound, complex or a compound-complex sentence. Though simple and easy to write, simple sentences alone can make an essay choppy. One can also put life into writing by using different sentence functions like statements, questions, personal feelings with stressed and emotional words. Using different sentence structures helps to vary the ways of explanation. See how you can blend the ideas in four simple sentences into one compound sentence, or in one complex idea. Observe the examples below.

a) I have not paid the school fees.

I went to school today.
I was asked to return home.
I didn't write the exam.

i) **Though** I have not paid the school fees**, yet** I went to school today; **but** I was asked to return home, so I didn't write the exam.

ii) I went to school today **but** I didn't write the exam **because** I was asked to return home **since** I have not paid the school fees.

iii) **When** I went to school today, I was asked to return home **because** I have not paid the school fees, **so** I didn't write the exam.

b) Joseph went through a lot of difficulties.

Joseph lost his parents.
Joseph worked hard to enter university.
Joseph managed to obtain first class degree.

i) Joseph went through a lot of difficulties **when** he lost his parents; **however,** he worked hard to enter university **where** he managed to obtain first class degree.

ii) **When** Joseph lost his parents, he went through a lot of difficulties; **however,** he worked hard to enter university **and** managed to obtained first class degree.

iii) **Though** Joseph went through a lot of difficulties **when** he lost his parents, **yet,** he worked hard to enter university **where** managed to obtain first class degree.

c) Education becomes expensive daily.

Parents and teachers do their best.
Students don't care.
Students get poor results.

i) **Since** education becomes expensive daily, parents and teachers do their best**; however,** students don't care **so** they get poor results.

ii) Parents and teachers do their best **since** education becomes expensive daily, **yet still** students get poor results **because** they don't care.

iii) Education becomes expensive daily **but** students don't care **so** they get poor results **even though** parents and teachers do their best,

Exercise: Join the simple sentences together to form a complex or compound- complex sentences. You are free to change the sentence position or replace words.

Paulina was born in a hospital.
Paulina was born somewhere in Freetown.
Paulina gets homesick anytime she hears the Krio language.

The space shuttle is a rocket.
The rocket is manned.
This rocket can be flown back to earth.
This rocket can be reused.

Mukeh taught English.
Mukeh taught with his father.
Mukeh taught for twenty-five years.
Mukeh was promoted as head of department.
The promotion was in 2017.

Oxygen is colourless.
Oxygen is tasteless.
Oxygen is odourless.
Oxygen is the chief life-supporting element of all plants.

Drug abuse is a dangerous phenomenon.
Drug abuse was introduced in our society by foreigners.
Drug abuse must be eliminated from our society.
Drug abuse is destroying the lives of our youths.

Many students are careless.
Many students are unserious.
Many students do not even listen in class.
Many students want to pass examinations.

B) **Vary Sentence Beginning:** One major way to construct sentence varieties is to begin your sentences with different parts of speech, phrases or clauses. :
Start with noun: Gambia is a small but powerful country.

Start with an adverb: Fortunately, Gambia is small but with a powerful leader.

Start with prepositional phrase: During his regime, the country enjoyed peace and rapid development.

Start with a participial phrase: Serving many years in power, he made the tiny semi-desert country great and stable.

Adverbial clause: When he was in power, the country enjoyed stability.

C) **Vary Sentence Length:** There should not be too many long sentences or too many short sentences in our writings. Too many long sentences will make writing dull and boring. Writing a long sentence requires the use of too many words; and when one is not careful, some words may be omitted or misplaced. Thus it will result into writing a faulty sentence or conveying a wrong message.

It is not also advisable to use too many short sentences because they can make an essay sound choppy. We must learn to use both long and short sentences in our writing. Varying the length of sentences can help a writer to create rhythm and lay emphasis on certain key ideas. We must learn to use all different kinds of sentences you have learnt before.

The short passage below is written in three different kinds of sentences. Observe them closely.

Short sentences

The whole family went to visit grandmother. She lived in the village. She became sick there. We have other relatives in the village. They called Dad. They gave him the information about her illness. He was in his office. He returned home. He told us. We went there immediately. The distance from home to the village was about twenty miles. The road condition was terrible. The vehicle also developed problems. So we spent more time on the way. We reached very late. Everyone in the village was asleep. We went straight to the hospital. Grandmother was sleeping. We didn't know what woke her up. She got up. She sat down in the bed. She was very happy to see us. She told the doctor to discharge her. They refused to discharge her. She insisted. They agreed to do so. The next morning, together with grandmother, we returned home in the city. It was the end of her illness. Grandmother brought back home the natural family funs and happiness.

Long sentences

The whole family went to visit grandmother in the village when she became sick there and other relatives we have in the village called and gave Dad the information about her illness when he was in his office. He returned home and told us, so we went there immediately to see her. It was a twenty-mile distance from our house in the city to the village, and the road condition was terrible and the vehicle also developed problems; so we spent more time on the way. We reached very late and everyone in the village was asleep, but we went straight to the hospital and grandmother too was sleeping but we didn't know what woke her up. She got up and sat down in the bed, and she was very happy to see us. So she told the doctors to discharge her, but the doctors refused to discharge her but she insisted; so they agreed to do so the next morning. Together with her, we returned home in the city and it was the end of her illness. So she brought back home the natural family funs and happiness.

Varieties of sentences with different lengths:

When grandmother became ill in the village where she was living, the whole family went there to visit her. Relatives from the village informed Dad about her illness when he was in his office. He returned home and informed us. We went there immediately. Though the distance was only twenty miles, yet the terrible condition of the road coupled with the problem the vehicle developed, we reached very late when everyone in the village was asleep. We went straight to the hospital where grandmother was sleeping. We didn't know what woke her up, but she immediately got up and sat in the bed. She was very happy to see us so she told the doctors to discharge her. When they refused, she insisted; so they agreed to do so. The next morning, together with grandmother, we returned home in the city where she brought back the natural family funs and happiness.

CHAPTER 9

ACTIVE AND PASSIVE VOICES

Voice in grammar is the feature of transitive verbs that tells whether the subject is acting or the subject is being acted upon. When the subject is acting, the verb is in the active voice; and when the subject is being acted upon, the verb is in the passive voice. **Active Voice:** The active voice refers to a situation where the subject performs the action. In an active voice, the subject comes first before the predicate; and it only transitive verbs that are used to indicate the active voice.

Passive Voice: The passive voice is used when the subject of the sentence is being acted upon. This means that the subject receives the action. To form the passive voice, we use an appropriate form of the auxiliary verb 'be' followed by the past participle of the main verb.

Here are some examples:

	Active Voice	**Passive Voice**
Present	The cat chases the rat	The rat is chased by the cat
Past	The cat chased the rat.	The rat was chased by the cat
Future	The cat will chase the rat.	The rat will be chased by the cat
Present perfect	The cat has chased the rat.	The rat has been chased by the cat
Past perfect	The cat had chased the rat.	The rat had been chased by the rat
Future perfect	The cat will have chased the rat.	The rat will have been chased by the rat

EXERCISE 1

Decide whether the following sentences are written in the active or passive voice. Then write the doer of the action on the line against each. If the doer is unknown, put a question mark (?).

1. Tom feeds his pig. active / passive_____
2. The dog is fed by Peter. active / passive_____

3. Fodei went to the forest. active / passive_____
4. The letter was written by Mary. active / passive_____
5. We hunted the thieves out of the village. active / passive_____
6. It rained very heavily yesterday. active / passive_____
7. The game had been won. active / passive__
8. The problem is solved. active / passive_____
9. They let the party failed to win the election. active / passive_____
10. The sea man risked his life. active / passive_____
11. The book was published. active / passive_____
12. The car has been hit by a stone. active / passive_____
13. It gets cold here during the winter. active / passive_____
14. Amie has destroyed her bicycle. active / passive_____
15. All the money has been stolen. active / passive_____

Forming a passive voice from an active voice

First, you must note that only verbs that take direct objects could be transformed into the passive voice. If the verb is transitive, the direct object will become the subject in the passive voice. The subject in the active voice will become the *object of preposition* in the passive voice, as '*by*' is inserted. A helping verb is also inserted so the simple predicate will become a verb phrase and move a step forward in the tense in the passive voice. Note also that the subjective pronoun in the active voice will change to the objective case and the number of the direct object in the active voice has to be taking into consideration. The number of the direct object plus the tense of the active voice will determine the helping verb that will be inserted in the simple predicate of the passive form of the sentence. Note the following examples:

Active		Passive
Peter killed one dog.	-	One dog **was** killed by Peter.
Peter killed two dogs.	-	Two dogs **were** killed by Peter.
She eats one mango daily.	-	One mango **is** eaten by *her* daily.
He ate three bananas.	-	Three bananas **were** eaten by *him*.

Observe the changes in the verb tenses and the pronouns when a sentence is converted from the active voice to the passive voice.

Verb tenses	Active voice	Passive voice
Simple Present Tense	Peter <u>appoints</u> him.	He <u>is appointed</u> by Peter.
Simple Past Tense	Susan <u>drove</u> her.	She <u>was driven</u> by Susan.
Simple Future Tense	They <u>will write</u> to Joe	Joe <u>will be written</u> to by them.
Simple Future Tense	We <u>are going</u> to <u>win</u> the game.	The game <u>is going</u> to <u>be won</u> by us.
Present continuous Tense	She <u>is speaking</u> Mende to me.	Mende <u>is being spoken</u> to me by her.
Past Continuous Tense	They <u>were winning</u> the game.	The game <u>was being won</u> by them.
Future Continuous Tense	We <u>will be breaking</u> them.	They <u>will be broken</u> by us.
Present perfect Tense	We <u>have given</u> him the pen.	He <u>has been given</u> the pen by us.
Past perfect Tense	The group <u>had taken</u> her today.	She <u>had been taken</u> by the group today.
Future perfect Tense	She <u>shall have chosen</u> us.	We <u>shall have been chosen</u> by her.

Use of Voices

It is advisable to use active voice because it is direct and economical. We also use active voice to point out and stress on the subject. Most writers prefer the voice as it makes prose more lively and active. An overuse of the passive voice makes a passage to be generally harder to understand and remember.

However, there are specific cases in English when the passive voice becomes more appropriate to use. Some of these cases are explained as follows:

1. Some writers prefer to use the passive when they want to avoid taking responsibility for what they do. For example, 'Some mistakes were made'. In this sentence, whoever made the mistakes is not mentioned.

2. The passive voice is used in scientific writing where emphasis is made on object or phenomenon being studied rather than the person or persons doing the study,

3. News reporters most times use the passive voice when they want to protect the confidentiality of their sources. In the sentence "It was reported that thieves broke into the store". In some cases the passive voice is used because the performer of an action is unknown or less important than the person who receives the action.

EXERCISE 2A

The sentences below are in the active voice. Change them into passive voice.

1. God created the heaven and the earth. _____
2. Gossipers and sycophants murder people. _____
3. I will do all the writing for God in heaven. _____
4. We bought all that was needed for the party. _____
5. Paul and Peter will take care of the class. _____
6. Our principal drove many students for fees. _____
7. My mother prepares delicious food. _____
8. His wife gives birth to baby boy every year. _____
9. I will teach English Lang. in grade twelve. _____
10. Our grandfather gave us some money. _____

EXERCISE 2B

The sentences below are in passive voice. Change them into active voice.

1. I was told by the chief to supervise the work. _____
2. The devil was sent by Satan to do what he likes. _____
3. I am loved by everyone I come across. _____
4. This book was written by a Sierra Leonean. _____
5. She is carried by Peter for the treatment. _____
6. This wonderful letter was written by them. _____
7. Everything on earth was created by God. _____
8. The little garden has been bought by Joe. _____
9. They were driven by the compound owner. _____
10. The old man was put into trouble by them and us. _____
11. Her trouble is carried by them, you and us. _____

CHAPTER 10

DIRECT AND INDIRECT SPEECHES

We use direct and indirect speech to pass information about an event that we witness or hear from someone else.

Direct Speech: This means that when the exact words of someone are used by another person to pass on his or her information to another person. Direct speech can be written or said in two different ways. Each of the ways requires critical punctuation technique.

Speaker - Statement Direct Speech

Here the speaker is identified first before the statement is said or revealed.

Tom said, 'My daughter is too playful.'
Fatou said, 'All the boys in my class are kind.'
She asked, 'Are all the girls in our class present here?'

Note that comma comes after *said, asked* etc; and then quotation opens. The first word in the quotation must be capitalized and the quotation must close after the end mark. Two or more sentences can be used in quotation.

Statement – Speaker Direct Speech

Here the statement is said first before the speaker is identified. The punctuation system here is slightly different from the above. As usual, the statement in the quotation must be capitalized and punctuated appropriately. The identifying phrase must be written separately. Observe the examples below.

'I am pleased to see you at my house.' Said Jaitta.

'Everyone in my class is clever.' The teacher said.

'Are all your parents at home?' Asked the old man.

'Watch out for the rolling stone!' Paul shouted.

Indirect Speech: This type of speech is made when someone reports another person's statement. In doing so, *said* or *said that* is often added to some of the exact words the statement owner used. Carefully observe the major changes that sometimes occur on the important personal pronouns, verb tenses, time and location of the subject or the object when direct speech is reported.

Important Pronouns:

Generally, the *first person singular* will change to the *third person singular*, and the *first person plural* will change to the *third person plural*. Take a mental look of the examples below.

Relevant Singular Pronouns	Relevant Plural Pronouns
I ... ... will become ... he, she or it.	We .. ... will become ... they
Me ... will become ... him, her, or it	Us .. ... will become ... ... them
My ... ... will become ... ... his, her or its	Ours ... ... will become . ... theirs
yourself ... ... will become ... himself, herself or itself	Ourselves .. ... will become ... ... themselves
Mine ... ... will become ... his, hers or its	

Observe the examples below

Direct Speech	Reported Speech
'I <u>own</u> the book **myself.'** Said Musa	Musa said that **he** <u>owned</u> the book **himself.**
Marian said, 'He **is coming** to see **me.'**	Marian said that he **was going** to see **her.**
'My baby disturbs **us** at night.' Said Amie	Amie said that **her** baby disturbs **them** at night.

'We went to visit our grandparents.' Fatou said	Fatou said that they went to visit their grandparents
'He gave us information about our family.' Di said	Di said that he gave them information about their family
'Mine is in my room.' Said Jattu	Jattu said that hers was in her room.
Job said, 'We work to please ourselves.'	Job said that they worked to please themselves.

Changes in the Verb Tenses:

To transform a direct speech into an indirect speech, the verb in the reported speech will go a step in to the tense. This means that the simple present will become simple past, and the simple past will sometimes become past perfect, or most often, remains the same tense. Please note that these changes are only necessary if the events/condition/situation that is reported has changed and it is no longer true. If the reported event is still true, change on the verb tense may not be necessary.

am, is … becomes … was

are … … becomes … were

shall … … becomes … should

will … … … becomes … would

can … … … becomes … could

may … … becomes … might

do, does … … becomes … did
was, were … … becomes … had been

isn't … … becomes … wasn't

aren't … … becomes … weren't

can't … … becomes … couldn't

hasn't, haven't … … becomes … … hadn't

don't, doesn't … … becomes … … didn't

won't … … becomes … … wouldn't

has, have … … becomes … … had

Observe the examples below

Direct Speech	Indirect/Reported Speech
Lucy said, 'We are in class.'	Lucy said that they were in class.
'My son has eaten his food.' Said Tad.	Tad said that his son had eaten his food.

Tom said, 'The boys <u>have done</u> their work.'	Tom said that the boys <u>had done</u> their work.
'They <u>shall pray</u> tomorrow.' Said the girls	The girls said that they <u>should pray</u> the next day.
Jobe said, 'I <u>can teach</u> grammar.'	Jobe said that he <u>could teach</u> grammar.
Rube said, 'My friends <u>may come</u> here.'	Rube said that her friends <u>might come</u> there.
'My team <u>shall win</u> prize.' Said Mata	Mata said that his team <u>should win</u> prize.
'I can't see my pen in the bag.' Said Nico	Nico said that he <u>couldn't see</u> his pen in the bag.
Yamu denied, 'It isn't mine!'	Yamu denied that it wasn't hers.
'We <u>aren't coming</u> to him!' Joe shouted	Joe shouted that they <u>weren't coming</u> to him.
'They <u>won't pay</u> the fees.' He refused	He refused that they <u>wouldn't pay</u> the fees.
'You <u>shouldn't worry</u> about us.' Faah warned.	Faah warned that you <u>shouldn't worry</u> about them.
'The food is delicious.' Jane said	Jane said that the food <u>was</u> delicious.
Paul said, 'I am too happy.'	Paul said that he <u>was</u> too happy.
The boys argued 'It <u>doesn't matter</u> to us.'	The boys argued that it <u>didn't matter</u> to them.
Cham said, 'You <u>don't want</u> to call me.'	Cham said that you <u>didn't want</u> to call him.
'They <u>will do</u> their work now.' Mother said.	Mother said that they <u>would do</u> their work then.
'I love my daughter.' Said the man	The man said that he loved his daughter.

Please note that the changes in the verb tense are not all the time applicable or necessary. It depends on situation from the time the speech or statement is said or uttered onto the time it is reported. If the reported event or situation remains the same, or if the reported event is a permanent truth, the change in the verb tense may not be relevant. So when the direct speech is in simple past and present tenses, it doesn't often change the tense when it is reported. It is assumed that the event, condition or situation reported is still the same.

Direct Speech	*Reported Speech*
'We <u>are</u> ready.' Said Moses	Moses said that they <u>are</u> ready.
'God is great.' Said the pastor	The pastor said that God is great.

Note: Don't change the verb tense if the situation or event in the direct speech remains true or the same onto the time it is reported.

EXERCISE 3

In the table below, there are direct and indirect speeches. Report the direct speech and change the reported speech into direct speech in the space against each sentence.

	Tom said that he was not around when I reached.
	Farrah said that you didn't care for them."
Binta said, 'My brother is going to punish me.'	
	Jobe said that they tried to pay themselves.
'We have come for our books and pens.' The boy said	
'I am here with mine and for myself.' Said John	
'Our boys are in the church for Easter mass.' He said	
	Fatou said that she worked for herself.
'They told us, but ours was not ready.' They answered	
	Sowe said that his team had to win the prize.

	The people said that they paid for their own benefit.
'I am sure we must pass this exam.' Haja said	
	Maaman said that he was talking to her when you called.

Words of nearness of place:

This … becomes … that
These … becomes … those
Here … becomes … there

Direct Speech	*Reported Speech*
This is your book.' Said the boy	The boy said that **that** was your book.
John said '**This is** your bag from Fandu.'	John said that **that is** your bags from Fandu.
'Musu's pen **is here** in the bag,' Said Tom	Tom said that Musu's pen **was there** in the bag.

It is important to note that the rule of nearness of place is not always applicable or necessary. It is greatly depending on the distance between the person reporting the speech and the place, object or event reporting about.

Words of nearness of time:

now … … … becomes … . then
today … … becomes … … that day
tomorrow … becomes … … the next day, the day after
yesterday … … becomes … … the previous day
last night … becomes … … the previous night
last week … becomes … … the previous week
next week … becomes … … the week after

These changes are only necessary or applicable when enough time has elapsed between the time the statement is uttered and the time it is reported.

Direct Speech	*Reported Speech*
'*I want* to go **now**.' Said Fodei	Fodei said that *he wanted* to go **then**.
Mary said '**Today is** my birthday.'	Mary said that **that day was** her birthday.
'I talked to them last week.' Lahai said	Lahai said that he talked to them the previous week.

Direct and Indirect Questions

We should know that a direct question should be in question form, and it requires question mark at the end. When reporting question, special care needs to be taken. In most cases, the introducing word will be '*asked*' instead of 'said'. When a question is reported, it requires no question mark, but full stop at the end. Observe also the position of the subject and the auxiliary verb in both direct and indirect questions. In direct question, it is **(*verb - subject order*)**. In indirect question, it is **(*subject - verb order*)**.

Direct question	Reported question
'<u>Is</u> she the head of the group?' Peter asked	Peter asked if she <u>is</u> the head of the group.
'Are there many people in town?' Tom asked	Tom asked if there <u>are</u>/<u>were</u> many people in town.
'When <u>are</u> we <u>living</u> for Freetown?' He asked	He asked when we <u>are living</u> for Freetown.
'<u>Do</u> you <u>know</u> who owns the school?' He asked	He asked if you know owner of the school.
'Can you drive a car?' Asked Tom	Tom asked if you could/can drive a car perfectly.
'Where are your friends?' the man asked	The man asked for the whereabouts of my friends.
'Where <u>are</u> my pens?' Jones asked	Jones asked where his pens <u>were</u>.

| 'Are you happy for the lunch?' Asked mother. | Mother asked if you were happy for the lunch. |
| 'Peter asked, 'Are you ready for the test?' | Peter asked whether you were ready for the test. |

Direct and Indirect Commands

A direct command always ends with an exclamation mark (!); while a reported command ends with full stop (.). To report the direct command, we use an infinitive or affirmative sentence. Note that reported commanded always end with a period. Eg:

Direct command	Indirect command
'Amie, switch off the light!' Her father instructed.	Her father instructed her to switch off the light.
'Paul, bring your books here!' Said Paul's father.	Paul's father told him to carry his books there.
'Tom, take my bag to school!' Said the teacher	The teacher told Tom to take his bag to the school!'

Direct and Indirect Requests

A direct request ends with full stop. When a direct request is reported, it will be introduced by a verb 'asked' or 'demanded'. We may not use 'please' most often.

Direct request	Reported request
'John, could you please take my bag home.' Abu requested	Abu asked John to take his bag home.
'Amie, could you please bring my food.' Said her father	Amie's father asked her to bring his food.
'I beg, don't go out tonight.' Her father pleaded	Her father begged her not to go out that night.

Note that in reported speech, these introductory words: **said**, **asked**, **requested**, **ordered** etc, can be alternated.

Said can be replaced by: *told, replied, agreed, reiterated, stated, announced, maintained* or *declared.*

Asked can be replaced by: *inquired* or *wondered*

Requested can be replaced by: *asked, implored, pleaded, advised or begged*

Ordered can be replaced by: *told, directed, demanded, instructed or commanded*

EXERCISE 4

Write the inverse or direct opposite of each of the sentences below; that's, if a sentence a direct speech, direct question, direct command or direct request, write the indirect form of it; and vice-versa.

1. "Where did you place my Bible?" Joe asked the boy.

   _____

2. "What were you asked to do?" Grandfather asked.

   _____

3. "What assurance have you that she will come?" asked the boy.

   _____

4. Peter asked whether we were happy with him.

   _____

5. The pastor asked if we actually believe in God Almighty.

   _____

6. I asked Massa if she will marry me.

   _____

REQUESTS

1. "Bring me some cold water to drink." Father requested.
2. "Juliet, please tell your father to call me." Mr Jusu requested.
3. Father requested "Please let somebody bring me a chair."
4. Massa, please show me some of your love." he requested.
5. Abu asked John to take his books home.
6. Massa told Paul to exercise some patient with her.

COMMANDS

1. Mama shouted "Get-up! Go inside and bring my cane!".
2. "The last person will not be allowed!" he threatened. …
3. Mrs Lamin ordered "All late comers should kneel down!". …
4. He instructed Joe to take his bag to the car park.
5. Papa commanded the boy to walk faster with his food.
6. Peter asked Tom to follow him from the market to home.

Question Tags

A question tag is a short *group of words with subject and verb end with question mark. Eg: **isn't he? aren't you? wasn't she? weren't they?** etc.* It normally follows a statement. Question tag is used when the speaker wants the listener to confirm that what he/she says is correct or true. A question tag consists of a **helping verb**, (a **negative adverb**), a **pronoun** with a question mark at the end. The helping verb and the negative adverb are written as single word with contraction. A tag that follows a negative statement contains no negative adverb. The pronoun in the tag must agree with the subject of the statement in person, number and gender. There are rules about the uses of question tags that need to be understood and followed.

Rule one: When the statement is positive, it must be followed by a negative question tag. Example

He went home yesterday, didn't he?
It is very cold, isn't it?
Your brothers are here, aren't they?

Rule two: If the statement is negative, the question tag should be positive.

We are not happy, are we?
She is not serious, is she?
They were not working in Banjul, were they?

Rule three: The ***helping verb*** and the ***negative adverb*** in the tag are often written together as single word with contraction. The verb in the statement must agree ***in tense*** with the verb in the tag. This means that if the verb in the statement is in simple present tense, the verb in the tag also must be in simple present tense. If the verb is in the sentence is in simple past tense, the one in the tag should be in the same simple past tense.

You **eat** bread every morning, ***don't*** you?
She **went** to school, ***didn't*** she?
We have no food, ***have*** we?

Rule four: If the statement is in the simple present tense and the subject is a third person singular, it matches with **does** or **doesn't** in the tag.

She **goes** to school, ***doesn't*** she?
He does not sleep here, ***does*** he?
Jarju **plays** football, ***doesn't*** he?
My mum does not eat 'nyebeh', ***does*** she?

Rule five: If the statement is in the simple present tense and the subject is not a third person singular, it agrees with **do** or **don't** in the tag.

You **run** marathon, ***don't*** you?
They **teach** in the 22nd July Academy, ***don't*** they?
We don't **go** for training, ***do*** we?
Papa and Mama do not quarrel, **do** they?

Rule six: When the statement is in simple past tense, it agrees with ***did*** or ***didn't*** in the tag. It doesn't matter whether the subject is third person or not.

They ate no food, **_did_** they?
She **prayed** for the exam, **_didn't_** she?
I **went** to see my mum, **_didn't_** I?
We **suffered** defeat, **_didn't_** we?
He paid no money, **did** he?

Rule seven: When *a verb phrase* serves as simple predicate in the statement, the helping verb will repeat itself in the tag.

Fatou **is** our prefect, **_isn't_** she?
The boys are happy, **aren't** they?
The milk **testes** sour, **_isn't_** it?
He **is** not healthy, **_is_** he?
We **are** not going, **are** we?
It **was** dead and buried, **_wasn't_** it?
They **were** tall and strong, **_weren't_** they?
He **was** not the champion, **_was_** he?
We **were** not in the party, **were** we?

Rule eight: Note that the verb, *am* always appear with the personal pronoun *I.* They form a very unique structure in a tag. Here, no contraction is used. The pronoun, **I** will appear between the verb, *am* and the negative adverb **not,** if the sentence is positive.

I **am** tired, *am* I **_not_**?
I **am** the queen, *am* I **_not_**?
I **am** not very beautiful, *am* I?

Note that when a verb phrase appears in a sentence, the first helping verb in the phrase will reappear in the tag.

We **are playing** the game, aren't we?
She **has been eating** the mangoes, **_hasn't_** she?
They **have been dancing** for two hours, haven't they?

EXERCISE 5

Write the appropriate question tag for each of the statements below.

1. Your father has a car,   Hasn't he?
2. I am the chief,   _____
3. We are not going to school,   _____
4. You do not play football,   _____
5. The president is in town,   _____
6. Nowadays, girls are not reliable,   _____
7. Many boys wanted her initially,   _____
8. I am not happy   _____
9. Thieves hate light and dogs,   _____
10. God loves sinners but hates their sins,   _____
11. Sinners will not enter into heaven,   _____
12. They have our books and bags,   _____
13. Mr Sama is not poor,   _____
14. Their own families are very rich,   _____
15. Its tail is not too long,   _____
16. There is no perfect being on earth,   _____
17. With God, all things are possible,   _____
18. Mujeh is intelligent and beautiful,   _____
19. They haven't gone home,   _____
20. She has not written any interesting book,   _____
21. This game is not very interesting,   _____
22. Everyone wants to be my relative,   _____
23. Sarah was once an intimate friend of Alice,   _____
24. This story is very interesting,   _____
25. Some teachers are half baked,   _____

EXERCISE 6

Write the appropriate statement (s) and response (s) against each question tag.
Observe the examples below. (open)

Statement	*Question tag*	*Response*
We are going home.	aren't we?	Yes, we are.
They are not singing.	are they?	No, they aren't.

1. _____, isn't she?
2. _____, wasn't he?
3. _____, were you?
4. _____, is he?
5. _____, am I?
6. _____, are they?
7. _____, was she?
8. _____, aren't we?
9. _____, wasn't you?
10. _____, didn't they?

PART 3

ENRICHING VOCABULARY

CHAPTER 11

RECOGNISING WORD ROOTS, PREFIXES AND SUFFIXES

To understand a language, one needs to acquire a stock of vocabulary items. The vocabulary items help users of a language to communicate with another and convey meaning in our day to day interaction with people. Vocabulary includes all those words whose meanings you can either recognise or you can deduce from the context. In order to acquire more vocabulary, you need to become an investigative reporter of your language and that of others. The more words one know in a particular language, the more he/she will be able to communicate in the language.

In order to understand most English words, you need to distinguish roots, prefixes and suffixes. Some simple definitions of roots, prefixes and suffixes are given with some examples.

Word Roots

As the name implies, a root is a word from which other words can be derived, usually through the addition of prefixes and suffixes. Most of the word roots in English are derived from Greek or Latin. Here are some common Latin (L) and Greek (G) roots with some examples.

Root	Meaning	Examples
-audi- (L)	to hear	audience, audio, auditorium
-bene- (L)	good, well	benevolent, benefit, benefactor
-bio- (G)	life	biography, biosphere, biopsy
-gen- (G)	race, kind	genealogy, gene
-geo- (G)	earth	geography, geometry
-graph- (G)	to write	graphic, photography, pictograph
-jur-, -jus- (L)	law	justice, jurisdiction

-manu- (L)	hand	manufacture, manual, manipulate
-path- (G)	feel, suffer	empathy, pathetic
-photo- (G)	light	photography, telephoto
-port- (L)	to carry	transport, portable
-tele- (G)	far away	telegraph, telepathy, telephone
-vid-, -vis-	to see	video, envision, visit

Prefixes and Suffixes

Knowing the meaning of prefixes and suffixes goes a long way in helping to decipher the meaning of unfamiliar words.

A **prefix** is a letter or group of letters added to the beginning of a word to change the meaning of the word to which it is attached. Prefixes carry specific meanings as in the examples below.

Prefixes of negation or opposition

Prefix	Meaning	Examples
a-, an-	without, not	apolitical, anemia
anti-	against	antibody, anticorruption
contra-	against	contravene, contraband
de-	from, take away from	demerit, declaw,
dis-	apart, away	disappear, discharge
il-, im-, in-, ir-	not	illegal, immature, indistinct, irrelevant
mal-	wrong	malpractice, maladministration
mis-	wrong, bad	mismanage, miscalculate, misbehave
non-	not	nonsense, non-alcoholic, non-human
un-	not	unfortunate, unhappy, unable, untidy

Prefixes of Quantity

Prefix	Meaning	Examples
bi-	two	bilateral, biannual, bicameral
milli-	thousand	millimetre, milligram
mono-	one, single	monologue, monogamy, monolingual

omni-	all	omniscient, omnipotent
semi-	half	semicircle, semicolon, semiconductor
tri-	three	tripod, trimester, tricolour
uni-	one	unicameral, unilateral,

Prefixes of time and space

Prefix	Meaning	Examples
ante-	before	antenatal, antedate
circum-	around	circumlocution, circumnavigate
hyper-	over, more than	hypersonic, hyperactive, hyperinflation
inter-	between	intermarry, international, interconnect
micro-	tiny	micrometer, microscopic
post-	after	post-war, postscript, post-natal
pre-	before	pre-arranged, pre-school, pre-war
re-	again, back	rewrite, redesign, review, reprint

Suffixes

A **suffix** is attached to the end of words and they are used to modify and extend the meanings and in some cases change the grammatical function or part of speech of the original word. Suffixes can for example change the adjective 'happy' to an adverb or a noun,

Adjective	happy
Adverb	happily
Noun	happiness

Noun suffixes

Suffix	Meaning	Examples=ds
-acy	state or quality	democracy, privacy, intimacy
-al	act of	rebuttal, refusal,
-ance, -ence	state or quality of	maintenance, eminence, prominence
-dom	place or state of being	freedom, martyrdom, wisdom

-er, -or	one who	teacher, player, investor, creator
-ism	doctrine, or belief characteristic of	tribalism, colonialism, patriotism
-ist	one who	organist, linguist, economist
-ity	quality of	veracity, opacity, obesity,
-ment	condition of	payment, bereavement, argument
-ness	state of being	kindness, politeness, seriousness
-ship	position held	professorship, headship, fellowship
-sion, -tion	state of being or Action	digression, transaction, creation

Verb Suffixes

Suffix	Meaning	Examples
-ate	cause to be	concentrate, regulate, capacitate
-en	cause to be or become	broaden, blacken, enliven
-ify, -fy	make or cause to be	unify, terrify, amplify
-ise	cause to become	civilise, specialise, criminalise

Adjective suffixes

Suffix	Meaning	Examples
-able, -ible	capable of being	commendable, capable, edible
-al	pertaining to	regional, political, tribal,
-ful	having a notable quality	colourful, beautiful, sorrowful, playful, careful
-ic	pertaining to	historic, poetic, mythic
-ish	having the quality of	foolish, clownish
-ious, -ous	of or characterised by	famous, nutritious, ambitious
-ive	having the nature of	festive, creative, massive
-less	without	endless, senseless, motionless

Synonyms and Antonyms

Synonyms: These are words that are very similar in meaning, whereas antonyms are words opposite in meaning. The lists below give some examples of commonly used synonyms and antonyms in English.

Words	**Synonyms**
Affect	influence, transform, moderate
Eligible	appropriate, suitable, qualified
Imminent	possible, likely, certain
Abundance	plenty, many, large in number
Acquaintance	associate, befriend, familiar with
Aerial	airborne, in-flight
Aggravate	magnify, worsen, exacerbate
Buoyant	cheerful, floating, happy
Cafeteria	restaurant, canteen
Campaign	crusade, promotion, movement
Trouble-shooter	peacemaker, problem solver
Catastrophe	calamity, trouble, upheaval
Changeable	unreliable, unstable, irregular
Coincidence	chance, concurrent, simultaneous
Condemn, criticize	disapproved of, denounce
Deficient, lacking	scarce, undersupply
Delinquent	criminal, crook, felonious
Descend	downward movement,
Deteriorate	depreciate, worsen, weaken
Distinguish	differentiate, tell apart
Enthusiastic	keen, fervent wholehearted
Entrepreneur	capitalist, industrialist
Disastrous	catastrophe, devastating, terrible
Insinuate	suggest, imply, indicate, intimate
Commotion	turmoil, upheaval, confusion
Pleasant	agreeable, gratifying, refreshing

Embarrass	molest, mistreat, humiliate
Exhibition	show, display, exposition
Fluorescent	shinning, bright, luminous
Forfeit	lose, give-up, surrender, sacrifice
Negotiate	agree, barging, consult
Mischievous	naughty, roguish, playful
Tantamount	equal, equivalent, similar
Minuscule	little, tiny, minute
Lieutenant	deputy, substitute, standby
Grievance	grumble, complaint, accusation
Harass	pursue, annoy, border, threaten
Hygiene	cleanliness, sanitation
Imagine	picture, visualize, dream
Fascinate	attract, motivate, captivate
Gauge	measure, weigh, judge
Indispensable	essential, necessary, vital
Interfere	obstruct, impede, hamper
Irrelevant	unrelated, not necessary
Irritable	annoying, tetchy, disliking
Opportunity	chance, prospect, possibility
Mortgage	credit, advance
Mediocre	average, middling, common
Threshold	doorstep, entrance
Fragile	delicate, easily broken
Endorse	approve, support, back
Intimidate	frighten, threaten, terrorize, bully
Awesome	impressive, fabulous, astonishing
Vague	unclear, fused, indistinguishable
Excellent	remarkable, splendid, superb
Crucial	very important, essential
Penniless	impoverished, bankrupt, hard-up
Decent	respectable, adequate, fair, suitable
Convict	offender, criminal, find guilty

Pessimistic	cynical, negative expectation,
Tranquil	calm, harmony, silence, serenity
Affluent	rich, wealth, well to do
Unrefined	crude, untreated, unprocessed,
Ludicrous	ridiculous, laughable,
Persuade	influence, convince, win over
Feeble	weak, frail, tender, flimsy
Illegitimate	illegal, prohibited, illicit, unlawful
Concede	admit, allow, grant
Impartial	unbiased, neutral, fair, objective,
Synthetic	artificial, unreal, fake
Believable	credible, realistic, convincing
Glimpse	peep, quick view, glance
Brave	fearless, heroic, valiant, bold
Protrude	stick-out, project, extend beyond
Ashamed	humiliate, mortify, embarrassed,
Speculate	conjecture, guess, wonder
Aggressive	hostile, violent, belligerent,
Limelight	public interest or attention
Impeccable	blameless, immaculate
Reluctant	unwilling, disinclined, hesitate
Investable	unavoidable, inevitable, necessary,
Ordeal	trail, torment, test, tribulation
Lucrative	profitable, well-paid, productive
Adversity	hardship, hard time, difficulty
Compete	contend, vie, race battle, try to win
Lure	bait, draw in, decoy, entice
Eligible	suitable, qualified, fit
Handicap	disability
Flatter	sweet talk, butter up, praise, cajole
Fastidious	choosy, demanding, hard to please
Sporadic	random, irregular, erratic
Judicious	conscious, careful, sensible,

Tangible	real, substantial, touchable, concrete
Larceny	theft, stealing, robbery,
Remorse	regret, sorrow, repentance, guilt
Impede	block, hinder, hamper, obstruct
Animosity	hostility, conflict, trouble

Words	Antonyms	Words	Antonyms
accept	reject	expand	contrast
adult	juvenile	hell	heaven
alive	die/dead	mountain	valley
ancient	modern	failure	success
arrive	depart	heavy	light
answer	question	fair	unfair
generous	cruel	false	true
gaunt	stout	familiar	strange
future	past	famous	notorious
frown	smile	fancy	reality
fertile	barren	guilty	innocent
feeble/weak	strong	good	bad
foe	friend	far	near
few	more	fat	thin
foolish	clever	first	last
freedom	captive	immense	tiny
foreign	native	inferior	superior
found	lost	ignorant	aware
here	there	join	separate
morning	evening	hide	expose/uncover
hero	coward	honest	dishonest
high	low	humble	proud
hollow	filled	junior	senior
bright	dark	lend	borrow
love	hate	loud	mute
asleep	awake	mad	sensible

assemble	disperse	merry	gloomy
bold	coward	miserable	improve
blessing	sin	miser	extravagant
bitter	sweet	long	short
large	small	maximum	minimum
better	worse	minority	majority
back	front	multiple	single
backward	forward	never	often
bottom	top	purchase	sell
bright	dull, stupid	opaque	clear
buy	sell	numerous	few
reveal	conceal/hide	none	all
cold	hot	north	south
clean	dirty	old	new
come	go	open	close
cheap	expensive	peace	war/trouble
exit	entrance	out	in
even	odd	permanent	temporal
enemy	friend	plain	coloured
educated	illiterate	pleasant	unpleasant
empty	full	polite	rude
ebb	come in	plural	singular
easy	difficult	poor	rich
depth	height	private	public
drunk	sober	present	absent
dry	wet	praise	blame
dwarf	giant	quiet	noisy
down	up	rapid	slow
early	late	senior	junior
east	west	sell	buy
deny	accept	wild	tame
condemn	praise	solid	soft
day	night	slow	quick
deep	shallow	show	hide

defeat	win	stationary	motion
defend	attack	steep	gentle
dark	shine	straight	bend
damp	dry	victory	defeat
together	alone	these	those
correct	wrong	top	bottom
confined	open/free	transparent	opaque

Idiomatic Expressions:

To throw dust in the eyes	- to deceive someone
Chicken hearted	- coward
Make both ends meet	- manage financially
Take the wind out of his sails	- to silence someone
Give cold shoulder	- show indifference or ignore someone by preventing discussion with him.
In the nick of time	- at crucial moment or end of time
Hen-pecked husband	- a husband ruled by his wife
Eagle eyed	- be observant
Play ducks and drakes	- wasting of money
What is a sauce for the goose is a sauce for gander	- the same rule applies to everyone
Sitting on the fence	- to remain neutral
To be on top of the world	- to be extremely happy
To have one's heart in one's mouth	- to be extremely frightened
To hold one's tongue	- to remain silent
With tail between the legs	- in a defeat and shame
Killing the goose that lays golden eggs	- destroying the source of future benefit for immediate but less benefit.

To speak with one's tongue in one's cheek	- to pretend
In someone's bad or good book	- out of favour or in favour of someone
To steer clean off	- to avoid
Take the bull by the horns	- tackle a difficult problem boldly or bravely
Every Tom, Dick and Harry	- ordinary people or everybody
Give the devil its due	- to appreciate one's effort
To make a head or tail of something	- to understand something
Fall foul of	- to come up against or be against
Hands in glove	- to be in good relation or united
Make a clean breast of	- to confess
Pass with flying colours	- to do very well or excellent pass
Smell a rat	- be suspicious of something.
Let the cat out of the bag	- reveal the secret
Put the cart before the horse	- to start at the wrong end
Do in Rome as Romans do	- to obey the rules and regulations of any society you find yourself.
A dog in manger	- someone who prevents others from enjoying something that is useless to him
Take a French leave	- to depart without permission or saying good bye
To bury the hatchet	- to make peace.
Paddle one's own canoe	- to mind or care for your own business
Swords of Damocles	- imminent danger in midst of prosperity
A wild goose chase	- a fruitless or futile search

Throw in the towel	- to give up the struggle or fight
To let bygones be bygones	- to forgive and forget
The game is not worth a candle	- it is more risk and expensive with less worth or benefit.
A nail in one's coffin	- an experience that can shorten life
Blood is thicker than water	- the tie of kindred is stronger than ordinary friendship
Low key	- simple, not costly or exorbitant
To face a showdown	- to face an important clash
A feather in one's cap	- an added prestigious responsibility
As fit as a fiddle	- to be very healthy
A forlorn hope	- a plan which has a very little likelihood of success
To nail a person down	- to obtain a definite promise from a person
Birds of the same feather flocks together	- persons of the same character move together
To get on someone's nerve	- to annoy someone or to make someone angry
A thorn in the flesh	- a continual cause of trouble or annoyance
A wet blanket	- someone who discourages others

PART 4

PUNCTUATION MARKS AND MECHANICS

Punctuation marks are other relevant symbols or signs that are used in writing, apart from letters. They play very important roles in writing and they have great influence on how a complete thought conveys a message. When punctuations are correctly used in writing, they help readers to easily understand the message. When they are incorrectly used, in most cases, they either present an ambiguous, different idea or a wrong sentence. There are end mark punctuations and other punctuations.

CHAPTER 12

END PUNCTUATIONS

End punctuation marks are used to separate complete thoughts in our writing. As a result, they always come at the end of a complete idea (a sentence.) There are three of them. They include **full stop/Period (.)**, **question mark (?)** and **exclamation mark (!).**

Full Stop/Period (.)

This is also known as period, and it is used in the following cases:

a) At the end of a declarative sentence or a statement. The following are some examples:

There are seven days in a week.
God is the creator of the universe.
Education comes first in term of national development.

b) It is used to close an imperative sentence that makes requests or give simple instructions.

Clean the house first before heating the water for tea.
Come closer and stand, so that you can hear clearly.

c) It is used at the end of an indirect or reported question.

He asked if we are going to visit the families in Kailahun this holiday.
Mum told me to ask when your dad will be at home tomorrow.
Ask whether they are going to spend the holiday here.

Question Mark (?)

This plays limited role in writing. It is used to end an interrogative sentence (direct question). This punctuation mark indicates that a sentence is requesting for information.

> What is your name?
> Who is your friend?
> Where are you coming from?

Exclamation Mark (!)

This punctuation mark is used to close an exclamatory sentence or an interjection. In other words, it indicates that a sentence gives command or a word expresses strong feeling. It is used to end any sentence that expresses strong emotion.

> Your presence here changes nothing!
> Watch out for the rolling stone!
> Don't let anyone in here!
> Remember to feed them when it is time!

Interjections could be separated from the rest of a sentence by either a comma or an exclamation mark; depending on the intended emphasis.

> Oh! What an enormous snake!
> Oh, it is only an empty bag.
> Wow! I have caught her at last.

EXERCISE 1

Use the most appropriate end marks in each of the following sentences

1. The chief told all the villagers to prepare for the farming season
2. Who told the chief to inform his people about the D-day
3. She asked whether we were there for the preparation

4. Get up and walk faster to help your mother
5. Who said I will not be the winner of this year's award
6. Ask them if they are ready to eat the food Priscilla prepared
7. We shall cultivate the land that is on the top of the mountain
8. Watch out, the thieves are around
9. He is a foolish man, he can do anything
10. Where are the boys that did this work
11. They asked me if Mr. Maddog is still our principal
12. They asked for all those that were ready to come outside
13. Give me some water to drink
14. Move backward and stand so that you can see clearly
15. Take my bag home quickly
16. Oh, it hurts me
17. Wow, my better-half is around now
18. Oh my God why have you forsaken me
19. Watch out, a very big black cobra is approaching
20. Danger, keep off

Other Uses of Full Stop/Period

Use period after most abbreviations:

- Use period after the abbreviation of personal names. Eg: F. Joe, M.B. Jah, F.M. Tuku, Mar. (for March), St. Peter (for Saint Peter)
- Use full stop after the abbreviation of titles used with names. Eg: Mr. Jusu, Mrs. Tongi, Lahai Jr. Dr. Mendy, Hon. Sowe.
- Use period within the abbreviation of time. Eg: A.M., P.M., B.C., A.D.
- Use period after the abbreviation of address Eg: Rd. for road, St. for street, P.O. Box 126

Note that abbreviations of government agencies, acronyms and widely used abbreviations are written without period. Such abbreviations are often capitalized.

Eg UNO, AU, WHO, IMF, ECOWAS, BBC, CNN, WASSCE, WAEC etc.

CHAPTER 13

OTHER PUNCTUATION MARKS

Comma (,)

This is one of the commonly used punctuation marks. It is used to separate words or groups of words within a sentence. Here are few ways comma is used.

A) **To separate items in a series: U**se comma to separate items in a **series.** Series is a group of three or more items of similar grammatical structures written one after the other. The items in a series could be words, phrases or clauses as in the following examples

   i) **Words in series:**

      <u>Nouns in series</u>: I bought pens, books, cap, belt and three T-shirts.
      <u>Verbs in series</u>: He can *draw, write, sing* and *dance* very well.
      <u>Adjectives in series</u>: The car park is very *crowded, noisy, dirty* and *dusty.*
      My friend is *short, black* and *gigantic.*
      She is *brilliant, determined* and *hardworking.*

  ii) **Phrases in series:**

      <u>Prepositional phrases in series</u>: He was stabbed *in the head, on the back, above the shoulder* and *under his arm.*
      <u>Infinitive phrases in series</u>: *To write books, to join politics* and *to run for presidency* are things I hope to do in future.

 iii) **<u>Main clauses in a series</u>:** We came, we saw, we fought and we conquered.

      Please note that it is only short independent clauses that can be separated by comma. Sometimes, they are separated by

semicolons. **Always make sure that there are three or more items in series.**

B) **Use a comma to separate two independent clauses in a compound sentence.** Eg:

1. I will start my studies early this term**, so** I will work hard to obtain a very good result.
2. They will respond to your call**, but** they will not make any contribution.
3. John has played his own part**, yet** no one has praised him.
4. I will come in the morning**, or** I will send you the books you asked for.

C) **Use a comma to separate interrupter:** Use comma to set off an interrupter within a sentence. Interrupter is an expression that will interrupt the free-flow of a sentence. Interrupters do not only stop the smooth run down of a sentence, but they may also contain irrelevant information. Common interrupters include subordinating word groups, appositives and words used in direct address.

i) ***Appositives:*** It is often a noun that is placed next to another noun and it renames, identifies or explains the noun. Commas are used to set off appositive and appositive phrase from the rest of the sentence.

Eg: My classmate, Ebrima, is a very good footballer.
Rev. Fr. Mendy, the pastor of our church, has bought a new car.
Sierra Leone, a small country in West Africa, has many minerals.
Book writing, a hobby my friend has chosen, is not an easy job.

ii) ***Words used in direct address:*** This is referred to the names or titles of people we call when we are directly addressing them.

Eg: Jusufu, please tell your father to call me.
Dad wants to see you, Jainaba.
Do you think, Fatou, your friends will be in the meeting?

iii) **Use a comma to separate subordinating word groups:** Use comma to separate nonessential phrases and clauses to form the main idea of a sentence. Non-restrictive subordinating word groups do not contain factual, specific or meaningful details about the main idea of a sentence. Such a phrase or a clause may be omitted without changing the main idea of the sentence. Two commas are needed if the expression to be set off is placed in the middle of the main sentence. Use only one comma to set off an interrupter that comes before or after the main sentence. Eg:

Maameh, *the girl I saw this morning,* did not listen to the teacher.
So Long a Letter, *the book I read two years ago*, was written by Mariama Ba.
Standing by the fence, I quickly glanced through the note before the exams commenced.

iv) **Introductory words, phrases and clause:** These are words or groups of words that introduce an independent clause. Use comma to set off words or groups of words that introduce a sentence.

  a) **words:** Eg: No, nobody is allowed to enter here.
     Yes, there is no time for it any more.
     Please, inform others about the meeting.

  b) **phrases:** Eg: Behind the door, there is a big box.
     In the middle of the forest, you can see the Luimbe tree.
     Happily jumping on her father, the girl brought the old man down.
     Frankly speaking, they won the prize.

  c) **clauses:** Eg: In the evening they arrived, everything was in place.
     When it started to rain, we all went into the houses.
     Your mother is around, I remember.

D) **Use a comma to separate items in conventional situation:** Use comma to separate the items in dates and addresses. Comma is also used after the salutations of informal and semiformal letters; and after the closure of any letter.

Eg: date- My first child was born on 22nd May, 1999.
The document, dated 19th December, 1975 was found in an old building in the village called Fandu, Kpombai Section, Kailahun District, Eastern Province of Sierra Leone.

Colon and Semi-colon (: & ;)

i)   Use colon to separate a list of items from the sentence (s) that follow. Eg:

We bought the following items: pens, books, erasers, pencils etc.
The bag contains the following: trousers, shirts, shoes, books, caps and belt.

ii) Use colon to separate a list of details from the introductory sentence. Eg:

Listen to how the drama unfolded: The stranger stood up before us and greeted, he told us his name and nationality; then he burst into long and loud laughter.

iii) Use colon between hour and minute. Eg:

The time for the English class 8:30.
We shall be leaving by 10:15 tomorrow morning.

iv) Use colon after the salutation of a business letter Eg:

Dear Sir or Madam:
To whom it may concern:

Uses of Semicolon (;)

This punctuation mark is made up of both period and comma, and it also performs the functions of both.

i)   Use semicolon to separate independent clauses that are not joined by **and, but, or, nor, for, so** and **yet.**

Eg: Fatou read her note for the exam; Isatou gave hers to her friends
Five students got A's; others got only credits.

ii) Use semicolon to separate two or more independent/main clauses in a compound sentence if one of the main clauses contains comma already; it doesn't matter which conjunction connects them.

Eg: Isha, Musu, Briama and Amara have gone to watch the film show; but Bintou, Ben and Paul are resting.

I invited the boys, the girls and the youths; and Paul called only the elders.

EXERCISE 2

In the short passage below, only the end marks are used. Commas, semicolon and quotation marks are missing. Identify where they should be and apply them correctly.

One hot afternoon I accompanied my grandmother to the previous year farm. We went to brush her vegetable gardens. She planted many different crops on all the ant-hills in the farm my father cultivated. Her best crops were pepper garden egg tomato bean and green. She planted plenty of them. On one of the ant-hills we saw a very big, long and black snake. I saw the snake first I pointed at it and shouted. Grandmother! A big snake! Where is it? She asked. Though she was an old woman yet she was strong and brave. She advanced towards the reptile and threw her short machete at it and hit it on the back. The snake became mad and jumped at her. I stood by to watch the drama unfold. Grandmother was very lucky to catch the snake by its head and held it firmly. Give me my machete! She turned to me and shouted. I was afraid to go near her. Don't be afraid the rest you see is just a rope. I hold the real snake the head. I timidly jumped collected the machete and gave it to her which she used to cut off the head of the black reptile.

Apostrophe (')

This punctuation mark is normally used to indicate possession or ownership. It is also used for the purpose of contraction.

Possession or relationship: Use an **apostrophe** and **s** to form the possessive case of nouns that do not end with **s.**

Anyone's guess, an hour's time, boy's room, father's plate, Peter's pen

Note that when the spelling of either singular or plural noun ends with **s,** we add only apostrophe to form the possessive case.

Eg: Moses' pen, Francis' book, my sisters' birthday, Mr. Harris' laptop, the boys' quarter

Pronouns like her, it, your, our and their form their possessive case by adding only **s** without apostrophe.

Eg: This shoe is yours. The pen is hers. That car is theirs. Those books are ours. Those are bicycles yours.

Contractions: This refers to an omission of letter(s) to allow two words to be written together as a single word without changing their meaning. Use only an apostrophe to indicate where letter(s) have been left out in a contraction.

Eg: I am … I'm, do not … … don't, were not … weren't, cannot … can't, is not … … isn't

EXERCISE 3

In the passage below, only the end mark punctuations are used. There are areas where commas, semicolons, colons, apostrophe and quotation marks are to be applied. Identify the areas and apply them appropriately.

My father sitting behind his machine called me this morning and sent me to the market in town. When I reached there I saw many people in the crowded noisy busy and dirty market. Dr Madman the famous crazy market crier pointed his iron bar towards me and asked. Why are you looking at me? How can you call yourself a perfect man when among your seven billion handworks in your own image, there is no perfect one? Tell me!

I felt threatened and I jumped into an old woman s tray full of items. The woman held me firm by my shirt and shouted above her voices. I can't take any beg but the money! Pay mi money! Some items destroyed were mirror ear-rings a tin of baby powder a pair of eye glasses and three spray bottles. When I paid for the damage goods the old woman laughed sang danced and clapped for me.

When I turned to go the mad crier again threatened me. You perfect being with imperfect parts and ways! Stand and wait for me! Stand let me come and wage a holy war on your imperfect soul that will take you to Purgatory through the perfect hell. I was completely baffled about his philosophical statements; I let them go. I remembered the paper where I listed the items that I went to buy. On the list were phone bread milk sugar and tea cups. Then I looked at my time. It was 10:10 AM. Look at him going with a document dated 19th December 1975 found in an old building in Fandu village Kpombai section Luawa chiefdom Kailahun district in the Eastern province of Sierra Leone! Again, it was Madman that was vibrating. I paid less attention to him instead I doubled up my steeps and escaped from the scene.

Uses of Quotation Mark (" ")

Use quotation marks to enclose a direct speech; that's someone's exact words

Eg: "All of you should finish your works today." Paul reminded us.

He said, "If you did not finish the work, I will punish you all."

Put a word or a phrase in a quotation mark if they are borrowed from another language. In such situation, the meaning of the word or phrase must be stated.

CHAPTER 14

CAPITALIZATION

Capital letters are very important in writing, as they draw reader's attention to the significant points in written material such as the beginning of new idea; and important words such as proper nouns or proper adjectives. They also make ideas clear when they are used correctly. When they are not used, or wrongly used, the ideas will be confused in a passage. Use of capital letters as follows:

Capitalize the following:

a) Capitalize the first letter of every sentence.

   Eg. There is dancing in the village today.

b) Capitalize the pronoun I, it doesn't matter where it appears in a sentence.

   Eg. He and **I** will come. **I** can play game.

c) Capitalize the proper nouns, it doesn't matter where it appears in a sentence.

   Eg. Sierra Leone, Hassan, Gambia, Blacky, December etc.

d) Capitalize geographical names (bodies of water, island, street, highway, parks etc.

   Eg Gambia River, MaCarthy Island, Jones Street, Brikama Highway, Bakau Park etc.

e) Capitalize the name of organizations, teams etc.

Eg. Language Club, Chelsea Football Club, Q-Cell, Senegambia

f) Capitalize the name of businesses, institutions, government bodies, Confederation, etc.

Eg. M. P. Trading, Njala University, National Power Authority, Kanifing Municipal Council etc.

g) **C**apitalize the names of nationalities, ethnic group, religion, religious books, holidays and followers, monuments, awards etc.

Eg. **S**ierra Leonean, Gambian, Wolof, Mende, Bible, Quran, Tobaski Holiday, Easter Holiday, Christians, Muslims, Statue of the 2nd Republic, Nobel Prize, Star of English Language etc.

h) Capitalize all proper adjectives.

Eg. Sierra Leonean writer, American president, Gambian laws, Nigerian movies, Mende **ethnic** group

i) Capitalize all titles that follow by proper nouns. Eg: Doctor Lahai, Professor Mansaray, President Bio, Teacher Momoh etc

EXERCISE 4

In the short passage below, all necessary punctuations are made. You can only do the capitalization.

mama salone is circular in sharp. the northeast, north and northwest shares border with guinea; the east and south borders with the south of liberia; and the Atlantic ocean locks the west and the southwest. it is politically divided into provinces and western area, districts, chiefdoms, sections, towns and villages. kailahun, kono and kenema districts are in the eastern province. bo, moiyamba, pujehun, and bonthe districts are in the southern province; while kpombali, port loko, koinadugu, kambia and tonkolili districts are in the north. freetown, the capital city and its environs are located in the western area. the staple food is rice; next to it are cassava, potato and yam. coffee, caocao and oil palm are the major cash crops the people grow. the major activities are farming, trading, fishing, mining and education. the currencies are leones and cents. there are many rivers and streams, swamps, low lands, savannah lands, forests, valleys, hills and mountains. additional natural resources include diamond, gold, bauxite, retile, stones and crude oil. green, white and blue are the colours of the national flag. there are christians, muslims, traditionalists and christmus peacefully co-existing in this anthem of west africa. inter-marriages are common among the eighteen ethnic groups which comprise of the seven million and more peoples living in the country. the two major political parties are sierra leone peoples party and all peoples congress party; Creole, mende and temne are widely spoken languages. Almighty God bless my beloved country!

EXERCISE 5

Write the capital letter (s) where necessary in the sentences below.

1. joseph and kaina are the only two sons of mr. and mrs. kasilio.
2. freetown and banjul are among cities in wast africa.
3. when i was in America, i lived in new york.
4. many african footballers play for premier league clubs.
5. jesus christ and prophet mohammed are true messengers of god.
6. president jammeh, the gambian hero, will never be forgotten.
7. torgbo and mamba are tallest mountains in kailahun district.
8. the boy, jeneba and i went to see doctor lahai.
9. united states of africa is the dream of most african patriots.
10. she lived in britain, germany and france before he returned home.

PART 5

ESSAY WRITING

CHAPTER 15

PARAGRAPH DEVELOPMENT

A paragraph is most often made up of group of sentences with or about similar idea. Sometimes single sentence can make a paragraph. Most paragraphs contain topic sentence and supporting sentences. Any good paragraphs contain introduction, development and conclusion. Always remember **PEED** when writing a paragraph. State a *Point*, advance *Evidence* to support your point and *Explain* the evidence to *Develop* your idea. There are two types of paragraphs. They are Functional paragraph and Paragraph Block.

Functional paragraph: This kind of paragraph does not contain a particular sentence that holds the main idea of the paragraph. All the sentences in this paragraph are unified, coherent, logically arranged and clearly connected. All single-sentence paragraphs are example of functional paragraphs. This kind of paragraph is often used for three different purposes.

a) Use functional paragraph to stimulate or sustain interest: That is, a few vivid sentences that work together to capture a reader's attention.
b) Functional paragraph is used to indicate dialogue: One principle of dialogue is that any time each speaker talks, a new paragraph begins even if it is only a single word he utters.
c) It could also be used to make a transition: That is, you use it in a way to help reader to move between the ideas of two topical paragraphs.

Paragraph Block: This type of paragraph contains **topic sentence** and the **supporting sentences**. A topic sentence always contains the main idea that will be developed into paragraph. Among the supporting sentences some will rename or explain the main idea in the topic sentence. Some will supply facts, statistics, examples, illustrations and other necessary details that will support the idea in the topic sentence.

Positioning of the topic sentence within the paragraph depends on the intention of the writer. If you want to wet your readers' appetites, place your topic sentence at the beginning of the paragraph. Place it in the middle of the paragraph when you want to give a background first before penetrating into heart of the topic. If you want to hammer home your message, or summarize the details of the idea you have stated earlier, you can place your topic sentence at the end of the paragraph.

Supporting sentences: They are called supporting sentences because they give sensory, facts, examples or details that can explain or prove the main idea in the topic sentence. Let your supporting sentence appeal to one of the senses: sight, hearing, feeling, taste or smell. Always remember that any supporting sentence must state one of these details or information about the main idea in the topic sentence:

Observe the examples below.

Topic sentence: *My late father was a famous tailor in our village.*

a) **Restate or re-explain the topic sentence:** This kind of sentence renames or re-explains the idea in the topic sentence but in different way.

   Eg: Kennie Masseh AI-Gbahan Lahai was a popular local tailor within our community and beyond.

b) **facts:** Facts are statements that can be proved with evidence. They support your main idea by providing proofs about it.

   Eg: He appeared very busy during the periods of festivities such as Tobaski, Ramadan, Easter, Christmas and initiation of traditional societies. He sewed for many people during any one of these periods.

c) **statistics:** These are also facts or instances that are usually stated in figures. It also supports the topic sentence as it provides vital details that can make the meaning clear. This is another form of fact.

   Eg: At least, he sewed for 74% of the ladies in the village during the last Christmas season before his sudden death.

d) **examples, illustrations or instances:** This is a specific thing, person or event that can demonstrate a point.

Eg: For that year's Christmas, he sewed for Mualaylay, Amuloma and Teigloma; three out of the four outstanding ladies' social clubs in the community.

e) **Use details:** These are the necessary parts of the whole that will add information that can make the point or the main idea clear by showing how all the pieces fit.

Eg: In their superb attires, the ladies sang and praised dad's name. They appeared very smart, decent and beautiful.

Here is the full paragraph.

My late father was a famous tailor in our village. He was a popular local tailor within our community and beyond. He appeared very busy during the periods of festivities such as Tobaski, Ramadan, Easter, Christmas and initiation of traditional societies. He sewed for many people. At least, he sewed for 74% of the women in the village during the last Christmas occasion before his sudden death. He sewed for Mualaylay, Amuloma and Teigloma; three out of the four ladies' social groups in the community. In their superb attires, the ladies sang and praised dad's name. They appeared very smart, decent and beautiful.

Unity and Coherence in Paragraph

The common features of any good paragraph are unity and coherence. There is unity in a paragraph when all the sentences are clearly connected and support or tell something about the main idea in the topic sentence. In other words, the specific details in the supporting sentences must be related to the main idea.

On the other hand, a paragraph is said to have coherence when the ideas are logically organized and clearly connected in a way that they make sense to the readers. Coherence is also created in paragraph if the reader is able to tell why and how ideas are connected; which can only be achieved through the effective use of *transitional* words or phrases. To create coherence, arrange your ideas in an appropriate order; and use the transitional words or phrases to keep the connection clear as you move from one idea or detail to another. There are many ways to organize paragraphs or essay, but the type of organization we choose depends on the topic or purpose.

Transitional Words

Transitional words and phrases understandably guide readers from one idea/sentence to the other. They are essential because they facilitate smooth run down and comprehension of ideas. They help writers to relate ideas in their works and readers to understand how ideas relate in pieces of writing. Transitional words and connectives may look alike but there is slight difference in their grammatical roles. Transitional words most often appear at the beginning of a sentence and go further to explain how ideas relate in a piece of writing. Whereas connectives most often appear between the words they join. There are ten different ways transitional words indicate how ideas relate as they are stated below.

a) **Restatement Transition**: - This includes: that is, in short, to repeat, to put it differently, in other words, in simple terms etc.

   Eg: Hundreds of fans occupied the field because their best players were on the bench. *In other words*, the fans did not want the game to play without their favourite players on the pitch.

   The people no longer respect their leaders' instructions; they even boo at them when they speak. *In summary*, they don't like their leaders any longer.

b) **Example Transition**: - This includes: for instance, specifically, to illustrate, thus, for example etc.

   Eg: It is actually true that corruption was rampant in the previous government. *For instance*, our First Lady alone was given Eight Billion Leone (Le 8,000,000,000) loan by our national bank.

No one can deny the fact that the modern technology is destroying our young generations. *For example,* it kills their precious times and teaches them a lot of immoralities.

c) **Conclusion and Summary Transition**: - This includes: finally, to conclude, in brief, to summarize, in closing, on the whole, at last, after all etc.

eg: In the then government, tribalism and regionalism were dominant; justice too was in the pocket of government officers and their relatives. Workers' meagre salaries were not regularly paid. *On the whole* corruption was rampant.

Unknown gunmen attack and murder defence less people in cold blood, women and girls are raped in broad daylight, shops are vandalized and items rooted. *In summary,* no one is secured in this country these days.

d) **Time Transition**: This relates ideas by indicating the sequence or order of their occurrence. They include: formerly, earlier, currently, later, afterwards, previously, immediately, then, subsequently, simultaneously, at the same time, in the future, until now etc.

eg. *At first,* it was a rebel war, *then,* came in Ebola and *now* it is mudslide that killed my people like flies.

In the past, I worked *at the time* learned *until now* I am not in good health condition.

e) **Addition Transitions**: - This includes: and, also, moreover, besides, first, second, third, furthermore, in addition, to begin with, next, finally, in the first place etc.

eg. Tijan Kabba ended the war; rehabilitate the country and the minds of the traumatized citizens; and *besides,* he minimized the rampant corruption that was responsible for the war.

I have acquired university degree, secured lucrative job and married. ***Moreover***, I am healthy and happy.

f) **Cause-Effect Transition**: - This includes: therefore, accordingly, consequently, hence, as a result, for this reason, thus etc

Eg. The previous government did very little for the people and embezzled huge amount of money. ***As a result***, the people did not vote for them again.

We all thought it wise to vote out the previous government and vote in this current one; ***therefore***, let us support it to succeed.

g) **Contrast Transitions**: - This includes: however, instead, yet, still, nevertheless, in contrast, on the other hand etc.

eg. I love you, I will educate you and help your family ***but*** I will not marry you.

He is popular, he has worked in United Nations Organization and he has wealth of experience, ***nevertheless***, he hasn't the constitutional right to become our president.

h) **Place Transitions**: - This includes: nearby, upon, above, beneath, alongside, beyond, on top of, in front of under etc.

Eg: It doesn't matter where I go to get victory over the struggle, ***to the right*** or ***to the left***, what matters is success.

It is not actually my business where money comes from, ***under*** the sea, ***on top of*** a mountain, ***above*** the sun; money is money, let it just be in my pocket.

i) **Comparison Transition**: - This includes: similarly, in like manner, likewise, by the same token, in similar fashion, in the same way etc.

Eg: When they came to power, they sacked all the south-easterners from government offices. ***Similarly, so***, their services were terminated when their government was voted out of power.

My parents took very good care of me, they put good manners in me and educated me. ***In similar*** fashion, I will take good care of my children and have them educated.

j) **Insistence Transition**: - This includes: yes, no, in fact, indeed etc.

Making education priority is ***indeed*** a reasonable idea, more especially when we have high rate of illiteracy in the country.

The government should let every child to attend school; ***in fact,*** it should be a punishable crime for any parent who fails to send his/her child to school.

CHAPTER 16

ESSAY WRITING

Essay writing is also known as continuous writing. It consists of letters, compositions, stories, speeches, debates and articles. This aspect of English Language examination carries the highest marks. Essay questions require candidates to express their abilities of writing to explain or narrate an event, argue out issues or to describe an object or event. Often, candidates are required to use numbers of words, and they are required to write an essay of *at least 450 words.*

What do the examiners look for in essay scripts?

Over the years, it has been proven beyond all reasonable doubt that candidates performed very poorly in English Language examinations conducted by West African Examinations Council. They often perform poorly in the continuous writing section. About Sixty to Seventy per cent of the marks for English Language for most examinations goes to this section. A good number of candidates fail English language because they do not know what the examiners look for when marking their scripts; and if someone doesn't know what you want, he/she hardly gives it to you. When examiners are marking English scripts, they take into consideration the following: content, organization, expression/text structure, sentence structure, mechanical accuracy, length of the script and format.

a) **Content:** In the IGCSE system, this aspect is called *Purpose and Audience*. This is referred to the information the question requests for. Examiners expect the candidates to write the correct information or message that is required. For instance, if you are asked to describe your best friend, don't only give abstract information about him/her that he/she cannot be recognized by even when he/she appears. Information such as his name, address, tribe, occupation, religion, nationality, academic background are less important in such essay and they earn the candidate less marks. They are just giving information about the friend instead of describing him. From the information above, one cannot just see the person and recognize him/her. They do not contain any information about the person's physical appearance or make-up. If you are describing someone and you leave out concrete information like his colour, size, shape, height and detail information about some specific parts, then the description is not complete; even though you may have given some other relevant information about the person. Both the concrete and abstract information are needed in describing someone or an object, but emphasis should be laid on the concrete information. This is because it helps someone to recognize the person or object when he sees him/her/it. So when a candidate fails to hit the nail on the head but just beats about bush on any question, he/she will lose some valuable marks.

b) **Organization:** Examiners expect candidates to present their answers in an orderly and organized manner. Some candidates will write good English and correct message, but in a disorganized manner. Candidates are therefore advised to put their points or ideas in logically organized and suitable paragraphs. Use one of the three organization styles discussed in the previous chapter. More details are given about them below.

Chronological Order: The details in a paragraph may be arranged in chronological order. This kind of order deals with paragraphs in which an incident that occurred is explained or an explanation of the steps in a process. Chronological order is simply the order in which things happen or the steps in which a process should be done. It is sometimes referred to as time order. It is also used in narrative essays, wherein events are told in the order in which they occurred. For example, assuming you are writing to explain the way a birthday party was celebrated. The first paragraph must probably be about the preparation for the celebration. Second paragraph will be about the morning activities on the very day of the celebration. The third paragraph may be on the afternoon activities and may be the fourth paragraph will on the very party itself in the evening hours. In short, you explain the activities in a sequential order.

Order of importance: The details in a paragraph may be arranged in the order of importance. In explanatory or argumentative essays, you may choose to put your facts or reasons in the order of importance or in the order in which they occur. A paragraph developed by facts or examples are all of equal importance. Simply, easily understood facts should come before those that are hard to understand. This is suitable for argumentative or cause and effect essay. It is about logical presentation of ideas; the most important idea comes first, second important one follows etc, down to the least.

Spatial order: This style is appropriate for descriptive essay. Here, ideas are presented according to the position of parts of the item or object you write about. Description appeals to the sight, so always the first thing to describe is the one that you see first or prominent to the sight. For example, if you are describing a school compound, you have to talk about the features of the school that are more likely to be seen before adding other details. For example, if the school has a fence, you will describe the gate first before moving on to describe other important features or structures that you will meet or see after the gate. One after the other, you can write about other important things in the school compound.

Note that anyone of these organizational styles needs to be accompanied with appropriate transitional words. Candidates that fail to put their ideas or points in appropriate order will lose reasonable marks. Remember too, that many writers do not use one method, but a combination of methods to produce an effective paragraph.

c) **Expression:** For IGCSE system, this aspect is known as ***sentence structure.*** One main aim of any essay question is to test the ability of candidates as to how best they can express themselves in English Language. It is largely based on the following: the use of appropriate registers or choice of and correct use of appropriate dictions or vocabularies, correct construction of different kinds of sentences structures and functions with different lengths and beginnings. When a candidate fails to effectively express himself/herself in essay writing, he/she will lose valuable marks.

d) **Mechanical Accuracy:** Candidates are expected to apply all the rules they may have studied during the grammar lessons. Examiners expect candidates to be grammatically disciplined and apply the grammatical rules such as appropriate use of capital letters and punctuation marks, correct spellings, verb tenses and concord (subject verb agreement or pronoun antecedent agreement). It is important to know that examiners look for mistakes instead of points when marking English scripts. More marks are allocated to this aspect than other areas; and it is this same area where most candidates loose marks. Candidates are therefore advised to read and understand the grammar rules and apply them correctly when writing the essay.

e) **Length of Script:** Candidates are required to write specific number of words for which marks will be awarded. A candidate who fails to write the required number of words will not gain all the mark allocated for essay. Note that if any candidate decides to write nonsense just for him/her to get the required numbers of words, he/she will be penalized under content, expression and mechanical accuracy. If on the other hand, a candidate used more words than required, only the ideas within the required numbers of words will be considered. Even if there are relevant points within the extra words/sentences, they will not be considered.

f) **Format of Letter:** It is referred to the laying out of a letter; that is where and how the parts of letters are written. Parts like address (s), date, salutation, (heading for formal letter), body of letter and conclusion are usually written in very special ways and with rules such as use of punctuation marks and capitalization, guiding them. This aspect is part of the organization. Candidates will gain full marks if they correctly apply these rules. Candidates will also be panelised for any mistake committed.

Link between Grammar and Essay

Grammar and essay are closely connected. Grammar deals with the study of rules that guide the use of language; while writing deals with the application of those rules. In writing, we apply all the rules we learn in grammar. Answering essay question demands candidates to express their writing skills to explain an event, to argue an issue or to describe an object. This includes all the rules we study in grammar: sentence structure and function, subject verb agreement, pronoun antecedent agreement, verb tenses, effective use of phrases and clauses, correct use of punctuation marks and capital letters etc; these rules have to be applied correctly. This is one of the reasons why grammar is considered as a major tool to excellent writing. Effective and efficient application of these rules will improve your writing skills and make the pieces of your writing magnificent.

Ways to Answer Essay Questions:

Understanding a question is very important. It is believed that how a question is understood and answered by a candidate determines the grade he/she will score. If one doesn't understand a question, it is likely that he/she will wrongly answer that question even when he/she may know the correct answer to the question. So candidates are advised to read any question over and again so that they will understand what the question asks them to do before attempting the question. Having knowledge on the question follows the understanding of the question. Understanding of the question will help to invoke whatever idea one has about the question, so the ideas will be put on paper in correct sentences. If you have no idea or very little knowledge on any question, do not attempt it first even if you understand the question. Always make sure that you have adequate knowledge on any question before you attempt it. Always first attempt the question that you know best before attempting other questions. Some essay questions will not demand candidates to write facts about their topics. Rather, it obliges them to effectively express themselves in writing. Most essay questions ask for personal opinion, creative or expository writing. To write a good essay, candidates must have broad ideas on the topic, sufficient knowledge on grammar and adequate vocabularies to express themselves. So if you want to be familiar with the rules and the skills of writing, you should write always. If you want to accumulate enough vocabularies that will enable you to express yourself accurately, and to have wide knowledge on topic matters, you should develop good reading habits. I advise you to read and write often.

CHAPTER 17

LETTER WRITING

Letter writing is different from other types of essays only in format. A letter has an address, date, salutation, body and conclusion. There are three kinds of letters. They are informal, semi-formal and formal letters. These letters are different from one another in format and language only. Informal letters and semi-formal letters have the same format, but different in diction or tone. On the other hand, a formal letter is different from the other kinds of letters in both format and language.

Parts of Letters

The following are the main parts of a letter:

Address: The address is normally written on the top right hand corner of the page. It is necessary because it shows the location of the writer of the letter. Every word in the address must start with capital letter except the articles (a, an, the) and prepositions. Each line in the address must end with comma. Full stop only comes at the end of the last line. It is important to note that punctuating an address is optional. But it is not advisable to punctuate some lines and leave the others. Punctuate all the lines if you choose to do so, or leave all if you don't want to punctuate.

A formal letter contains two addresses. The second address is often written on the line below the date, but on the left hand side of the page. There are two ways to write addresses; *vertical straight line style* and *slant style*. If you are using vertical straight line style, make sure that the first letter of all the lines must be in vertical straight line. Eg:

> 10 Maada Lahai Street,
> Gbenyama Section,
> Nyandehun Mambabu, Kailahun.

On the other hand, if you choose to use slant line style, the first letter of each line must be situated under the second letter of the first word in the line above as shown in the example below:

10 Kanni Lahai Street,
Gbenyama Section,
Nyandehun Mambabu
Kailahun

Date: This is another important part of a letter. It is important as it indicates the time the letter is written. It is normally written on the line below the first address. The first letter of every month must be capitalized. Always punctuate the date. Comma comes after the month and full stop comes after the year. Eg: 23rd February, 2019.

Salutation: This is a form of greeting. It is important in two ways. Firstly, as greeting, it serves as a key to open communication. Secondly, it also shows the relationship between the writer of the letter and addressee. In informal and semi-formal letters, the salutation is written on the line below the date, but on the left hand side of the page. In formal letter, it is written below the second address. Always skip a line before writing your salutation in a formal letter. Capitalize the first letter of salutation and put a comma at the end.

Eg: My dearest friend, Dear father, but use colon at the end of a salutation of formal letter.

Eg Dear Sir/Madam: etc

Heading: It is only formal letters that have headings. The heading serves as title to the letter; and it is important because it gives the reader a clue about the main message of the letter. Like the address, all the words in the heading, except articles or prepositions, must be capitalized. Capitalize articles or prepositions only when they come at the beginning of the heading. Do not forget to underline your heading when it is written in small letters. But, if it is written in block letters, do not underline them. Always make sure that it is written on the line below the salutation, in the middle of the two margin lines. The heading and the second address of formal letter are always found in the question.

Body of letter: In the body of a letter, the writer clearly presents his/her message. Depending on the length of the message, the body has to be divided into paragraphs. For this reason, always remember to start the body of your letter with a paragraph. Begin every new idea with a new paragraph.

Conclusion: This is also known as the closing of letter. Like the salutation, the conclusion can also indicate the relationship between the writer and addressee. The conclusion of the different types of letters are different from one another. For formal letter, it is always either ***Yours faithfully, Yours sincerely*** or ***Yours truly***. For informal or semi-formal letter, it largely depends on the relationship between the writer and the addressee. The conclusion can be written on either the left or right hand side of the page, below the body of a letter.

Types of Letters

Informal letter: This is also known as a friendly letter. It is most often written by and to people of the same age group, and for informal purposes. In most informal letters, writers use informal language such as jargons, slangs, contractions, phrasal verbs and abbreviations. Sometimes, people ignore some of the parts of letter stated above, or they write them in different ways or location on the page. But for examination purpose, you are advised not to do so because the examiner may not understand your jargons or slangs as your friends do.

Semi-formal letter: This kind of letter is written to elderly relatives or friends. It is perceived that the writers of this kind of letter are most often younger than their addressees. For this reason, the language will not be as informal as in an informal letter; nor does it have to be too formal as in formal letter. In other words, the language used in this kind of letter must be polite, simple and clear.

Formal letter: This is also called official or business letter. The format and language are different from the other kinds of letters. Besides the other parts the other letters carry, a formal letter has second address and a heading. This second address must contain the following: official title of the addressee; this should be written on the first line, the name and location of the office or institution should be written on the next lines below respectively. It is not advisable to use personal name of the addressee even if you know or relate to him/her well.

The salutation is always ***Dear sir or madam***. If you know that the addressee is a male, use *sir*; and use *madam* for female. Use both if you are not sure of the sex of the addressee. Always use a colon at the end of the salutation (:).

The heading of a formal letter serves as a suitable title for the letter; therefore, it should not be written as a full sentence, and it could be carved out from the question. It must be compressed into a phrase.

The language must be completely polite and formal. No jargon or slang is allowed. Only nationally or internationally approved abbreviations are allowed in this kind of letter. It is advisable to write the full meaning of any abbreviation when you use it for the first time; after which, you can continue using the abbreviation. It must be brief and to the point.

Writing of Formal Letter

There are two different kinds of formal letter. There are personal and non-personal formal letters. Personal formal letters are written on behalf of the writer himself/herself alone. For instance, letter of application for a job or admission in an institution are examples of personal formal letter. Non-personal formal letters are those we write on behalf of an organization or people including or excluding the writer. For instance, if the head boy writes a letter of apology, requesting or complaining on behalf of the school, or if you are an NGO worker and you write to inform government about a problem you discovered in a particular community; such a letter is referred to as non-personal formal letter. Observe few examples below.

There are explanations followed by examples:

Question: *Assuming you have completed your schooling and you are looking for job; fortunately, you come across an advertisement for the position of secretary in Q-Cell Mobile Company in the Foroya Newspaper. Write and apply for the job.*

Old Jeshwang,
Kanifing Municipality,
Serrekunda.
22nd May, 2016.

The Managing Director,
Q-cell Mobile Company,
State Avenue,
Serrekunda.

Dear Sir/Madam:

APPLICATION FOR THE POSITION OF SECRETARY
In your first paragraph, state what you want and the source where you got the information about the job.

Eg:

I write to apply for the position of secretary in your company, as the vacancy was advertised in the Exclusive Newspaper on Friday 17th May, 2015. *Or*

I am highly interested in the position of secretary in your company as the vacancy was advertised on the national television, Monday night 24th July, 2018.

In the next paragraph, tell the addressee who you are. Talking about yourself including three areas: personal information, academic history and job experience. The personal information includes your age, tribe, religion, marital status and nationality. You may add your sex if your name cannot identify your sex. Here, the activities are similar to form filling in IGCSE.

Eg: I am twenty-two years old, Sierra Leonean, Mende by tribe. I am a faithful Christian, married with two children. *Or*

I was born twenty-two years ago in a village called Nyandehun Mambabu in Kailahun district, eastern province of Sierra Leone. I am a Mende by tribe and a faithful Catholic; married with four children.

For the academic history, state the following: names of the schools/ institutions you attended, the years of entry and leaving, the achievement you made and the certificates (results) you obtained. This must constitute its own paragraph.

Eg: I started my schooling in Roman Catholic Primary in Nyandehun in 2002. In 2005 when I was in grade five, I became the class captain. I was also a member of the school football team and the drama group. In 2006, I participated in a debate organized by the Ministry of Education. I won the prize of the best speaker. I sat to the Selective Entrance Examination or National Assessment Test in 2007. I was able to secure very sound result which helped me to gain admission in the National Secondary School in Kailahun ...

(Note that some examining bodies such as WAEC, will demand for particular number of words your essay must contain. It is in this area you have to work hard to get the number of words. You are at liberty to name more schools/institutions and give more information about your activities and achievements in each institution so that you can get the number of words.)

In your next paragraph, state the job experience if there is any. It will include the job title(s), name(s) of the office(s), position(s) held, achievement(s) made and the years you did the job(s).

Eg: In 2012, I secured a job in the office of Africel, where I worked as Assistant Secretary in the office of Public Relations. I used to organize sensitization programmes on radio and television to inform the public about the activities and promotions of the company. After a year of effective work, I was promoted to Assistant Public Relations Officer.*(Give more experience where necessary)*

In your next paragraph, state your referees. Here are some necessary information you need to give about your referees: Provide names (s), addresses and the contact numbers of people who could be contacted for confirmation of information you have given. If you state their office address, don't forget to state their official title or position. You can name only two or three referees. Note that your referees should not be your relatives.

Eg: Mr. Mambu B. Sheriff, Program Director, Paul Lahai International Youth Organization, contact number: 8455/2677; Mr. Joseph Ejeku Boima, Secretary General, Africel Mobile Company, Kailahun. Contact number: 191275; and the photocopy of my documents enclosed with this letter can testify th claims.

Conclude your letter with commitment to hard work so that the aims and objectives of the company could be achieved.

Eg: If I am fortunate to gain the employment in your company, I will work hard so that the aims and objectives of your company will be achieved.

Close your letter with one of the followings: Yours faithfully, Yours Sincerely or Yours truly; then you pen down your signature first before writing your full name below it.

Eg:

Yours faithfully,
(signature)
Gibao Ngaima.

Another example question:

Assuming your parents are civil service workers. Dad has been promoted and transferred. He has decided to move together with the rest of the family when the first term just ended. In the new community, write and apply for admission in one of the schools.

10 Jones Street,
Blackhall Road,
Kissi,
Freetown.
23rd February, 2019.

The Principal,
Saint Augustine High School,
George Brook,
Dwazark Farm,
Freetown.

Dear Sir:
<u>Application for Admission</u>

Just state what you want in the first paragraph.

Eg: I am delighted to write and apply for admission into your school/institution.

OR

It pleases me to request for an admission in your noble school/institution.

Briefly say something about yourself and give reasons for your transfer to this community in your next paragraph.

Eg: I am a seventeen-year old Sierra Leonean; faithful Christian and Mende by tribe. My family and I lived in Basseh for more than seven years. I am a grade 10 pupil form Basseh Senior Secondary School. My parents are civil servants; dad was promoted and transferred here six months ago.

Now the rest of the family has joined him. I need a vibrant school like yours to continue my schooling ... *(Give more reasons)*

In form of praise, you can give reasons why you choose the school.

Eg: Before our transfer to this community, I have heard a lot about the excellent performance of your school in both national and international examinations. Since then, I developed the interest to taste the quality education your hardworking teachers impart to the learners. Or I am a science student and your school has one of the equipped laboratories in the community. ... *(Give more reasons)*

In the next paragraph, state your referees. Here are some necessary information you need to give about your referee (s): Name(s), addresses and the contact numbers. If you state office addresses, don't forget to state their official title or position. You can name only two or three referees. Note that your referees should not be your relatives.

Eg: Mr. Andrew Jusu Koroma, Head of English Language Department, contact number: 0191269; and Mr. Vicent T Bangali, Head of Geography Department, contact number: 0270916; all in Basseh Senior Secondary School.

Conclude your letter with a promise to obey the rules and regulations of the institution.

Eg: If I am fortunate to gain admission in your school, I will abide by all the rules and regulations of your school and work hard to obtain a good result so that the good name of the school will continue to flourish.

Close your letter with one of the following: Yours faithfully, Yours Sincerely or Yours truly; then you pen down your signature first before writing your full name.

Eg:

Yours truly,
(signature)
Mujeh P. H. Lahai

Example of non-personal formal letter:

Question: *As a concerned citizen and an NGO worker, you have witnessed an outbreak of a plague in a certain community. Write a letter to the Ministry of Health informing him about the matter. Throw light on the other health related problems the community is facing and suggest possible solutions to the problems.*

108 Pademba Road,
Old Jeshwang,
Kanifing
Serrekunda.
19th December, 2018.

The Honourable Minister,
Ministry of Health,
Brookfields Hotel,
Banjul.

Dear Sir:

A Sudden Outbreak of Epidemic Diseases

As usual, hit the nail on the head. State exactly and precisely the information you want to relay in the first sentence. State and briefly describe the specific problem(s). Continue by explaining the stage of the situation in this paragraph.

Eg: There is a sudden outbreak of an epidemic disease in Bartima Community. Following the flood caused by the heavy rains, dysentery, malaria and cholera related calamities have broken out in this community. Within the last two weeks, about seventeen people have been admitted by these epidemic diseases. The community has only one small health centre which is less equipped with few unqualified and less experienced workers. This centre is now filled to capacity with patients. More new cases come daily. No life is currently safe in this community.

It is important to explain at least a major cause of the problem because it can help in mapping out an immediate strategic solution. While stating the problems, you can also give brief descriptive information about the community that may serve as a link to the problem. This will include the location and estimated number of people living there, facilities available and their health related issues.

Eg: Pa Musa Konomoie, one of the elders of the community, described the plague as natural disaster waiting to happen. According to him, the heavy downpour of rains only ignited the outbreak, but one major cause of this problem is over population and lack of certain hygienic facilities. There are about twenty-one thousand people dwelling in this community which contains less than four hundred houses. Most of the houses are without toilets. There are only eleven public toilets with five water wells which often dry up. The garbage collectors too are not effective; most of the drainages are filled with rubbish. Flies from the heaps of the garbage disperse bacteria to house hoods.

State and explain the effects of the problems on the community. Remember that some effects are immediate and direct, others may be long-term and or indirect.

*Eg:-***Death:** As I stated earlier, this epidemic has already destroyed many innocent souls. More and more are being admitted on daily basis; some are in very critical condition. Panic has gripped the community since the outbreak started. Urgent action is very necessary at the moment.

Recommend and explain possible solutions to the problems. Certain problems need more different approaches/solutions; some approach may be immediate and direct; some may be long-term and indirect solutions. To be objective and organized, one needs to mention the immediate solution first under the recommendation. It is good to use appropriate paragraph to summarize the main ideas in the topic. Don't forget to identify the roles of government, NGOs, community authorities and members.

This problem needs urgent attention; if not the worst may be inevitable and it will come soonest. This community needs enough medicines and trained and experienced medical personnel to work with those on the ground to calm down the situation. They will work with community leaders and members to keep their environments tidy and educate them on how to keep their foods and maintain their cooking utensils by keeping them clean and safe.

Yours faithfully,
(signature)
Joseph P. Elogima Boima.

CHAPTER 18

WRITING ARTICLES

An article is another form of essay writing. To write an article means to give critical analysis of the subject matter in question. The major things involved in article writing include the following:

-Selecting the appropriate title for an article is the first step. It is interesting to learn that the title could be carved from the question. An appropriate label of any article will help readers to have a clue about the message it contains.

-Definition of the topic: Most article topics deserve to be correctly and convincingly defined in line with what is being said about the topic. It is possible for some particular article to have more than one definition, depending from which angle the writer looks at the topic. If there are varieties of your article topic, clearly specify the one you concern about.

-Some articles are cause and effect topics. When you write on this kind of topic, your next step will be to state and explain the causes. State each cause and clearly explain it. Mention at least five causes. Just after you state and explain the causes, identify and clearly explain the direct and indirect, (immediate and long-term) effects/results/impacts on the people or and the society. There are two ways to do this: Some people write each cause followed by its own effect; some will write all the causes before writing the effects.

To be objective, you have to suggest possible solutions as recommendation to any problem you identify or mention. When making your recommendation, remember that some solutions may be immediate while others may be long-term. Also, remember to identify and explain the roles that government, organizations, local authorities and individuals will play to bring about the solution. Observe the examples below.

Write an article for publication in a national newspaper on the rampant drug abuse among the youths in your community.

Step one: Get an appropriate title for your article from the question.

<u>Rampant Drug Abuse in the Hellish Aacutay Community</u>

Step two: Introduce your article first by clearly defining and specifying the topic. Specification of the topic is necessary if there are varieties of it; it helps to narrow the topic down. You can also estimate the extent, weight or gravity of the problem. Remember to indicate the category of people involved in the abuse, the specific drugs that are abused and how the abuses occur.

One very serious problems the world is facing today, which is as dangerous as terrorism, is the abuse of drugs by teenagers and youths. The abuse of drugs by young people in our society has become the order of the day; and the number of these drug abusers is increasing on daily basis. Hard drugs such as marijuana, cocaine, brown-brown and some other narcotic drugs like kola nuts, cigarettes, amphora, 'attaya' and alcohol, are often abused.

Among the youths and young people of Hellish Aacutay community today, smoking, inhaling and taking-in of these drugs is very rampant. Some drug abuse is done ignorantly; others are done consciously. Whatever way one looks at it, abuse is an abuse. Every nation heavily depends on her young people for her future development activities. So if the lives of those living in Hellish Aacutay are buried in drugs, this means the future of our Aacutay and many other parts in the world are in jeopardy. The peace and security of our society is under constant threat. The authorities and parents need to take an immediate and drastic action in order to put the ugly situation under control.

What I refer to as drug abuse in this article is the misuse of any drug (common or narcotic drugs). Whenever a drug is taken for a wrong purpose, at the wrong time or more than the required dosage, that drug is said to have been abused.

There are two kinds of drugs. They are common drugs such as paracetamol, septrin, penicillin, panadol etc; and narcotic or hard drugs such as marijuana, cocaine, brown-brown, cigarettes, alcohol, 'attaya', 'amphora', kola nuts etc. For the purpose of this article, I am only concerned with the abuse of narcotic drug and not the common drugs.

Step three: State and explain the causes of the drug abuse. State and explain what lures people into the drug abuse.

Eg: There are a number of factors that are leading the young people into drug abuse. They include peer pressure, depression and frustration, for pleasure sake, for criminal intention etc.

- **Peer Pressure: Peer Pressure is defined as an influence of peer group over a member or members of the group to do or behave the way the group wants.** About sixty-five percent of those who abuse and have become addicted to drugs were initiated by their friends. They are influenced by their friends. **Sociologists believe that peer pressure exists, and it is believed that either persuasively or forcefully, group members will directly or indirectly copy the attitude, value, belief or behaviour of other influential members. It is believed that a good number of drug abusers were initiated into the game by their friends; who too, may have been lured in it by other friends. In peer group, influential members continue to lure their friends to do what they want.**

Step four: State the effects of drug and explain them.

Eg: The abuse of drugs has got very adverse effects on the abusers particularly and the society as whole. Some of the effects include perpetual violence and crime, ill health (madness), drop out from school, economic problem, suffering to death and creating of an unhealthy and backward society.

- **Perpetual violence and crime:** Perpetual violence, robbery and prostitution are always common among drug abusers' thus paving way to increase of crime rate in the society. In any community where narcotic drugs are abused, security of lives and properties is always under threat and stability and peace will seem to be fragile. From petty theft to armed robbery, prostitution and violation of other by-laws are renowned features of narcotic drug abused in society. Sometimes, teenagers or youths under the influence of drugs will attack people, community properties and even security officers. The abusers themselves will sometimes point their guns at one another and kill themselves. Innocent citizens may also lose their lives in such violence.

-Step five: State or suggest ways how the problem could be solved. Name the participants: the state, NGO's, religious groups, community leaders, parents and the abusers themselves; explain their different roles and how these roles will be executed.

Eg: There is no problem without a solution. Drug abuse is seen to be a huge problem which needs global effort if it is to be put under control. The government, NGOs, authorities and individuals in the very communities where the abuse occurs have to do something to control it. Formulating and enforcing by-laws, organizing sensitization sessions and instituting rehabilitation programmes for youth in the communities.

–   **Formulation and enforcement of policies:** To combat or minimize drug abuse in our society, policy makers have to formulate by-laws that will enable the law enforcement officers to pursue the criminals and deal with them appropriately. Such laws will not only target the abusers, but should also target the producers, distributors and sellers. Community members should be persuaded to aid the efforts of the securities and authorities by supplying in relevant information.

The last stage is to conclude your article. An appropriate functional paragraph is needed here to summarize all the causes, effects and recommendations.

PART 6

COMPREHENSION AND SUMMARY EXERCISES

Both comprehension and summary questions test the candidates' reading and understanding and writing ability. Summary goes further to test how candidates can deduce or explain in their own words the main point of a given paragraph/passage. So if a candidate is to answer questions correctly on these topics, he or she must be able to read clearly so that he/she can understand what he/she reads. To read clearly means to read according to the punctuation marks; without repeating, counting or miss-pronouncing the words in the sentences. To inculcate perfect reading habit, it is advisable for candidates to read always. One can also overcome reading problems by listening to newsreaders on national and international media and copy their skills.

It is also important to note that it is not in all cases that one has to attach a dictionary meaning to certain key words in the passage. Rather, learn to attach meaning to words according to the way they are used in a given sentence or passage.

CHAPTER 19

COMPREHENSION PASSAGES

Before attempting any question on comprehension passage, it is good to read and understand the message in the passage first; then you can read and comprehend the questions on the passage. Skim the passage to find the answers to the questions. Mark any sentence you believe contains the answer (s) to any question. Read the questions again and then the passage. This time, carefully read to understand the passage; lay emphases on the sentences or paragraphs you believe contain the answers. Write your answers in your own words. Though you will not be limited to number of words or sentences, yet, try to be as brief and clear as possible. Capitalize and punctuate your sentences correctly. Remember that you have four different sets of questions to answer in most comprehension exercise.

a) The first set of questions will be on the content of the passage. These questions are only answered correctly if the content of the passage is clearly understood.

b) The second set of questions will be on grammatical structures. To answer these questions, one must study and understand the phrases and clauses in the grammar section. It is advisable for a candidate to start with this set of questions. The reason is that they do not require reading and understanding of the passage.

c) The third set of questions will be on figurative expressions. There are ten common figures of speech one needs to study and understand before you answer this set of questions. They include simile, metaphor, hyperbole, personification, irony, euphemism, idiom, and paradox. WAEC often targets these commonly used figures of speech.

d) In another set of questions, you will be required to supply words or phrases similar to other words in the passage. Before giving any similar word or phrase to replace another word in the passage, consider not only the dictionary meaning of the word, but also the meaning the word as it is used in the passage. This means giving the meaning of the word as it is used in the context. Also, take into consideration the part of speech of the word, the tense or the number of the word. If the word to be replaced is a noun and it is singular, make sure that you use singular noun to replace it. If the word is verb and it is in past tense, use another verb in the same tense to replace it.

Comprehension (1)

Read the passage below carefully and answer all the questions that follow it.

When Sombo was informed by her father about her marriage to Pa Marabou in the next two months, she totally became **disgruntled** and she shed crocodile tears. The fourteen-year old girl went through turbulent and sleepless night. Throughout the following day, she was very quiet and remorseful like someone that is bereaved. In the evening, she refused to eat. She was not only lack of the knowledge about marriage, but she had not also set eyes on her sixty-seven year old future husband.

When Yea Maama, Sombo's mother who was not also happy about her daughter's early marriage, noticed her daughter's distress, she went around her to encourage her. Sombo asked her mother to **sensitize** her about the **institution** she was going to join. "My daughter, marriage is difficult to explain. All I can tell you is that you are going to stay with a man for the rest of your life, work for him and **produce** children for him as I stayed with your father and produced you for him." "Did you know my father before meeting him?" The poor girl asked again. "It was not a matter to know the man. It is purely fathers' decision; most times, we the mothers are not even consulted. Even when we are told, it will only be for our hearing not for our saying. In this male dominated society, whatever men say is final. The day I saw your father, that day I became his wife and that day, I realized the reality of this male **chauvinistic** world." Her mother responded slowly.

The D-day came. Early in the morning Yea Maama ordered Sombo's siblings to catch her big cock and kill it. Sombo went to fetch water from the nearby stream. When she returned, she saw seven elders sitting in her father's veranda. Two of them (an old man and an elderly woman) were strangers, though she later **recalled** to have seen the old man in one or two occasions before. He is a witch that her **quarrelsome** father hired to protect him and the rest of his family when he was in conflict with the rest of the villagers for a very small piece of land seven years ago. In the past, he had almost quarrelled with every family in the village. The others were her father, the village chief, the village Imam and two others; all of them were indigenes of Kpakpambu village.

In a jubilant mood, Yea Maama's friends were helping her with food preparation in the kitchen behind the house. <u>The glutinous fire was leaking the bottom of the big black pot</u>. The ignorant Sombo quietly went to her mother and enquired as what was going on. Her mother, who remained mute, was half happy and half sad. She was happy because a woman must be happy on the wedding day of her first child. Beneath her happiness, there was shadow of her distress. Her trauma would plaster on her face any time she remembered that her teenage daughter was going to Pa Marabou as a replacement of the debt that her husband was unable to pay.

1. How did Sombo receive the news about her marriage?
2. Explain what Sombo's mother told her about marriage.
3. Why was Sombo's mother not happy?
4. Who was Pa Marabou?
5. Describe the relationship between Sombo's father and the villagers in the past.
6. Name the figures of speech in these expressions as they are used in the passage.

   i) *shed crocodile tears*
   ii) *she was very quiet and remorseful like someone that is bereaved*
   iii) *The glutinous fire was leaking the bottom of the big black pot*

7. State the grammatical name and functions of the underlined groups of words as they are used in the passage.

   i) *who was not also happy about her daughter's early marriage*
   ii) *whatever men say*
   iii) *when she returned*

8. Use a word or a phrase to replace the underlined words as they are used in the passage.

    i)   *disgruntled*
    ii) *sensitize*
    iii) *institution*
    iv) *produce*
    v)   *chauvinistic*
    vi) *recalled*
    vii) *quarrelsome*

Comprehension (2)

Read the following passage carefully and answer all the questions on it.

I can vividly remember my predicament in my first year as a new teacher. On the first day in class, I told my students that they were mature enough to comport themselves in an exemplary manner without bordering them with *stringent* rules. I wanted them to like me and so I allowed them a lot of freedom. Unfortunately, I lost class control, and the students exploited the situation to disrespect me. Some would leave their seats without permission, freely throw objects like pens, rulers or crumpled pieces of paper to classmates or talk with others.

During the long vacation, I made myself busy reading books on discipline and consulting seasoned colleagues for help. When we resumed school the next session, I had formulated *strategies* on maintaining discipline. There were laid-down rules such as: Students are to be *courteous* and silent when the teacher or a student is speaking to the class. Students are to ask for the teacher's permission to leave their seats for anything; students are not to leave the class during lessons.

After giving the class the rules that I knew were *essential* for class control, I made sure the students followed them to the letter. I virtually enforced discipline myself instead of sending students to the Principal's office for disciplinary action as I did the previous year. After about a month, I realized that my efforts were *yielding* results.

Then, two months before the Christmas holidays, I began to relax some of the rules. One of them read as follows: "Whenever any student wants to leave the class for any reason, he should come up for permission, provided he does this without disturbing other students." About one week later, I told the students that because they were not disruptive, they could whisper to one another, open or shut windows quietly without my permission.

Indeed, <u>before the second term holidays</u>, we had a classroom where students would come in and go on recess as they finished their class assignments and also where small group discussions on project work took place. Where a student in one group talked too loudly to disturb others, he/she was *cautioned* by the group members, not me. Teaching then became a pleasure and I felt my students had matured greatly by learning to conduct themselves in a more acceptable way.

a) Why did the writer not give his students rules initially?

b) What was the outcome of the writer's desire for the students to like him?

c) How did the students react to the writer's loss of class control?

d) What did the writer do to change the unfortunate development in the class?

e) What helped the writer to formulate measures to maintain discipline in class?

f) " ...<u>before the second term holidays</u> ..."

    i) What grammatical name is given to this expression as it is used in the passage?

    ii) What is its function?

g) " ...I made sure that the students followed them to the letter."

    i) What does the writer mean by this statement as it is used in the passage?

h) For each of the following words, use a word or a phrase to replace the underlined words as they are used in the passage.

    i) stringent,

    ii) strategies,

    iii) courteous,

    iv) essential,

    v)   yielding,

    vi) cautioned

Comprehension (3)

Read this comprehension passage carefully and answer all the questions on it.

As I watch Matthew step out of the plane, I concluded that diligence, intelligence and luck had turned him from the rustic pauper of twenty-five years earlier to a high professor. Here was a village boy of yesteryear, an orphan from earlier life, cheated out of his heritage by his half-brothers and uncles whose actions forced him to <u>fend of</u> himself. So how did he become an internationally acclaimed computer wizard?

<u>When his well-to-do father died three years ago</u> after his mother, he had just gained admission to a fee-paying secondary school. Had his parents lived, that would not have been a problem. But his <u>immediate</u> relatives were more interested in sharing assets than handling liabilities. They shared the three buildings in the city, as well as several cocoa plantations with hundreds of oil palms. None <u>considered</u> it the right to take care of the poor boy. Left in the lurch, he clung on a classmate <u>who had longed to work in the city</u> as a petty clerk. They moved to the city. Both were <u>engaged</u> by a big-time retailer in all sorts of goods, which he gave out to the boys to hawk on the busy roads. There were no salaries; all they had were commissions on each day's sales. Matthew and his friend could be out in the street from 6:00 a.m. till almost midnight. That way, they were able to <u>keep body and soul together</u>.

But Matthew soon decided that his returns could cater for a little more than that. His <u>yearning</u> for education was still very keen; he cut short his daily schedules at 4:00 p.m. to attend the evening school organized by some secondary school teachers. He made a very rapid progress. Often, after class, he would return to the street. He never fared worse than any of the other learners, most of whom attended classes after the normal school.

In time, he sat to and passed all his school certificate examination papers with flying colours. Indeed, his result was among the best in the country.

An oil company which had a policy of sponsoring the university education of the best students in various disciplines awarded him a scholarship. Thus, his university education in computer science was fully sponsored. Eventually, he emerged as the best graduate in the university. The training made him a top 3-D computer programmer in engineering and architectural designs in the sub-region.

So, as he stepped out of the plane, returning from one of his international conferences, I could not, but reach the conclusion I had made earlier.

a) Where was the writer when he arrived at the conclusion with which he opened the passage?

b) What tragedy had beset Matthew early in life?

c) What worsened Matthew's plight?

d) How did Matthew solve the problem of acquiring secondary school education?

e) What element of luck contributed to Matthew's success?

f) " ...keep body and soul together ..."

    i) What figure of speech is used in this expression?

    ii) What does it mean?

g) "When his well-to-do father died three years ago ..."

h) " ...who had longed to work in the city ..."

    i) What are the grammatical names given to these expressions as they are used in the passage?

    ii) What are their functions?

i) For each of the following words or phrase, find another word or phrase which means the same and can replace them as they are used in the passage.

    i) fend for

    ii) considered

iii) immediate

iv) engaged

v) yearning

vi) eventually

Comprehension (4)

Read the following passage carefully and answer the questions on it.

Although the Sakabu people needed kerosene for lighting, they also depended on it more for food preparation. However, <u>constant</u> fuel scarcity made the commodity hardly affordable where it was available. Searching for dry wood from the forest became <u>necessarily</u> the order of the day.

Early one morning, Amara and his younger brother, Musa, armed with cutlasses and axes, joined other people <u>who were more familiar with the forest</u>, to go and search for fire wood. It soon dawned on them that this "essential commodities" had been driven so far away that people had to wander into <u>the heart of the forest</u> before they can find a huge branch of tree that looked dry. Convinced that it was, they went into action, each cutting from his/her own side.

Scarcely had they started when Musa suddenly jumped up from his position and exclaimed "Goodness!"

When Amara <u>enquired</u> what had happened, he explained that the ground on <u>which he was standing</u> was lifting him up. This sounds <u>peculiar,</u> so Amara went closer to examine the ground. It appeared level and was full of dry leaves. There was no sign of anything other than the bear ground. <u>Mockingly,</u> he asked him to return to work, adding that his <u>phobia</u> about the forest was changing into an illusion. Nevertheless, Amara struck the ground with his cutlass, cutting through it to reassure his brother that there was nothing to fear. But before he could leave, they noticed blood trickling out of the cut on the ground and they scampered away, developing goose-fresh. <u>Whatever the blood was trickling from</u> was unknown at the moment.

<u>As they watched from distance</u>, they realized that there was a writhing movement and gradually, a curled creature stretched out in full length of about three and half feet. The earthly but <u>splendid</u> design of the snake became visible, and it started what was like its last struggle away from the spot. Its pace was decreasing with every effort to crawl on while more blood was being lost as a result of the deep cut it had received.

Whether it was shock or fear that prevented Amara from finishing up what he started, he can't say. But though they <u>accomplished</u> their aim of going to the forest that day, he was hunted by the guilt of an unwilling murderer many days after.

QUESTIONS

    a) Why was kerosene important to the Sakabu people?
    b) State two reasons why the people sought an alternative to kerosene.
    c) What lifted Musa?
    d) What did Amara start and could not finish?
    e) ... the heart of the forest ...

        i) What figure of speech is contained in this expression?
        ii) What does it mean?

    f) ... who were more conversant with the forest ...
    g) Whatever the blood was trickling from ...
    h) ... as we watched from distance ...
    i) ... which he was standing ...

        i) What grammatical name will you give to these expressions as they are used in the passage?
        ii) What are their functions?

    j) For each of the following words, find another word or phrase which means the same and that can replace them as they are used in the passage.

        i) constant
        ii) necessarily

iii) enquired
iv) peculiar
v) mockingly
vi) phobia
vii) splendid
viii) accomplished

Comprehension (5)

Read this comprehension passage carefully and answer the questions on it. *(2010)*

Miss Lahai one day announced in class that she wanted one of us to live with her to help her with the domestic works at home. There was a rush to volunteer which took her completely by surprise. When she recovered and quieted our excited shouting, there was a moment during which none of us dared breathe, as she <u>scanned</u> the eager faces. <u>What made her to choose me</u> I have never found out; but I had noticed before that she was partial to me. "All right Fodei." She said. "You can come; but first run along and get your father's consent."

My parents were only too glad to have one mouth fewer to feed and my brothers and sisters to see the back of one who <u>inevitably</u> had begun to assume an air of superiority when talking to them.

Miss Lahai's bungalow was a stone's throw from the school. That very evening saw me installed on a mat in a corner of her veranda. I was unable to sleep as I was excited at the thought of the good fortune that had come on my way. To be in earshot of Miss Lahai's English all day, to have access to her books, to <u>nurse</u> the possibility, overwhelming even in thought of going with her frequently to Nyandehun Mambabu; all these <u>visions</u> kept my eyes widely open and my brain racing until very late that night. With my wrapper pulled right over my head and happy beyond all description in my heart, <u>I smiled myself to sleep.</u>

I learnt a very great deal in Miss Lahai's bungalow. Apart from improving my English, I learnt about the world outside, and began to sense that there were barriers much higher and less easily gauged than those of mere language and colour, between my own people and those from whom she sprang. The smiling teacher in the daytime often became the <u>brooding</u>, restless, ill-tempered spinster in the evening. Her bungalow was shared by another lady, a doctor, also a Sierra Leonean, who travelled to and fro between two villages on a bike. I noticed that when not at work or talking about it, these two women showed no signs of being happy. As I grew up with them, I found myself wondering what had made them leave their own country and come to live this strange life among people whose ways were totally different from theirs.

QUESTIONS:

a) Why was Miss Lahai completely surprised?

b) Why was Fodei's family happy to allow him to go and stay at Miss Lahai's bungalow?

c) State the overwhelming thought that kept Fodei awake.

d) What did Fodei find difficult to understand about the two ladies.

e) Mention the identical traits in these two ladies' behaviour.

f) " ...What made her to choose me ..."

    i) What grammatical name is given to this expression as it is used in the passage.

    ii) What is its function?

g) "I smiled myself to sleep."

    i) What is the meaning of this expression?

h) For each of the following words, find another word or phrase which means the same and can replace them as they are used in the passage:

    i) scanned

    ii) inevitable

    iii) nurse

    iv) visions

    v) gauged

    vi) brooding

Comprehension passage (6)

Read this passage carefully and answer all the questions on it.

It was little past 10:00 am but the medium-sized hall that served as a prayer house was already brimming with people from different parts of the metropolis, who had come to seek cure or answers to their problems. The majority of these lots were those with seemingly intractable mental health conditions. The superintendent of the prayer house in question was often spoken of in whispers as possessing uncanny spiritual powers to exorcise evil spirits. It was also believed that he had answers to numerous illnesses that need orthodox medication. Wednesday of each week was set aside for these healing sessions.

On this particular Wednesday, noisy supplications to the Most High and ceaseless invocation of His name to free those supposedly held captive by alleged evil spirits had reached fever pitch. Suddenly a middle-aged man broke loose from the crowd and ran as fast as his wobbly legs could permit. Some male workers from the prayer house gave him a hot chase.

At first, bemused by-standers rained curses on the fleeing man, wondering why a man in his right senses would in broad daylight rob a house of God. They obviously mistook the man for a robber fleeing from the scene of his crime. But he was not. Minutes late, he was caught and chained on feet and hands, despite his struggle against his captors who intermittently lashed him with horse-whip. As he was being violently dragged along the street, the man ceaselessly muttered incomprehensible words that sounded like the muttering of a colony of baboons. Then, a clearer picture of the situation dawned on the on-lookers. The man after all, was not a thief and had stolen nothing; rather, he was mentally deranged.

The above incident is a common occurrence in many parts of the country. It aptly underscores the devastating mental health conditions plaguing a sizeable number of people in recent times. It also points to the unspeakable and inhuman treatment which people with such health disorders suffer at the hands of self-style spiritualists. This is the usual lot of mental patients whose family members refuse to take advantage of orthodox treatment.

QUESTIONS

a) What brought the people to the prayer house?

b) State the functions of the superintendent of the prayer house.

c) What was wrong with the onlookers' assessment of the run-away man?

d) Mention two instances of inhuman treatment in the passage.

e) What is the writer's attitude towards the treatment of the lunatics in the prayer house?

f) *'... like the muttering of a colony of baboons ...'*

What figure of speech is used in this expression?

g) *'... whose family members refuse to take advantage of orthodox treatment.'*
   i) What grammatical name is given to this expression as it is used in the passage?
   ii) What is its function?

h) For each of the following words, find another word or phrase which means the same and which can replace it as it is used in the passage:

   i) intractable,
   ii) exorcise,
   iii) supplications,
   iv) wobbly,
   v) bemused,
   vi) intermittently,
   vii) deranged

Comprehension passage (7)

Read the following passage carefully and answer all the questions on it.

The school is an institution purposely designed for educating children. It has a dual function: educational and the social functions. The first function aims at the development of the individual and the second deals with the nurturing of the citizen. Whether these two aims can be pursued side by side have puzzled educationists.

There must always be a closed connection between the education of an individual and the progress of the society. One of the effects of education on a child is the formation on his/her ideals. It is this which ultimately determines the direction in which the society moves. For this reason, when we think about education, our minds go at once to school, and the importance of roles played by other agencies tends to be underrated. Parents go so far as to leave the discipline of the child entirely to the school; so that when a child offends at home, he is reported to his/her teacher for correction. This is a wrong view of the duty of the school.

It is the duty of the parents to ensure that their children attend school regularly and provide for them the various materials needed for their school work. It is also a duty of the home to augment the work of the school by enabling the child to prepare whatever he needs for the school.

It is now generally recognized that it is the duty of the state to give every opportunity of education to the child if he/she has the necessary talents. It is its duty to provide schools of all grades and money for their up keeping. In addition, it should supervise the schools to protect children from inefficient and misleading teaching. The school is therefore an agent of the community in the work of educating the young. The teacher is the servant of the community and his duties are the most sacred that a citizen can be called upon to discharge.

QUESTIONS

a) State the two aims of the school.
b) What three roles are parents expected to play in the education of their children?
c) State three specific contributions expected from the state towards educating children.
d) According to the writer, what is the connection between education of children and progress of a society?

e)   What's the writer's attitude towards teaching?

f)   … *that a citizen can be called upon to discharge.*

  i)   What grammatical name can you give to this expression as it is used in the passage?

  ii) What is its function in the sentence?

g)   For each of the following words, find another word or phrase which means the same and can replace it as it is used in the passage:

  i)   nurturing,

  ii) ultimately

  iii) underrated

  iv) regularly

  v)   grade

Comprehension (8)

Read the following passage carefully and answer the questions on it.

Normo Faama today ranks as the 16th poorest community in Kemaina chiefdom, with a GNP of less than Le 5,000. Those with jobs in the few surviving farms and newly established NGOs are probably numbered among the lucky ones. More than half of the population survives on less than Le 50 a day. They include most of the 'Nana' smokers and the 'Akpetehsi' drinkers who are the residents of urban slums where an average family lives in a one-room shack without running water, electricity or a toilet. Their wages are pitifully low and most of them are casual labourers.

Taking a bus to and from their working places every day would cost them more money than they earn. They have therefore devised a way to circumventing the problem. Long before the first cock-crow, thousands of workers start the long trudge from the slums to the farms in the forests. Drifting out of the mud lane between the densely packed shacks more and more people join the trail of workers that snakes up the hill. Poverty, the people tell you, is their community's biggest problem.

The greatest contradiction, however, is that every month a new luxury shopping mall springs up. The rank between the "alaijoes" – those who drive flashy Mercedes vehicles – and the have-not widens. There is <u>an abundance</u> of natural resources and money to be made of course, but a small number of people continue to make it by fair means or foul. So as it was in the beginning, so it is and ever shall it be world without end.

Questions

a) In what two ways is poverty manifested in the lives of the people of Normo Faama?

b) Give an instance of a contradiction in the situation described in the passage.

c) What is the writer's attitude towards the situation in the passage?

d) Give a reason to support your answer.

e) How do the workers overcome the problem of transportation cost?

f) ... *without running water, electricity or a toilet*

    i) What grammatical name is given to this expression?

    ii) What is its function in the sentence?

g) ... *the trail of workers that snakes up the hill*

    i) What figure of speech is contained in this expression?

    ii) What does it mean?

h) For each of the following words, find another word or phrase which means the same and which can replace it as it is used in the passage:

    i) casual

    ii) circumventing

    iii) trudge

    iv) densely

    v) an abundance

Comprehension Passage 9

Marriage as an institution is facing its greatest threat ever in the twentieth century. Ever, since the first man and woman were joined together, the institution has been beset by many problems as it is today. This trend, which started in the western world, has spread into many countries, and it is still spreading to the remaining parts of the <u>globe.</u>

The most disturbing problem is the high rate of divorce which is *spreading like wildfire*. It is no longer a social <u>stigma</u> for women to fill forms to indicate that they are divorced; men also proclaim their liberty from the shackles of matrimony with pride. Little wonder that young couples resort to separation and eventually divorce at the slightest disagreement.

The availability of an <u>alternative</u> aggravates the seriousness of the problem. Instead of entering into matrimony, many couples simply choose to live together. Even the courts now respect such common law marriages and respect the rights of partners in such associations. The great advantage of this accord to the partners is the fluidity of the associations and the ease with which one or both can call off the marriage. Besides, very many countries now <u>enact</u> laws that recognize the rights of children born out of wedlock. This single factor has helped to shoot up the number of such children in civilized communities. A recent <u>survey</u> in an urban college shows that about forty per cent of the students were born out of wedlock.

Not less among the factors hastening the death of the marriage institution is the rising cost of living. Nowadays, it is essential for both partners to be gainfully employed to be sure of a reasonably decent level of existence. The marriage itself costs so much that many young people simply remain single, raising one or two kids from ladies <u>who are willing collaborators against the institution of marriage</u>

Question

a) What does the author mean when he refers to marriage as an institution?

b) What do the words ***liberty*** and ***shackles*** mean, as it is used in the passage?

c) Mention one advantage of this system.

d) " *... spreading like wildfire*"

What literary device is contained in the extract above?

e) ... who are willing collaborators against the institution of marriage

    i) What grammatical name you can give to expression above?

    ii) What is its function?

f) Find a word or phrase which can be used in place of the following words as they are used in the passage:

    i) globe

    ii) stigma

    iii) alternative

    iv) enact

    v) survey

Comprehension Passage 10

The second semester examination came and went and the students were now leaving for the Easter holiday. The few who loitered about were either those who had exhausted their pocket money and had no means of going home; or fun-loving students who wanted a last-minute frolic on the campus.

Inside his room, Alie sat bleary-eyed on the bed, wondering what he was going to tell his parents. He still found it difficult to believe that he had been rusticated for cheating in an examination; it was unbelievable to his father noting that he was the most intelligent of all his children. Had he not beaten most of his intelligent rivals throughout his primary and post-primary education? Had he not won the award reserved for the most outstanding student in the faculty of Engineering at the end of his first year at the university? That was a feat that earned him the respect of other students in the faculty and had made his course-mates elect him unanimously as their leader. This same feat helped him in the third year and was expected to do the same cheating now in his fourth year. But now, he had been given a package for cheating in an examination. Only a year to go and he would have become a chemical engineer. "<u>Engineer Alie Okon</u>", people would have called him. Now he had been caught red-handed incheating. What devil ever got into him to make him cheat his last examination?

He could never forget the <u>incident</u>. It had been such a shameful affair. He had written on a piece of paper with an empty pen so that no <u>obvious</u> mark might be left on it. Only on close examination could one notice any <u>imprints</u> on the paper. A casual observer would only see a plain and harmless piece of white paper, but the invigilator was eagle eyed. The moment he took out the paper from his pocket to copy the answer to a correctly anticipated question, the invigilator was onto him. He scrutinized the paper and discovered his trick. He did not hesitate to send him out of the examination hall, in spite of <u>pleas</u> from his shocked mates. Later, Alie mentioned the problem to his friends in the Axe confraternity, but rejected their suggestion of writing a threatening letter that such a letter would only serve to expose his identity as a secret cult member. Alie did not want to blame the invigilator. The man was just doing his duty. It was unfortunate that he was the only one caught in this "common prank" of cheating

a) State two problems that worried Alie as he sat in his room.
b) How did Alie's mates honour him for his brilliance?
c) What goal had Alie set for himself before now?
d) What evidence is there in the passage to show that Alie was a brilliant student in the university?
e) Why did Alie refuse the suggestion to write to the authorities?
f) Had his father not said that he was the most intelligent of all his children? What literary device is contained in the expression above?
g) " … that earned him the respect of other students in the faculty"

    i) What grammatical name would you give to this expression as it is used in the passage?
    ii) What is its function?

h) For each of the following words, find another word or phrase which means the same and which can replace it as it is used in the passage:

i) exhausted,
ii) reserved,
iii) Incident,
iv) obvious,
v) Imprints,
vi) Pleas.

Comprehension Passage 11

On my trips to Freetown, it was my practice to befriend a passenger at the car park; I thought a best way to ensure that I was not alone during the trips. Every Sunday morning, I would leave my family in Kailahun and go to work in Freetown, and then return on Friday evening. Policemen were my favourite passengers since I <u>realized</u> that their presence in my car gave me confidence on the road. Next in preference were well-dressed ladies whom I regarded as respectable and time conscious individuals; I enjoyed engaging them in lively conversations. That was the <u>pattern</u> until one fateful day I was taught a never-to-be-forgotten lesson. Early that morning, I picked up middle–aged, well–dressed lady. I <u>presumed</u> that she was a self-respecting, high–class woman, apparently on a business trip. No sooner had she settled in the car, then she fell asleep. Within ten minutes, she began to snore. At first, I tried to rouse her but this proved <u>futile</u>. So I left her alone. Soon, I noticed <u>that she was drunk</u>. The odour of liquor was still heavy around her. I discovered that my judgment had been wrong. But the worst was yet to come.

I soon arrived in Freetown. I shook her up and she opened her eyes widely, she yawned, looked around and asked me for her handbag. I thought I had not heard her correctly; so I looked questioningly at her. She repeated her statement, "Yes young man, I mean you should give me my handbag." Of course, I asked her what she was talking about. She emphasized, "You have taken my handbag. You have to give it back to me; otherwise the whole of Freetown will step into this."

I still could not decide whether she was serious or simply joking. I parked by the roadside and told her to get down. But then she went for my tie and started shouting. In a twinkling of an eye, many people had surrounded the car. She continued to shout that I have stolen her bag containing some money. Nobody believed me when I tried to explain what had happened. I was <u>urged</u> to give her some money and <u>let sleeping dogs lie.</u> I told her to release my tie to enable me to take out my wallet. She did and I emptied the content of my wallet into her hands. As she stepped out, one of the men shook his head, peered into the car and said: "Young man, I know what happened. I know her. She is Cecilia Siabatu Kamara, a daughter of the most wicked and corrupt politician. She is one of the most notorious <u>tricksters</u> around. You are lucky she accepted that small amount of money from you."

a) Why did the writer have to ply the route from Kailahun to Freetown on a regular basis?

b) For what reason did he choose to pick up a passenger on each trip?

c) Why did he prefer policemen to other types of passengers?

d) What particular fact made him immediately regret picking up the woman on that fateful day?

e) Quote a sentence that describes the character of the woman.

f) " … that she was drunk"

   i) What grammatical name is given to this expression as it is used in the passage?

   ii) What is its function?

g) "Let sleeping dogs lie"

   i) Which figure of speech is used in this expression?

   ii) What does it mean?

h) For each of the following words, find another word or phrase which means the same as they are used in the passage.

   i) realized,

   ii) pattern,

    iii) presumed,

    iv) futile,

    v) urged,

    vi) tricksters

Comprehension Passage 12

Mr. Ogun, it was that man who wooed me for school. That was decades ago. I had resisted <u>vehemently</u> and even ran away to hibernate with my maternal grandmother. I had told Granny that I wanted to spend a few days with her. By night fall, my father, who suspected that I was hiding there, came to take me away. The following morning, he dragged me all the way to school where Mr. Ogun received all fresh students. I swore secretly that I would <u>abscond</u> at the first opportunity, but throughout the day, Mr. Ogun kept a watchful eye on fresh pupils. He had a smiling face and looked very friendly. As soon as he had registered our names, he led us to the field to play. Of all the children, I was <u>probably </u>the only one who looked forward to an opportunity to abscond. Mr. Ogun seemed to have read my mind; he used my name in the songs he composed as we marched round the field. He once held my hand and marched along with me. As we went on, he announced: "What a smart fellow my friend is!"

In the classroom, Mr. Ogun told me to sit in front and he stated: "My smarter will keep the pieces of chalk and the duster." <u>Gradually</u>, I was mellowing in my plan to abscond; I began to think that I could give school a try. At the end of that day, my father was around to take me home. Perhaps he decided not to take chances. During the first week, my father took me surprise. Every morning, as I produced the pieces of chalk from the cupboard, Mr. Ogun smiled broadly, nodding approvingly. Before we left the classroom for recess, for games or for home, I dutifully kept the materials safe, and as soon as we returned, I produced them. It took sometime before I realized that my role was crucial since the pilfering of such materials was common in all the other classes.

My father soon stopped bothering about me as I would get up from bed, take my bath, and get into uniform without any <u>prodding</u>. My love for school was deepening, especially when I discovered that I was among the few that always did well in most test. And Mr. Ogun would praise me to the skies.

Towards the end of the school year, we learn that Mr. Ogun was going on transfer to another school. How <u>devastated</u> I felt now, at last was the time to abscond from school. But then, I simply could not take the crucial step because <u>my bond with school had become very firm.</u>

- a)   What evidence is there in the passage that the writer's experience took place long ago?
- b)   Mention two things that Mr. Ogun did that won the writer for school.
- c)   What was the benefit of the duty performed by the writer to his class?
- d)   What do you think the writer implies when he stated that he dressed up for school without any prodding?
- e)   Why couldn't he carry out his plan to abscond when his mentor had left?
- f)   … that my role was crucial …

    - i)   i). What is the grammatical name given to this expression as it is used in the passage?
    - ii)   ii) What is its function?

- g)   … my bond with school had become very firm.

    - i)   What figure of speech is used in this expression as it is used in the passage?
    - ii)   What does it mean?

- h)   For each of the following words, find another word or phrase which means the same and which can replace each as it is used in the passage.

    - i)   vehemently,
    - ii)   abscond,
    - iii)   Probably,

279

    iv) gradually,

    v) prodding;

Comprehension Passage 13

When the principal introduced Mr. Njobe as our new Mathematics teacher, we did not think much of him. He did not look very likeable nor did he appear to be an achiever. Nothing was spectacular about him apart from the fact that he was a South African. Most of us who knew the goings-on in his country regarded him as one of the <u>luckless</u> refugees from the apartheid regime. After the mild clapping, we forgot about the man with gaunt, hungry looks.

During his first lesson in our class, it struck me that not once did he <u>consult</u> the textbook. Rather, to teach the properties of the square and rectangle, he made us measure the top of our tables, the classroom doors, and other objects around. From there, we discovered <u>that these objects had opposite equal sides</u>, and all the angles were equal. We did not have to learn these from books; he made us find out. When later I consulted my textbook, what Durrell, the great mathematician, wrote came very much alive. I started to see Mr. Njobe as equal to Durrell. With time, we began to like his teaching. He taught with zeal and usually through play like methods. His class was always lively and full of jokes. For instance, to teach us the properties of a circle, he instructed us to bring out the bowls which we used for the midday meal. During the lesson, he made each one measure the distance round his bowl. Incidentally, almost every bowl was different in size. We laughed at the sizes of the different bowls while we <u>meticulously</u> measured them throughout the lesson, there was much laughter. Finally, he told each student to divide the distance round the bowl by the distance through the centre. Imagine our <u>amazement</u> when we realized that all the bowls were the same. This, he explained, is the base in all computations regarding the circle. That was fifty year ago and I have not forgotten. <u>He actually tamed mathematics for us,</u> <u>terrifying</u> as it was.

Then, one day, we learnt that Mr. Njobe was on admission in Wesley Guild Hospital. The representatives we sent to convey our good wishes were refused entry into the intensive care unit; they were told that his condition was <u>critical</u>. We virtually went into mourning for weeks but just as we were writing him off our mind, one hot afternoon, his car crawled into the school compound. As he stepped out, students swarmed out, carried him shoulder-high and danced round the school, chanting spontaneously Njobe, welcome! Mathematics, welcome!

a) Describe the appearance of Mr. Njobe on his first day in the school.
b) With what concept of South Africa did the writer associate Mr. Njobe?
c) What did the students' mild clapping suggest?
d) What is unique about the new teacher's method of teaching?
e) ' ... that these objects had opposite equal sides ... ''

   i) What is the grammatical name given to this expression as it is used in the passage?
   ii) What is its function?

f) "he actually tamed Mathematics for us'

   i) What figure of speech is used in expression?

g) For each of the following words, find another word or phrase which means the same and which can replace it as it used in the passage:

   i) luckless,
   ii) consult,
   iii) meticulously,
   iv) amazement,
   v) terrifying,
   vi) critical

Comprehension Passage 14

Part of my one-year study programme in Britain involved visiting several places of historical importance, especially those related to pre-colonial African history on which I was researching. One was the home of William

Wilberforce, the 19th century anti slave trade statesman. The house has been turned into a museum by one of the several organizations that fought the scourge. Among the most outstanding features of the museum were the several statues of slaves in different postures; black slaves being captured in their native homes, chained together, led to the port for sale, packed in the slave ship and forced to work on plantations. The sculptures were particularly remarkable in that they illustrated very movingly, the bane which Wilberforce threw himself against.

As a black man, I could not help shedding tears when going from room to room on two floors. Then there was a period of pandemonium which I, unwittingly caused. I was on the first floor, about to cross the lobby, when I came face to face with another visitor, a white man. When he saw me, a wave of fright swept through him. His eyes were immediately bloodshot. He shouted out of fright and ran back. Quickly, he made for the staircase, sped down to the ground floor, and took to his heels.

All this while, I remained still *at a loss* as to the cause of his action. He stopped shouting only when he got into the bus that brought his group. Meanwhile, others around him, realizing the cause of his fright, came to tell me that I was the cause. They *laughed it off* when they told me that he had thought I was one of the statues and suddenly turned into a human being. I discovered the reason for his fright when I entered the room which he just left. I found that one of the statues looked exactly like me. Whoever did the wax model perhaps have my picture. It was my height, my shape, my complexion. Indeed, the exact replica of me.

I realized what had happened. I was the only black present in the building. The man had not expected a live black person to be in the museum. Thus, the sudden sight of a black person moving around, with the stature and face of one of the statues, should certainly frighten him. I wondered what could have happened if I had pursued him down the staircase.

Questions

    a)   Why did the writer visit the museum?

    b)   What did the statues of slaves depict?

c) How would you describe the state of the white man as he struggled to land himself on the bus?

d) What does the writer mean when he says ... ***at a loss***?

e) What does the writer mean when says "***laughed it off***"?

f) What was the role of Wilberforce, according to the passage?

g) Quote a sentence to support your answer.

h) ***took to his heels***.

   i) What literary devise is contained in above?

i) ... if I had pursued him down the staircase.

   i) What is the grammatical term for the words above?
   ii) What is its function?

j) Find a word or phrase which can take the place of each of the following as used in the passage:

   i) courge,
   ii) unwittingly,
   iii) bloodshot,
   iv) suddenly,
   v) sight

CHAPTER 20

SUMMARY PASSAGES

Summary: Summary question demands a candidate to read and understand both the passage and the questions, identify the key ideas the question (s) demand for and briefly write them in your own words. Summary is considered to be the simplest of all questions on most English language exam, because the answers to the questions are always found in the passage. All a candidate is expected to do is to identify the answers and briefly write them in his/her own words in simple and clear sentence (s).

Before attempting any summary question, carefully read and fully comprehend the passage and the questions. Understand the key word (s) in the questions and memorize them. Skim the passage to identify areas where those key words or ideas about them are. Sometimes the key words in the question will be replaced by another word in the passage. Note also that the key word(s) may not be stated in certain paragraphs but relevant information about them will be stated there. Read around the key words and understand what is said about them. In phrases, collect the pieces of ideas and pen them down. In your own words, put the ideas in brief, simple and clear sentences to answer the questions. Remember that you are limited to number of words or sentences, don't go beyond the number. Let's learn from the example below.

Read the sample summary passage carefully and answer the questions on it.

According to Lawumi, the attack launched on Owu by the Allied Forces was a punishment on the people of Owu for their arrogant attitude towards Ele Ife. The ancestors of Owu people came from Ele Ife in the person of Lawumi herself. As a granddaughter of Oduduwa, the progenitor of the Yoruba race, she married Ansunkungbade, the founder of Owu. They gave birth to two children in the persons of Sango and Anlugbau. Her grandfather, Oduduwa, also gave Ansunkungbade a crown and made Owu the seventh kingdom of the Yoruba land. According to Lawumi, Owu people forgot this history and they attacked Ele Ife.

Another reason why the Allied Forces waged war on Owu was because of the defiant attitude of Owu people to their gods. They never obeyed the instructions of their gods. For instance, king Akinjobi and his wife, Erelu, were advised by the gods not to allow Djemu, their first son, to live. The gods described him as an unlucky boy who had come on this earth with bad luck; and that if they allowed him to live, he would seduce a woman and that would bring trouble on them. They ignored this instruction and allowed the boy to live. Because of their stubbornness, the people of Owu also failed to call Anlugbua to come to their rescue as he instructed them to do when he was leaving the earth. This again shows that the Owu people were defiant to their gods.

Owu had also launched a revenge attack on Apumu market when it was under the control of Ele Ife. In the battle, Iyunloye, a wife of Gbenagbena Ogunade, a famous artist, was captured and brought to Owu. Prince Djemu made her his wife. Okunade became mad with anger. He abandoned his tools and career as an artist, and took up arms to revenge for his beautiful wife. He became the leader of the Allied Forces who matched and launched the onslaught on Owu city. This is another reason why the Allied Forces attacked the people in Owu city.

Question: In three sentences, one for each, give three reasons why the Allied Forces attacked Owu city.

Step-1: Identify the key words in the question. The key words in the question are (*reasons, Allied Forces, attacked*)

Step-2: Skim read the passage, identify the key words or relevant information about them and pen them down.

According to Lawumi, the attack launched on Owu by the Allied Forces was a *punishment* on the people of Owu *for their arrogant attitude* towards Ele Ife. The ancestors of Owu people came from Ele Ife in the person of

Lawumi herself. As a granddaughter of Oduduwa, the progenitor of the Yoruba race; she was married to Ansunkungbade, the founder of Owu. They gave birth to two children in the persons of Sango and Anlugbau. Her grandfather, Oduduwa, also gave Ansunkungbade a crown and made Owu the seventh kingdom of the Yoruba land. According to Lawumi, Owu people forgot this history and they attacked Ele Ife.

Another reason why the Allied Forces waged war on Owu was because of the *defiant attitude of the people* to their gods. They *never obeyed* the instructions of their gods. For instance, king Akinjobi and his wife Erelu were advised by the gods not to allow Dijemu, their first son, to live. The gods described him as an unlucky boy who has come on this earth with bad luck; and that if they allowed him to live, he would seduce a woman and that would bring trouble on them. They ignored this instruction and allow the boy to live. Because of their *stubbornness*, the people of Owu also *failed to call Anlugbua* to come to their rescue as he instructed them to do when he was leaving the earth. This again shows that the Owu people were defiant to their gods.

Owu had also lunched a *revenge attack on Apumu market* when it was under the control of Ele Ife. In the battle, Iyunloye, a wife of Gbenagbena Ogunade, a famous artist was captured and brought to Owu. Prince Dijemu made her his wife. Okunade became mad and abandoned his tools and career as an artist and took up arms to revenge for his beautiful wife. He became the leader of the Allied Forces who matched and launched his onslaught on Owu city. This is another reason why the Allied Forces attacked the people in Owu city.

i) *as punishment for the arrogant attitude,*
ii) *defiant attitude of the people,*
iii) *never obeyed,*
iv) *stubbornness,*
v) *failed to call Anlugbua,*
vi) *revenge attack on Apumu market*

Step-3: Read around these key words and understand what is said about them. In your own words, briefly write the ideas in simple and clear sentences as answers to the question.

Answers:

1. The allied forces attacked Owu city to punish the people for their arrogant attitude towards, Ele Ife, the home community of Lawumi.
2. The city was also attacked because the people were defiant and never obeyed the instructions of their gods.
3. It was a revenged attack because the Owu forces attacked Apumu market before and captured Iyunloye.

Summary passage (1)

Read the summary passage carefully and answer the questions on it.

People are usually unwilling to make changes in their lives after being accustomed to certain life style. However, this can cause many problems, as changing circumstances often make a change in life style inevitable. Take for example, people who leave their country and go abroad for various reasons. Such people will inevitably face many challenges. First they have to adapt to a new culture and habits that may be completely different from what they were used to in their own country. They will also have to adapt to the weather and may need to learn a new language completely different from their mother tongue, which they used more frequently before their relocation.

Again, at some point in live, some people may have cause to change their career. The reason for this may be varied and need not to concern us here. But career changes inevitably necessitate the acquisition of a different set of skills and experience in the new job; a new routine and adaptation to new friends and colleagues at work. In the face of economic recession and related circumstances, people may lose their jobs as the organizations they work for try to adjust to the adverse situation by retrenching many of their workers. (Terms such as "downsizing", "right sizing" and "restructuring" are the modern-day euphemisms for this phenomenon!) A worker who suddenly loses his or her job obviously has to adjust to a new life style – at least until a new job comes along.

Closely relate to job loss is retirement. Many people carry on at their jobs as if they will remain in that job forever. But retirement is inevitable not only for paid worker but also for self-employed. Retirement in most cases means a change from an active working life to more secondary life style. It often requires giving up official property such as accommodations and vehicles and the replacement of a regular salary with a modest pension, which may not be regular. For people who may not be prepared for retirement, the prospect of it to them is often viewed with apprehension.

Outside the work domain, other changes inevitably continue to take place. For example, at some point in live, young men and women will come together and get married and start their own families. The transition from bachelorhood or spinsterhood of course means adaptation to a spouse, raising children, and discarding many of the habits, often reckless and impulsive of unmarried life.

Finally, as painful and undesirable as it is, death is inevitable. The untimely loss of a loved one – a wife, a husband, a parent – often turns people's life upside down and necessitate a drastic change in lifestyle. Many people never anticipate such a loss, and if unfortunately, it does occur, it can be quite devastating. In conclusion, people have to be ready for many changes that may occur in their lives; as change is inevitable and there is no grantee for anyone that life will be stable forever.

Questions:

In four sentences, one for each, summarize any four **factors** that can cause **change** in **life style** as discussed in the passage.

Summary passage (2)

Read this summary passage and answer the questions that follow.

No one can deny the fact that anyone who wants to be successful in learning the English Language needs a good English dictionary. Such a dictionary should be a source of information about the language – information that is not generally available in grammar books. It should not only contain a list of words and their meanings, but also a lot of information that can help a learner to speak and write good English.

In order to use a word correctly, the reader needs to know how to link it with other words in the sentence. He should also know the structures that often proceed or follow it, and whether it is formal or informal. This will help to choose what word is appropriate for a particular context. A dictionary is, therefore, an invaluable aid to reading as well as writing skills.

If the meaning of a particular word in a passage impedes the overall comprehension of the main ideas presented in it, then the dictionary should be used. Most teachers must have observed a wide spread tendency among their students to attack a new passage by reading it word by word, stopping to reach for a dictionary whenever they come across a word they do not know. This is a wrong approach; the dictionary should be used only as a last resort. The main objective of reading a passage is not to define specific words but to understand the ideas and concepts of the passage. The frequent use of a dictionary tends to focus the reader's attention on words when he/she should be concentrating on understanding the main ideas of the passage. Efficient reading implies obtaining the greatest amount of information from the passage on the shortest time possible. The frequent use of a dictionary takes too much time – time that can better be employed in getting an overall understanding of the passage.

Instead of turning to the last resort, the reader should continue reading. Very often, the meaning of an unfamiliar word can be guessed from the context in which it is used. The passage may give a definition, cite examples or describe a circumstance surrounding the use of such a word well enough for him/her to know what it means. After reading the whole passage, the reader may realize that he/she has understood the important ideas presented without knowing the meaning of every word. If, after reading the entire passage, the reader is still unable to guess the meaning of a word from the context, then he should study the structure of the word. The word may be a compound word which, when broken into its component parts, can be easily understood.

If, after exhausting these approaches, the reader still does not understand the meaning of a word, and if this word is vital to the comprehension of the whole passage, then and only then, he/she should refer to a dictionary.

Questions

a) In one sentence, state the purpose of a good dictionary.
b) In two sentences, one for each, state the two disadvantages of constantly referring to a dictionary when reading a passage.
c) In three sentences, one for each, summarize the three steps that a reader should take before referring to a dictionary.

Summary passage 3

Read this passage carefully and answer all the questions on it.

For some, grass is just the green stuff outside the house that they have to mow. For farmers and footballers, it is indispensable. For children, it is the ideal playground. For those who live in most urban area, they have very little to do with grass and the product made from it.

Grass makes up a major part of the vegetation that covers the earth; and no wonder, since it is the most adaptable plant grown on earth, growing in polar region and deserts, in tropical rain forests and wind-swept mountain slopes, entire vegetation area are dominated by grass.

Unlike many other plants, grass grows not at the tip, but in growth areas above the nodes. New shoots might start from stems growing horizontally on or under the ground. So when the lawn mower or the cow cuts away the tip, or fire rages through the field, grass keeps growing; whereas many other plants stop. Furthermore, with most grasses, if the stem is bent over by wind or trodden by foot, it can raise itself erect by growing on the side facing the ground. For this reason, grass usually recovers quickly after being damaged, which gives it an edge over other plants in the fight for sunlight.

Grass is not only the most abundant plant, but it is also the most important flowering-plant family on earth. A botanist once described grass as the foundation of our food. It is 'like a dam protecting mankind from famine.' Try to remember what you ate today. Did you start with a bowl of cereal made with millet, rice, oats or sorghum? If so, then, you ate grass seeds. Grass is not only good for food, however. If your house is made up clay and straw, it is grass that gives them the necessary strength. In different parts of the world, roofs are thatched with grass. One of the advantages of such roofs is that they keep the interior of the building cool, regardless of the external temperature.

Grass covers and adorns much of the earth. Apart from the beautiful, peaceful and relaxing sight of a green grass meadow or a well-kept lawn, grass is a major oxygen supplier because of the sheer mass of the green vegetation that it produces. Finally, its fine roots perform the all-important function of protecting the soil from erosion. Keeping its versatility in mind, we are not surprised to learn that the usage and cultivation of grass has a long history.

Questions

a) In two sentences, one for each, summarize the two reasons why grass forms a major part of the earth's vegetation.

b) In four sentences, one for each, summarize any four ways in which grass is useful to humans.

Summary passage 4

Read this passage carefully and answer all the questions on it.

Nearly every evening, after Mr. Bockarie, a traffic warden returned from work, he would sit with his work-mates to discuss that day's work experience. During all such discussions, Mr. Bockarie's nephews always listened with keen interest. On and on these evening conversation went until surprisingly to the nephews, their uncle's friend, Mr. Salia, brought out a bundle of Le 10,000 notes. The two men decided to share the money because other police officers were not on duty when some drivers, who were caught with some narcotic drugs, decided to grease their palm so as to escape the hooks of the law.

Immediately after sharing the money, Mr. Bockarie told his wife, Jamie, to go to market and buy Le 200,000 worth of meat. This was a rare occurrence in that household. The two men ate and thanked God for allowing such law-breakers to travel all the way unchecked by other road traffic officers. They talked, laughed and bade each other goodbye for that day; but ensured that they had arranged to mount the police check-point at the most strategic position the next day.

Before he left for work the next day, Mr. Bockarie had parked a brand new Mercedes Benz car in front of the house and instructed his nephews to wash the car and watch over it until he returned.

Children, being what they are, took that opportunity to gossip among themselves whether or not their uncle had received his gratuity before the actual time or that the road traffic deal had brought in a windfall. Following this curiosity, whenever Mr. Salia visited their uncle, they always made sure that they got the gist of their discussion. Haplessly for the two officers, the children heard their conversation that a friend of the first driver who offered the huge bribe was to come by that same way toward late evening two days after.

Mr. Bockarie's nephews thought of capitalizing on this rare occasion to make some money for themselves. After all they want to be in vogue. On that fateful day, the eldest nephew dressed himself in his uncle's police uniform, as he was a chip off the old block. This happened while his uncle was having his siesta. He marshalled his brother and friend and they took the 'police check' sign with them.

They actually succeeded in controlling the traffic for some time, as those who knew Mr. Bockarie to be busy –like, merely greeted him and continued their journey. As soon as they had 'reaped flesh' off their targeted lorry drive, they were now prepared to leave. All of a sudden, bad luck befell them. One bus driver, whose driving license had been confiscated by the real Mr. Bockarie, accosted the 'Mr. Bockarie look alike' and politely demanded his license. Knowing that he was impersonating, the other two quickly responded that that day for checking alone; so he should come for it the following day. The two young voices, coupled with the fact that they were not in uniform aroused suspicion.

The matter was reported to the nearest army barracks; and the three young boys were arrested and interrogated. The officers were shocked at the revelation that the boys were following the footsteps of their uncle.

Questions

   a) In two sentences, one for each, state what aroused the curiosity of the boys and their finding.
   b) In two sentences, one for each, state what the boys did that exposed their uncle.
   c) In two sentences, state how Mr. Bockarie's extravagance put him into trouble.

Summary passage 5

Read this passage carefully and answer all the questions on it.

For many years now students' general performance in English Language examinations has been on a sharp decline. Very many people erroneously believed that teachers' inability to adequately test the students is one major cause of this unwanted situation.

Nonetheless, some have cited students' inability to read fluently, let alone they understand clearly what they read as a root cause of this massive failure. Their low level of vocabulary and sub-conscious neglect of basic examination rules further contributed to the picture painted above.

For very many obvious reasons, the teachers find it difficult to give students class work or assignments; since they have to evaluate the work of about seventy or eighty students per class. The worse is that less than ten percent of the students have the required textbooks for continuous practice. Sometimes, some of those who have the textbooks cannot read them fluently, thus complicating the issue of comprehending the text.

It is indeed an oversight to make mention of where this problem catapults from without taking the efficiency and commitment of the instructors into account. Are they fully baked or half baked, if baked at all? There are certain instances where they may fail to discharge their duties effectively either because of ill-preparedness or lack of knowhow or both. When the afore-mentioned is properly handed, then the dedication and tactical approach to the job come to the fore.

A large class can be split into smaller groups so teachers will truly assess the tasks given to them without missing their teaching periods. This can really be done if the teachers are not 'over loaded' with periods as often the case with some toddling privately owned schools, whose primary aim is to maximize profit at the detriment of the very students that pay the fees.

Very pertinent is the issue of tolerating vernacular speaking in schools, especially at lower levels. The medium of communication should be the English Language so as to foster their understanding of the language and the mastering of word application after they have been taught to read. Actually, any child who does not know how to read should not deserve a place in the next grade. But when schools have adopted the principle of 'let my people go', keen competition has eroded among students. This breeds mass failure. Until there is a collective effort to correct these errors at this stage, the poor performance of students in English Language will continue unabated.

Questions

a) In three sentences, one for each, state the factors which make teachers' work difficult.

b) In three sentences, one for each, state the three factors that cause massive failure in English Language.

Summary Passage 6

Read this passage carefully and answer the questions on it.

The influence of speech on the development of thought is a fascinating subject which has long attracted the attention of educationists, psychologists and linguists. We know enough already to realize that growth of intelligence partially depends on the use of language; for example, the more the baby hears structured language, the more rapidly his mental faculties will develop.

Speech is the foundation on which every language is built. The child begins to learn a language first by hearing and then imitating speech patterns. He has to listen to a great deal before he can begin to make out the meaning of what is said. A child brought up in complete silence would scarcely be human, for we are human in so far as we communicate through speech with others. But we begin to make out the meaning of what is said after listening for some time. A child brought up in complete silence would scarcely be human, for we are human in so far as we communicate through speech with others. But we begin by understanding far more than an ear able to express: the passive acquisition of a language precedes its active use, and that is why children are so dependent upon adults. It is surprising how quickly an infant will grasp the meaning of simple phrases constantly repeated. Baby talk may be emotionally satisfying to the loving adult but it is misleading and useless to the child, and is best avoided.

Speech is also essential for the psychological well-being of the child; it is well known that sick children who are left to themselves get well much more slowly than those whose emotional and psychological needs are met by friendly, sympathetic and intelligent conversation each day. Hospitals, where human relation is good, cure patients much more quickly than one where human relations are not so warm. A study of patient–nurse relationship in some hospitals noted that patients recovered more speedily in those hospitals where they enjoyed warm human relations than those where they do not. We become human and stay human through the faculty of language.

The silent man is regarded with suspicion and hostility. He may become an object of fear if he persists in refusing to speak. Lonely people tend to become morose and ill. Their ages quickly deteriorate if they are isolated from the rest of the community, whereas the old grandmother who is an active and respected member of her children's families can remain alert until the day she dies. There are, no doubt, other factors at work, such as unspoken love and affection, but speech plays a major role in cementing these bonds of affection. Married people who can talk easily as well matters a great deal in the context of our daily lives.

In the past, speech revealed a man's social origins. It was a badge that marked him off from other men; especially those considered superior. Bernard Shaw's Pygmalion develops this theme brilliantly. In the preface to the play, Shaw wrote: "As soon as an Englishman opens his mouth, he makes other Englishmen despise him." That remark is less apt today, although it still carries an uncomfortable sting.

Question

a)   In five sentences, one for each, summarize the importance of speech.

Summary Passage 7

Read this passage carefully and answer the questions on it.

Have you ever wondered how books get published before reaching the reader? Perhaps you assume that the author is solely responsible for designing, printing and getting the books distributed to readers. Actually, in most cases, it is not the author who originally conceives the idea of a book; rather, it is the publisher, based on the results of a market research, who decides on the type of book to publish. So usually, the concept of a book begins with a market research which is an exercise that is carried out to establish the type of books that would sell fast among a specific group of readers.

The task of hunting for a good writer follows. The publishing house goes out to source for a good writer, usually among the academics in the secondary or tertiary institutions. Sometimes, however, such a writer is found in other professions. For instance, for a good law book, a senior advocate might be best to consult. Discussions are held with the chosen writer to map out precisely the level of the language and purpose. The writer or writers will then write the manuscript and submit to the publisher.

When the manuscript is submitted to the publisher, it is subjected to rigorous screening to establish whether it is good enough to the taste of the readers. Its suitability or otherwise is assessed. If it is found unsatisfactory, it is simply returned and that is the end of the matter. However, if it is found publishable, whatever amendments recommended by the assessor will be done by the author as guidelines to update the work.

When the final manuscript had been accepted, it is further subjected to editorial board; most of these are themselves experts in English Language as well as specialists in the particular field that the book covers. In most cases, they take a critical look at the language, as well as the currency of the content. So, where outdated facts are identified, the editorial board does the rectification. Furthermore, editors are good at economizing words; very often they cut down on the length of the material.

Whatever leaves the table of the editorial division goes into the publishing section. This has the task of doing the final typesetting, providing the pictures and illustrations where needed, and arranging for a printing press to handle the final production of the book. Contrary to what most people often assume, a printing press is not the same as a publishing company. Indeed, most publishing companies do not have printing presses. A printing press charge money for the printing and production of the number of copies demanded by the publishers. Once the payment has been made for the printing, and the copies have been delivered by the printer, the role of the printer ends.

The publisher's marketing division takes over the copies, advertises the book, goes out to the potential users and makes sales. Advertisement may be done on the radio and television networks, in newspaper and on billboards. The staff of the marketing division may meet schools and the ministry of education to get the book adopted. The wider the publicity the higher the sales are likely to be.

Questions

a) In five sentences, one for each, summarize the five stages in the publication of a book.
b) In one sentence, state how the publishing house creates awareness for a book

Summary Passage 8

Read this passage carefully and answer the questions on it.

The press is a general term for all types of printed newspapers and periodicals. It is an asset as a menace to society. Like many things in this world, it has its good and bad sides. Even though it has bad sides, no society can shut it down and thrive. The press has its aims and objectives which it follows, come what may. Anyone who wants to be abreast with current affairs or notable events in his country must resort to reading printed material, apart from watching the television.

In fact, the press serves more people than the electronic media do. Newspaper and periodicals go where the television cannot. Printed material goes even to the remotest areas of a country. Institutions of learning disseminate information. However, not all cities, towns and villages have these institutions, but the print media can be used to disseminate information to people in these areas.

Government, institutions and organizations have their policies, programs and activities for the smooth running of their affairs. At times, only those in authority reap the benefits. Subordinates are often afraid to criticize the authorities. Their best bet is to resort to the print media which become their mouthpiece. Thus, what the oppressed cannot do, the print media do without fear or favour.

The press is also at beck and call of anybody who wants its services. Many a time, one sees people job-hunting. They roam the streets of cities and towns; go from one office to the other: move from one employing authority to another only to be told that vacancies do not exist. To be candid, they do not need to waste time and energy seeking jobs.

All they need to do is comb the advertisement columns of newspapers and periodicals and they will be informed about available jobs. However, the press can be nuisance in a society. How many times have we found newspaper and periodicals publishing false and unauthenticated stories? Such stories spread like wild fire. They stir trouble and bring about disunity in societies. The publishers are often out to enrich themselves by churning out false information. For some newspaper and periodicals, reckless and dangerous gossip is their stock-in- trade. No one can deny the fact that moral decadence has gripped our world. It is true that even adults contribute to this menace in our societies. Many of our children and youth go for that which is morally low.

The truth is that the press contributes to a very large extent to loss of morality in our societies. There are publishers who specialize in the production of pornographic material which even our children and youths can afford to buy. Publishers of newspapers and periodicals, therefore, should constantly be conscious of their crucial roles in the society and should always strive to use the media for the promotion of peace, orderliness, progress and prosperity, and not for negative and destructive ends.

Questions

a) In four sentences, one for each, state four positive roles of the press, according to the writer.

b) In two sentences, one for each, state the two negative roles of the press, according to the writer.

Summary passage 9

Read this passage carefully and answer all the questions on it.

It is now fashionable to hear discussions mainly about the disproportionate representation of males and females in the population. It is indeed not uncommon to hear people say that for every man there are about two or three women; so, every man can marry more than one woman. This theory is, of course, more popular among adherents who favour the seeming glamour of the polygamous way of life. The big question is: How correct is this theory, and what are the facts?

The stark reality is that in any normal populations, out of every one hundred conceptions, about fifty-three to fifty-five are for boys, and about forty-five to forty-seven are for girls. So there are potentially more boys than girls in any normal population. However, because of many factors some of which are not fully clear, the foetus of a boy is far more fragile than that of a girl. So there are more miscarriages of male children than of female ones. So by the time the children are born, the ratio between boys and girls has been reduced to about fifty-two boys to forty-eight girls. As infants, boys are more delicate than girls. Boys are less resistant to certain killer diseases and girls have a higher chance of surviving. The result is that before adolescence, at about the age between nine and eleven years, boys and girls are virtually at par in the population.

Throughout adolescence, from the age of twelve to nineteen years, boys continue to fall victims of many ailments at a much higher degree than girls do. Besides, boys' tendency to be more adventurous, more daring and risk-taking, expose them far more to mishaps. Some of these do reduce their representation in the population. So, by the end of the age of adolescence, there are slightly more girls than boys. The reduction, thereafter, in the number of males continue progressively. Men are the breadwinners, the soldiers, the travellers. It is during their middle age that very many men die tragically as soldiers in their boots, so to say. The net result of this is that by the time they are in mid-thirties and forties, there are more women than men.

Finally, in their late forties and fifties, far more men than women die of cardiac diseases like hypertension, heart-attack and anxiety. This is the period when there are clearly more widows than widowers.

On the whole, therefore, there are more females than males but certainly not in the proportion claimed by adherents of polygamy. During their marriageable years, there are about eleven wives to ten husbands – that's husbands and wife of the same age. That in some communities, one man could marry as many as fifteen wives is a result of the fact that men normally marry from among the ladies younger than they are. This, more than any other factor, allows some men who are inclined to polygamy to have their way.

a) In five sentences, one for each factor, summarize the factors responsible for the progressive reduction in the number of males as against females from conception to adulthood.

b) In one sentence, state why some form of polygamy is possible in any normal population.

Summary passage 10

Read this passage carefully and answer all the questions on it.

Of all banes confronting the economies of the developing nations, not in the least in seriousness is inconsistency in policy. Apart from the quite obvious factor or frequent changes or governments in these countries, a phenomenon which invariably tolls the death knell of existing policies each time a government is swept out of office; even stable governments themselves seem to have a knack to modifying policies frequently. A leader of government is often regarded as radical and hence popular, when he shakes up his cabinet. Such shake-ups often lead to the change of policy.

Quite often, such avoidable changes reflect the shifts in the leaders' friendship patterns in the third world countries. A position at the top attracts large number of friends, a phenomenon which engenders keen rivalry for attention among the friends. Back-biting is hence not uncommon, and a favourite who is today regarded with an office may easily get the boot tomorrow.

Besides the poor economic situation, a common cause of social unrest brings about frequent changes in policy. An economic policy which does not produce the expected result within a short time is usually thrown out, often with the initiators of the policy. Sadly, though the fault lies not so much with the policy as the factors both within and outside, beyond the operators. The truth here is that failure tends to rush leaders into taking rash actions which result in further damage.

Finally, quite a number of the sharp changes are dictated, or at least influenced from outside. In a situation where a weak country decides to embrace a stronger one, it has to contend with some dictation from the stronger partner. To reach an agreement with another country necessarily means modifying operations at home in so far the agreement affects activities.

Frequent changes in policy harm development far more than is realized. Apart from the financial wastage brought about by the sudden abandonment of projects when new rulers assume offices, the resulting sense of insecurity scares off foreign investors. Besides, inconsistency of the policy hinders the concentration of effort on specific projects. Moreover, the frequent abandonment of projects mid-stream, especially those being executed under international agreements, tends to suggest to aid donors and leaders that the beneficiaries are not serious. Potential donors and leaders prefer dealing with serious-minded and committed leaders.

a) In three sentences, one for each, state the factors responsible for frequent changes in policy.
b) In three sentences, one for each, state the results of the frequent change in policy.

Summary passage 11

Read this passage carefully and answer all the questions on it.

We have often heard students making wild assertions that the staff members of public examining body are their worst enemies. Some, in fact, see the officials of these public examining bodies as wicked souls scheming day and night to devise ways of failing them. How correct are these assertions? The facts will speak for themselves.

The task of setting an examination paper begins long before the examination day. Indeed, months or years before the seasoned experts of the various subjects are given the teaching and examination syllabus and requested to set questions. These are compiled for subsequent scrutiny. Then another set of experts is set to examine the questions critically, make the necessary modifications and come up with the questions that conform to the acceptable standards. The result of this exercise is a set of polished and unambiguous questions that are very fair to those being examined. These questions are then securely stored.

The next stage is the registration of candidates. This stage involves not just the examining body, but also the candidates, their parents, their principals and some other members of the public. This is so because apart from the candidates to fill in the forms, their principals have to endorse them while the parents have to provide the registration fees. Any mistake or inaction on the part of any of these may ruin the chances of the candidates. If for instance, a candidate makes mistake in his choice of subjects or in filling his form, or if the principal does not submit the registration fees at the right time, the chances of the candidate will be jeopardized.

Next is the conduct of the examination itself. Again, more officials from outside the examining body than from within are involved. Think of the supervisors, the invigilators and even the security officers. They are definitely more in number than the staff of the examining body and any one of them could take an action that might result in the failure of candidates. Take the invigilator for instance. If he is negligent, a candidate could swap answer scripts under his very nose, and when this is detected by the markers, the results of the candidates may be cancelled.

Probably, the most hated person to the candidates is the marker whom they, in their ignorance, regard as a wicked drunkard who are delighted in failing them. What candidates do not realize is that an examiner is trained to score points strictly according to a carefully prepared making scheme from which he must not deviate. It is his/her constitution. Besides, his work is consistently checked by his team leader and the chief examiner. Should he be discovered to have marked inaccurately, he could be removed. So, contrary to candidates' opinion, the examiner is a seasoned teacher, a careful scorer, a person always on his guard.

The final stage comes with the collation of results. This stage is mainly computerized, and computers do not make mistakes. A candidate's results may not be processed if he is involved in a malpractice, if he/she has used a wrong examination number or no number at all, or if he fails to write all the papers that make up a subject. So when a result is withheld, the fault is mostly that of the candidate.

How then should we view the activities of the public examining bodies? Definitely, we should view them with understanding, sympathy and appreciation.

a) In one sentence, summarize the writer's purpose in this message.
b) In two sentences, one for each, state how the actions of the candidate and the invigilator can jeopardize the candidate's chances of success.
c) In three sentences, one for each, summarize the steps taken by examining bodies to ensure that candidates are given a fair chance of success.

Summary passage12

Read this passage carefully and answer all the questions on it.

Are you scared of speaking before a large audience or even making a few suggestions in public? There is no need for this. You can deliver an effective speech in public. Here are few pointers.

Perhaps the most important step is to be sure of what you are going to say. This sounds obvious enough, but it is amazing how many people get up to speak when in fact they have very little to say. After one inconsequential point, they discover they have run out of steam. So to make sure you speak well, have enough points to speak about, examine them in depth and digest them thoroughly. The more points you have, the more conversant you are with them, the more confident you will be.

How do you present your speech? Certainly, before you begin, you will be a little uneasy. Even the most experienced speaker feels the same way before beginning his speech. This is not bad; in fact, it is a good tonic for successful speech. To overcome this, do not rush headlong into the task. Rather, it pays to breathe in and out heavily, deeply and calmly. Then, slowly, calmly and carefully, begin your speech in clear and confident voice. This is when you are going through the salutation. 'The Chairperson, Honourable Guests of Honour, Distinguished ladies and gentlemen … … It is an honour for me to stand before this august gathering and … …' By the time you would have gone through all these rituals, you would have reached a point of emotional equilibrium. You should now be sufficiently calm to go on with your speech.

Somewhere at the beginning and at a strategic point in your speech, you should introduce flavour into what you are saying. You would not want to serve tea without sugar after all. So you should inject some humorous remarks once in a while. But this calls for a skill. To start with, you cannot introduce humour indiscriminately; otherwise, you might sound like a jester. Experienced speakers often introduce humours early in their speeches presumably to ease the tension in the hall. But these jokes must be brief, purposeful and closely related to the point.

Many speakers are scared by the countenance of their audience. Not all their looks are friendly. However, there are bound to be few friendly ones, and it is advised to pick them out, and look at them from time to time and ignore the hostile ones. Looking at friendly faces will keep you at ease.

You are advised to write your own speech in full, and after which, you should read it several times before the day. You get a willing listener to criticize your delivery. Do this several times until you almost recite it. Notice that we are not advising you to memorize it because you could forget vital areas due to anxiety. Writing out the speech and practicing it would make you much familiar with the contents, and indeed with the words.

Speech making is an art. While it is true that some are gifted in speech making, it is more correct that anyone who doesn't suffer from speech handicap can learn to deliver effective speeches. Thus one can become a master in this art.

a) In one sentence, state the intension of the writer.
b) In five sentences one for each, summarize the five steps in giving a good speech and the reason for each speech.

Summary passage: 13

Read this passage carefully and answer the questions on it.

Poverty! Can anyone who has not really been poor know what poverty is? I really doubt it. How could anyone, who enjoys three square meals a day, explain what poverty means? Indeed, can someone who has two full meals a day claim to know poverty? Perhaps, one begins to grasp the real meaning of poverty when one struggles really hard to have one miserable meal in twenty-four hours. Poverty and hunger are cousins, the former always dragging along the latter wherever he chooses to go.

If you are wearing a suit, or complete traditional attire, and you look naturally round in your apparel, you cannot understand what poverty entails. Nor can you have a true feeling of poverty if you have some good shirts and some pairs of trousers; never mind that all these are casual wear. Indeed, if you can change from one dress into another, and these are all you can boast of, you are not really poor. A person begins to have a true feeling of what poverty means when, apart from the tattered clothes on his body, he doesn't have any other, not even a 'calico' sheet to keep away the cold at night.

Let us face it. How can anyone who has never slept outside in the open, appreciate the full harsh import of homelessness, claim to know poverty? Yet, that is what the real naked poverty is. He who can lay claim on a house cannot claim to be poor. Indeed, if one can afford to rent a flat, or a room in a town or in a city without the landlord having cause to eject him, the individual cannot honestly claim to be poor. The real poor man has no roof over his head; this is the reason why poor people are found under bridges, in tents or simply in the verse opened air.

But that is hardly all. The poor man faces the world as a hopeless underdog. In every bargain, every decision or in every invent involving him and others; he is always reminded about his failure in life. Nobody listens alternatively when he makes a point; nobody accepts his opinion merits consideration. So in most cases, he learns to accept that he has neither wisdom nor opinion.

The pauper's lot naturally rubs off on his child who is subject not only to hunger of the body, but also to the mind. A pauper lacks the resources to send his child to school. Even in communities where education is free, a poor man's child still faces an uphill task because the hunger of the body impedes the proper nourishment of the mind. Also, denied access to modern communication media, a child of a poor man has very little opportunity to understand the concepts he is taught. His mind is rocky soil on which the teacher's seed cannot easily germinate. Thus embattled at home and then at school, a pauper's child soon has very little option but to drop out from school.

That is still not all. Weakened by hunger, embattled by cold and exposure to elements, feeding on contaminated water and rotten food, a poor person is easy target to diseases. This is precisely why the poorest countries have the shortest life expectancies while the longest life expectancies are recorded in the richest countries. Poverty is really a disease that shortens life!

    a)   In six sentences, one for each, summarize the problems of the poor man.

ESSAY AND LETTER WRITING QUESTIONS FOR PRACTISE

Q1.   You are the head boy or head girl of your school. Write out a speech you will deliver during a thanksgiving ceremony.

Q2.   It has been realized that nowadays, young people dress indecently. As a concerned citizen write a letter to the editor of a local or national newspaper to highlight this issue and suggest what needs to be done to minimize the trend.

Q3.   You are the chief Speaker in a debate on: *"**Life without our parents is difficult.**"* Write out your speech for or against this assertion.

Q4.   Your elder brother who is living in the village has written you a letter to express his desire to move to the city to seek out for job. Write a reply letter, advising him to stay put in the village and state at least three things he can do there to make his stay worthwhile.

Q5.   Write a story to illustrate the saying: "You reap what you sow" Your story should be good enough for publication in a school magazine.

Q6.   Recently, you visited a village and discovered that the inhabitants there still consume well water. As a concerned citizen, write a letter to the permanent secretary of the Ministry of Health about your discovery and suggest ways of improving the quality of water for the villagers.

Q7.   You are the chief Speaker in a debate on the topic: "Absenteeism is a major factor responsible for students' failure." Write out your speech for or against this assertion.

Q8.   Write an article for publication in a national newspaper on high cost education in your country. State what should be done to remedy the situation.

Q9.   Not long ago, you received a letter from your uncle who wants you to outline your educational ambition so that he may assist you. Write a reply to his letter, thanking him and outlining your plans.

Q10.   Write a story, real or imaginative to illustrate the saying: "A patient dog eats the fattest bone." Your write-up should be good enough for publication in a local newspaper.

Q11.   Write an article for publication in your school magazine on the effects of drug abuse on the youths in your country.

Q12.   There have been reports that people in your area no longer feel safe due to certain factors like criminal activities, immoral behaviour and unhygienic aspects. As a concerned resident, write a letter to the Chairman of your Local Council, highlighting these factors and suggest what should be done to control the situation.

Q13.   You are the Chief Speaker in a debate on: "Divorce is a major contributor to loss of morals in our society." Write out your speech for or against this assertion.

Q14.   Write a story to illustrate the saying: "A stitch in time saves nine."

Q15.   You have been sent on indefinite suspension for the part you played in a recent disturbance in which valuable school property was damaged. Write a letter to the principal of your school describing the part you played and apologizing for your involvement.

Q16.   Write an article for publication in a national newspaper on why you think a woman should be your country's next president.

Q17.   Write a letter to your elder brother working aboard and describe the hardship you and your parents are facing at home. Ask him to render you some financial assistance.

Q18. You are the chief speaker in a school debate on the topic "Public secondary schools are better than the private ones." Write your speech for or against the topic.

Q19. Tell a story that ends with the advice: "Cut your coat according to your cloth."

Q20. You have just taken part in a local festival in your village. Write an article for publication in a cultural magazine describing the festival: state its origin and importance to your people, and the specific role you played.

Q21. You are in the final year of secondary school. Write a letter to your uncle, who is an influential person in society, telling him what you intend to do next and asking for his assistance.

Q22. You have just returned in to the city from your village where you spent the last holiday. In an article suitable for publication in your school magazine, compare life in your village with that in the city.

Q23. There was a riot in your school resulting in extensive damage; the Ministry of Education ordered the school to be shut down. Write a letter to the Minister of Education, explaining the causes of the disturbance, and appealing for the School to be re-opened.

Q24. As your contribution to a debate, write arguments for or against the proposition. "We are happier that our fore-fathers."

Q25. Narrate an experience you have had or heard about that illustrates the saying. "Where there is a will, there is a way."

Q26. Your brother is about to enter secondary school. Write a letter to him, stating at least three problems he is likely to face in the school and suggest ways of solving them.

Q27. Write an article for publication in your school magazine: 'The evil effect of the examination malpractice in our society.'

Q28. Write a letter to your local government authority and comment on three health hazards in your area. Make suggestions as how the situation will be improved.

Q29. You are the main speaker in an inter- school debate. Write your speech for or against the motion: "Corrupt public officers deserve capital punishment."

Q30. Write a story ending with: "He reaped what he sowed." The story should be suitable for publication in your school magazine.

ANSWERS TO EXERCISES

CHAPTER 1

EXERCISE 1

Underline the nouns in the sentences below.

1. My best <u>game</u> is <u>politics</u>.
2. <u>Timoh</u>, <u>Joseph,</u> and <u>Amina</u> are best of <u>friends.</u>
3. <u>Evolution</u> is <u>part</u> of <u>nature</u>
4. The <u>enthusiasm</u> is in the <u>air</u>.
5. <u>Sunday</u> is the coldest <u>day</u> of the <u>month</u>.
6. My <u>brother</u> is a prominent <u>lawyer</u>.
7. Is it <u>time</u> to go, <u>Fodeiwa</u>?
8. The <u>horse</u> is in <u>Fandu</u>.
9. The <u>chair</u> is old and is missing a <u>leg</u>.
10. When will the <u>boys</u> arrive?

EXERCISE 2

Underline all the nouns in the paragraph below.

On my <u>way</u> to <u>school</u> this morning, I witnessed a serious <u>fight</u> between two <u>in-laws</u>; both were elderly <u>men</u>. It was in <u>Bakau Car Park</u> and there were huge <u>crowd</u> excitedly watching, shouting, laughing and clapping for the <u>fighters</u>. They fought for some <u>money</u> that was given to them by a <u>driver</u>. The two <u>men</u> had helped the <u>driver</u> to load his <u>vehicle</u>, so he gave them some <u>coins</u> and <u>Leones</u> as <u>compensation</u> for their <u>effort</u>. According to one <u>by-stander</u>, the <u>man</u> who handled the <u>cash</u> attempted to hide with it. He was later found behind one of the abandoned <u>cars</u> in the <u>corner</u> of the <u>park</u>, eating <u>Nyebeh</u> and <u>bread</u> he had bought with the <u>money</u>. When he failed to produce the <u>money</u>, the other <u>man</u> hit him with an iron <u>bar</u>. He was bleeding and swimming in the <u>pool</u> of his <u>blood</u>. <u>Police officers</u> were immediately called to the <u>scene</u>. The bleeding <u>man</u> was taken to the <u>hospital</u> while the other <u>man</u> was arrested and taken to the <u>police station</u> for <u>investigation</u>.

EXERCISE 3

Underline all the proper nouns in the short passage below.

On Friday morning, <u>Alfred</u> left for <u>Kailahun</u> to go and play football for his club, Kailahun <u>United</u>. Kalahun United played the match with <u>Kambo Warriors</u>, the famous club in the country. Kailahun United has <u>Amara, Osman, Tommy</u> and <u>Sharr</u> as its star players. The <u>Head of State</u> donated Le 500,000 to each of the teams. <u>Mr. John Jusu</u> from <u>Nyandehun</u>, was the referee for the match. When he blew his whistle to start the game, <u>Modou</u> of Kailahun United passed the ball to <u>Lamin</u>. From him the ball went to <u>Mustapha</u> who crossed it to <u>Tamba</u>. <u>Bubacca</u> of Kambo Warriors, the man of the match, scored the first goal in the tenth minute. At the end of the ninety minutes, it was Kambo Warriors three, Kailahun United two. The National Stadium was jam packed with jubilant fans from all angles of the country. Among them were <u>Muslims, Christians, ChristMus</u> and free thinkers, all sat together to watch the match.

EXERCISE 4

All the common nouns in the short passage below are underline.

The <u>youths</u> nowadays have no <u>patient</u> about <u>life</u>. This may be one of the <u>reasons</u> why most of them live in a regrettable <u>life</u>. When they run into one another's <u>life</u> today, they will propose <u>marriage</u> tomorrow, and then the next <u>day</u>, they are <u>couples</u>. They do not ask for any parental <u>advice</u> or <u>blessing</u>, nor do they give themselves enough <u>time</u> to observe each other. Such <u>marriage</u> is always temporal. My <u>brother</u> engaged in one such <u>marriage</u> in the past. He met the <u>girl</u> in a night <u>club</u> when he was celebrating his eighteenth <u>birthday</u>. Two <u>weeks</u> after, he informed the <u>family</u> that he had met a <u>woman</u> he loved and wanted to marry. To our greatest <u>dismay</u>, he did not even know the actual <u>name</u> of the <u>girl</u>, her <u>tribe</u>, her <u>home</u> or the <u>name</u> of single <u>member</u> of her <u>family</u>. Realizing this, our <u>father</u> thanked him and asked him to lead us to the girl's <u>family</u> which he was unable to do. He was ridiculed.

EXERCISE 5

Underline all the compound nouns in the short passage below.

Nowadays, <u>football</u> game is the best in the world. It is written about in every <u>newspaper</u> around the globe. The <u>grandchildren</u> of my <u>brother-in-law</u> have vowed to have it as future career. Their late <u>grandmother</u> loved to play <u>volleyball</u> and <u>basketball</u>. She had many <u>playmates</u> when she was in the game. On the Marry-go-round day in Kailahun, she won several prizes. Among them were <u>toothbrushes</u>, <u>tablecloth</u>, <u>gunpowder</u>, <u>laptops</u> and <u>penknife</u>. When these <u>grandchildren</u> decided to play <u>football</u>, I expected them to be famous in future; more especially when their <u>landlords</u> of the <u>households</u> have constructed them the pitch and bought them a <u>cupboard</u> full of the necessary <u>textbooks</u> about the game. Among the books, there were some with <u>teaspoons</u> and <u>baseball</u> pictures on the covers. They were the most important ones for their training. Now, Kailahun hopes to produce world first class <u>footballers</u> in future. <u>Fodei Lahai</u> told us that last year, he saw these promising boys on <u>Tobaski Day</u>, <u>Christmas Day</u> and on <u>Easter Day</u> merry-go-rounding in and around <u>Fandu Neiwuibu</u> in <u>Nyadehun Mambabu</u>, Kailahun district, Eastern province of <u>Sierra Leone</u>.

EXERCISE 6

Underline all the collective nouns in the short passage below.

Most <u>communities</u> in the world today are pruned to violence. Youths of these days can be easily fashioned into destructive weapons that will destroy their own <u>society</u>. Within the process, most of them can even destroy their own lives. For instance, two days ago, a <u>mob</u> of youths attacked and killed a trader for not selling to them what he hadn't in his shop. In another incident, some <u>groups</u> among the spectators attacked one another after common argument had broken among them. The <u>audience</u> in Community Centre in Kailahun set fire on the building when one of the actors left the stage earlier than expected. Why the world is so violent these days? Is it because of the way families bring up their children? Psychologists and sociologists must work hard to find out how peace in society must be maintained. One thing we must do is to ask the <u>congregations</u> in the churches and mosques to pray for world peace.

EXERCISE 7

Underline all the collective nouns in the sentences below.

1. My <u>family</u> is part of the <u>congregation</u> that worship in this church.
2. The violent <u>mob</u> demonstrated against the act of the <u>crew</u>.
3. The <u>team</u> did not play to the expectation of this <u>society.</u>
4. This <u>community</u> set up the <u>committee</u> to monitor the work.
5. The destruction of the <u>swarm</u> was the <u>staff</u>'s decision.
6. I was part of the <u>band</u> that entertained the <u>harem</u> of the king.
7. The light from the <u>galaxy</u> exposed the <u>gang</u> of thieves in hell.
8. Maintaining <u>groups</u> within the <u>club</u> may lead to division.
9. I saw our couple in the huge crowd that came to welcome us.
10. <u>Herd</u> of cattle destroyed the <u>colony</u> of termites.

EXERCISE 8

Underline the concrete nouns in the sentences below.

1. The action of the <u>actors</u> did not please the <u>audience</u> at the <u>theatre</u>.
2. The consumption of the unpleasant <u>food</u> causes illnesses.
3. A <u>community</u> with many happy <u>families</u> is less violent.
4. Most <u>lovers</u> love entertainment but hate tedious jobs.
5. I see no honour in the behaviour of these days' dignified <u>people.</u>
6. God created the heaven and earth for all <u>mankind.</u>
7. <u>Football</u> has become the major game in the <u>world</u>.

EXERCISE 9

Underline all the concrete nouns and circle the abstract nouns in the short passage below.

My grandfather, Kennie Fodei Lyhai, the then paramount chief of Luawa chiefdom in Kailahhun district, was a philosopher. One **afternoon**, he expressed to me the **confusion** and **concern** about **creation**.

"**God Almighty**, together with His **angels**, created this universe and everything in it. He did the **creation** through the **words** in His own **language**. It is only we the humans **God** used his **hand** to create. That makes us very special from all the other **creatures.** That is even the **reason** why He gave us **dominion** over everything He created. This also shows that He loves us more than any other **creature**. **Love, loyalty, honesty** and **perfection** are among the **things Almighty God** demands from us in return for His **love** for us. **Love** and **perfection** are the greatest of all. **Allah** wants us to love one another and be perfect like Him. But how can this be possible? Will the **life** be normal if it happens as He wants? For instance, all of us are made in His own **image**, but no one is perfect like Him. Again, if we are all perfect like Him, and we love one another like ourselves, how can the lawyers, judges, police, criminals, doctors and clergy men get their daily bread? There will be no **crimes**, so those who live on **crime** will have no **source** of income; no **case** will go to court for lawyers and judges. There will be no **sickness** for doctors to treat and get money. There will be no need for **religion** since everyone will be perfect and commits no **sin**. This is the great **wonder** about Him that no one can understand." "Anyway, let us pray for His **mercy** to rain on us on the **Judgment day**." I told him slowly when he finished speaking.

EXERCISE 10

1. A proper noun names a specific person, place, animal or thing; a common noun refers to the general name of persons, places, animal or things.

2. A compound noun refers to two or more words used to refer to the same person, place, animal or thing; a collective noun names a group or collection of persons, animals or things.

3. A concrete noun names an object that can be recognised by one of our senses; an abstract noun names an idea, a quality or characteristic.

EXERCISE 11

Proper noun	Common noun	Collective noun	Compound noun	Abstract noun	Concrete noun
Peter	bread	family	grandmother	Beauty	bread
Banjul	butter scot	mob	laptop	marriage	butter scot
Easter	water	committee	butter scot	honesty	
Sunday	grandmother	crowd	teaspoon	ignorance	
Serrekunda	laptop	congregation	football	freedom	
God	doctor	audience		happiness	
New York	angel			air	
Tom	teaspoon			patriotism	
Head of State	community			peace	
Tuesday	football			prayer	
Kailahun	table			sin	
John	sin			opinion	
	children				
	holiday				
	prayer				
	boy				

EXERCISE 12

Fill in the blank spaces with the singular or plural of the noun against each

Singular	Plural	Singular
leaf	leaves	Sunday
piano	pianos	furniture
box	boxes	child
Reverend Father	Reverend Fathers	head of state
plier	pliers	man

church	churches	Crisis
country	countries	secretary
plateau	plateaux	Noise
ox	oxen	lorry
thief	thieves	foot
biography	biographies	testimony
lady	ladies	chief
deer	deer	beach
datum	data	information
hero	heroes	syllabus
In-law	in-laws	Friday
tomato	tomatoes	stadium
mouse	mice	Hoof
phenomenon	phenomena	Half
toy	toys	Team
evidence	evidence	Proof
politics	politics	breakfast
mango	mangoes	woman
	foxes	roof
self	selves	Story
lorry	lorries	Luggage
part of speech	parts of speech	man of war

Plural	Singular	Plural
Sundays	synopsis	synopses
furniture	Tourays	Tourays
children	linguistics	linguistics
heads of state	passer-by	passers-by
Men	news	news
crises	tomato	tomatoes
secretaries	toothbrush	toothbrushes
noises	basis	bases
lorries	donkey	donkeys

Feet	glass	glasses
testimonies	battery	batteries
chiefs	wife	wives
beaches	radius	radii
information	Mansaray	Mansarays
syllabi	radio	radio
Fridays	criterion	criteria
stadia	knife	knives
hooves	body	bodies
halves	pygmy	pygmies
teams	foot	feet
proofs	key	keys
breakfasts	medium	media
women	focus	foci
roofs	ass	asses
stories	fish	fishes
luggage	body	bodies
men of war	figure of speech	figures of speech

EXECISE 13

The sentences are singular, make them plural.

Singular	**Plural**
1) A cat is a small animal.	Cats are small animals.
2) There is a bird up the tree.	There are birds up the trees.
3) The boy has a book in his bag.	The boys have books in their bags.
4) Only a pupil and a teacher are here.	Only the pupils and the teachers are here.
5) That girl has a bicycle.	Those girls have bicycles.
6) His tooth is aching.	Their teeth are aching.
7) A man is coming with a dog.	The men are coming with dogs.
8) I heard a story about him.	We heard stories about them.
9) Here is a mouse in a box.	Here are mice in the boxes.
10) She is washing her foot in a bowl.	They are washing their feet in the bowls.

EXERCISE 14

Write the possessive forms of the phrases below

1. Boys' room
2. Men's association
3. Class's money
4. Monkey's tail
5. Thomas's book
6. Peter and Paul's pen
7. Tom and Med's pens
8. Fodei's mother
9. Tom and Fatu's brother
10. The family's property
11. Moses's bag
12. Girls' club
13. African children's day
14. Teachers' meeting
15. The principal's office
16. Mr. Peter's house
17. The dogs' food
18. Children's game
19. My mother's photos
20. God's words
21. The principal's car
22. The teams'
23. Father's blessing
24. Christians' beliefs

EXERCISE 15

	Word	**Word class**	Noun form
eg	Laugh	verb	laughter
1	develop	verb	development
2	peaceful	adj	peace

3	Honest	adj	honesty
4	Happy	adj	happiness
5	friendly	adj	friend
6	Pray	verb	prayer
7	capable	adj	capability
8	Quiet	adj	quietness
9	Treat	verb	treatment
10	Foolish	adj	foolishness
11	patriotic	adj	patriotism
12	Free	adj/verb	freedom
13	hopeless	adj	hope
14	faithful	adj	faith
15	Timely	adj	time
16	enslave	verb	enslavement
17	bravely	adv	bravery
18	Intelligent	adj	intelligence
19	Gentle	adj	gentleness
20	ungodly	adj	ungodliness
21	breathe	verb	breath
22	honorary	adj	honour
23	Able	adj	ability
24	Create	verb	creation, creator, creature
25	popular	adj	popularity

	Word	**Word class**	Noun form
eg	inform	verb	Information, Informant
26	True	adj	truth
27	sinful	adj	Sin, sinner
28	communicate	verb	communication
29	entertain	verb	entertainment
30	Lead	verb	leader, lead
31	Participate	verb	participation, participant

32	beautifully	adv	beauty
33	advise	verb	advice
34	Die	verb	death
35	responsible	adj	responsibility
36	Do	verb	doer
37	Sad	adj	sadness
38	Mad	adj	madness
39	effective	adj	effectiveness
40	understand	verb	understanding
41	appreciate	verb	appreciation
42	Environmental	adj	environment
43	depend	verb	dependence, dependant
44	explain	verb	explanation
45	difficult	adj	difficulty
46	totally	adv	total, totality
47	license	verb	licence
48	necessary	adj	necessity
49	prepare	verb	preparation
50	advocate	verb	advocate, advocacy

EXERCISE 16

Underline the nouns that function as subjects in each sentences below.

1. <u>Kailahun</u> is my home town.
2. <u>Father</u> usually brushes his cocoa and coffee farms.
3. <u>Fandu</u>, a village in Kailahun district, is a nice place to live.
4. <u>The indigenes</u> are very peaceful, brave, wise and educated.
5. <u>That region</u> is the backbone of Sierra Leone.
6. In the past, <u>Kailahun</u> enjoyed very attractive culture.
7. <u>Several people</u> from that area appear prayerful and hardworking.
8. Who gave <u>you</u> this information about the home of this writer?
9. Am <u>I</u> not speaking the true about Kailahun?
10. <u>We</u> search for the truth that will set us free.

11. Do <u>you</u> know the boys that fought for me?
12. Here are <u>the boys</u> I told you about yesterday.
13. There is <u>a boy</u> in this school that can fight me.
14. Do <u>your family</u> eat Benachi and Nyebeh?
15. Who is <u>the man</u> that pays your fees every year?

EXERCISE 17

Underline the nouns that function as direct objects in the sentences below.

1. The Smiling Coast has admirable <u>leadership</u>.
2. The clever gentleman has made plenty <u>achievements</u>.
3. This small semi-desert nation receives many <u>visitors</u> every year.
4. Some of these visitors perform <u>wonders</u> in this peaceful nation.
5. Some citizens hate the <u>visitors</u> for the wonders they perform.
6. When I knocked <u>the door</u> of the desert house, it opened.
7. One must take his <u>time</u> to deal with some desert dwellers.
8. They love the <u>way-farers</u> from far away homes.
9. I love <u>The Gambia and the Gambians</u>.
10. We speak both <u>French and English</u>.

EXERCISE 18

Underline the direct objects and circle the indirect objects in the sentences below

1. In my school, one old man tells the **pupils** <u>stories</u> every day.
2. He will ask <u>them</u> to tell **their parents** the <u>stories</u>.
3. This man sometimes buys his **children** some <u>bread</u> to eat.
4. Some children send **him** <u>gifts</u> from their parents.
5. When they come, he opens **them** his <u>gate</u> to enter.
6. My grandfather wrote my **dad** many <u>fork tales</u>.
7. When I was young, my grandmother bought **me** many <u>toys</u>.
8. He sent **us** invitation <u>cards</u> for his birthday party.
9. When I was in Kailahun, I wrote **them** this <u>letter</u>.
10. The government awards honest **citizens** <u>contracts</u>.

EXERCISE 19

In the short paragraph below, underline the prepositional phrases and circle the nouns or pronouns that function as object of preposition.

I went to **town** this morning to buy some food for my **family**. In the supermarket, I spoke to my old **friends** briefly. I returned to my **car** and quickly jumped into **it** as time was not in my **favour**. By the **car** there was an old woman. She talked to **me** in a low **tone** and pointed to her empty **belly**. With **me**, was very little amount. I took One Hundred Dalasi from the **wallet** in my **bag** and gave her. She prayed for abundant **blessing** from **God** in **Heaven** to rain on **me**. I put her in my **car** and drove her to her **resident**. At home, her family received her happily and thanked me a lot for my **generosity**.

EXERCISE 20

In the sentences below, the appositives are underlined and the predicate nominatives are bold.

1. That tall man, the noble prize winner, is our new **manager**.
2. Mr. Juanar, Paul's brother, is the former managing **director** of SALWACO.
3. Bob Marley, legend of Reggae, died on 11th May, 1980.
4. John Peter Mendy is my best **friend**.
5. My best friend is **John Peter Mendy**.
6. Ensa, the winner of the competition, is **my brother**.
7. My brother, the dancer, is **Mambu**.
8. He is our English **teacher**.
9. The world biggest reggae star, Bob, died but left massage for his fans.
10. Mr. Jusu Koroma, the new chief, is that smartly dressed **gentleman**.

EXERCISE 21

	Subject	Direct Object	Indirect Object	Object of Preposition	Predicate Nominative	Appositive
1		ball				
2						Wife
3	Amie	French				
4	G. Giama					
5	Tom	story		devil		
6	Paul			police		
7		box	Musa			
8		story				
9	football	glass				
10	Mr. Mendy	History				
11	God	Man and woman				
12		letter	mother			
13	music		happiness			
14	Paul	bird			boy	
15		story		Fatou		
16	Earth				home	
17		Elizabeth				
18	Mr. Joepi			Car		
19		football	Joseph			
20	Joseph	car				
21	girl		Plate			
22						friend
23			Fodei			
24		Amie				
25		essay	Peter	school		
26	Timy	Game				
27	Jekujar				criminal	Friend
28		Boy				
29	Pat K			team		Head
30	Mr. Lahai	pen	daughter			
31	students			class		
32	prefect					Jattu
33	People			John		

34	Mr. Jarju	car	Jeku			
35	buffalo	bridge		river		
36	man			God		Paul
37		the pot				
38	guys				bosses	
39	father	event, Tommy				
40	Joe	bible	mother			
41				kitchen		
42	dog	snake				
43	Papa	Mama				
44						chief
45	father					
46	Ebrima				brother	
47	boy					
48		idleness				
49	girl					
50	Massa Sama				heart to heart	

EXERCISE 21

Proper Noun	Common Noun	Abstract Noun	Collective Noun	Compound Noun
Christmas Day, Kailahun, St John Catholic Church, Labour Day, Christianity, God Almighty, **Common Noun** service, passers-by, marry-go-round, good-bye, life	families, community, crowd, compound, mob, banning, team, religion, society, church, home, grandfather, row, grandchildren, mother-in-law, bag,	Christmas Day, Labour Day, banning, Christianity, religion, peace, happiness, unity, love, service, God Almighty, marry-go-round, good-bye, days, life	families, community, crowd, mob, team, society **Common Noun** pictures, days, friends, football, pastor, toothbrush,	Christmas Day, St John Catholic Church, Labour Day, grandfather, grandchildren, marry-go-round, good-bye,

EXERCISE 22

Write the antecedents of the underlined pronouns below

	Antecedents	pronouns
1.	We, John	our, his
2.	Peter, our	your, we
3.	they	their
4.	we	our
5.	Binta, our	who, us
6.	... ...	We, her
7.	they, us	their, we
8.	I	my
9.	it	it
10.	Children	they
11.	They	their
12.	Mother, us,	she, our Fatou

EXERCISE 23

1. them, me
2. Him, us
3. She, they
4. They, we
5. He, us, her
6. Me, them
7. He, us
8. She, us
9. We, them
10. They, us, them
11. She, him
12. I, them

EXERCISE 24

1. mine,
2. his,
3. hers,
4. ours,
5. their,
6. Its,
7. Yours,
8. Hers,
9. Its,
10. It

EXERCISE 25

REFLEXIVE PRONOUN:	*INTENIVE PRONOUN:*
2). ourselves,	1). himself,
3). ourselves,	5). herself,
4). himself,	7). themselves,
6), herself,	8). themselves,
10), myself,	9). myself
12). himself,	11). itself,
14), yourself	13). yourself

CHAPTER 2

EXERCISE 1

In the short passage below, action verbs are underlined and non-action verbs are bold.

This morning, I **did** not get up from bed early. The reason **was** that I went to bed very late last night, because Kailahun **was** celebrating SLPP victory. It **was** too late when I went to the tap to fetch water for bath so that I **will** prepare for the day's activities. The only tap in our area, Kebawana, **was** parked full of people who **were** all very anxious to **get** water and make haste to schools and working places. Few lazy children **were** reluctantly playing, singing and running about. While I stood in confusion thinking what to do next, I quickly remembered the burst pipe at Gbanyawalu around the house of my friend. I last passed by the area three days ago, and it **was** at night. I decided to run to the place and collect my water there. I took to my heels as faster as my legs **could** allow me. When I reached there, the damaged pipe **was** fixed. I returned to where I **was** but from a far distance, I saw nobody there. I **was** happy and confused. I **was** happy because I thought I **could** easily get the water and go home soon; but again I wondered as how the large crowd I left few minutes ago **could have** all filled their containers and left so soon. To my greatest dismay, the tap **was** not running any longer when I reached there.

EXERCISE 2

Action Verbs	Linking Verbs
1.tasted,	2. tasted,
4. smelt,	3. smelt,
5. looked,	6. looked,
7. grow,	8. grow,
9. felt,	10. felt,
12. sounded,	11. sounded,
13. Appeared	14. appeared

EXERCISE 3

	Action verbs	Helping verbs	Linking verbs
1	talk	Will	… … … … …
2	love	Is	is
3	… … … … …	… … … … …	is
4	help	can, could be	… … … … …
5	… … … … …	… … … … …	was

6	… … … … …	… … … … …	are
7	… … … … …	… … … … …	are
8	works	… … … … …	… … … … …
9	worked	Has	… … … … …
10	considered	… … … … …	… … … … …

EXERCISE 5

In the sentences below, the verb phrases are underlined, helping verbs are bold while the main verbs are in italics.

1. I **will** *go* home and tell them about the meeting in school tomorrow.
2. Tee-man **has** *told* everyone to inform the people about the meeting.
3. I believe everyone has to do so when we all return home after school.
4. They **will be** *monitoring* the boys who **will be** *cleaning* around.
5. The meeting **will have been** *completed* before the bell rings for lunch.
6. Some students **were** *eating* their lunch when the teacher **was** *calling* them.
7. The boys **will be** *playing* the game while the girls **will be** *cleaning* around.
8. Those who **have been** *playing* the game **will** not *attend* the meeting.
9. Mr. Doup, who **has** *taught* for five years, **was** *ringing* the bell.
10. They **had** *finished* the work three days before my father came.

EXERCISE 7

Transitively expressed verbs	Intransitively expressed verbs
2. stopped,	1. travelled,
5. pulled,	3. stopped,
7. asked,	4. walked,
9. obeyed,	6. opened,

10. checked,	8. come,
11. Asked,	12. climb,
15. pushed,	13. Move,
18. continued,	14. did,
19. spent,	16. moved,
23.see	17. closed,
	20. arrived,
	21. reached,
	22. were welcomed,
	24. tired

EXERCISE 9

#	BASE	PAST	PARTICIPLE
1	slide	Slid	slid
2	make	Made	made
3	slink	slunk	slunk
4	smell	smelt	smelt
5	dig	Dug	dug
6	dream	dreamt	dreamt
7	speed	Sped	sped
8	feed	Fed	fed
9	fly	Flew	flown
10	find	found	found
11	dwell	dwelt	dwelt
12	fling	flung	flung
13	get	Got	got
14	grind	ground	ground
15	run	Ran	run
16	sleep	Slept	slept
17	jump	jumped	jumped
18	ring	Rang	rung

19	*fix*	*Fixed*	fixed
20	*hang*	*Hung*	hung
21	*burn*	burnt	*burnt*
22	*hold*	*Held*	held
23	bid	*Bid*	*bid*
24	*bite*	Bit	*bitten*
25	*brake*	*broke*	broken
26	*catch*	caught	*caught*
27	*cut*	*Cut*	cut
28	*hurt*	Hurt	*hurt*
29	hit	*Hit*	*hit*
30	clothe	*clothed*	*clothed*
31	leap	*leapt*	*leapt*
32	feed	*Fed*	*fed*
33	*sit*	*Sat*	sat
34	*spell*	*Spelt*	spelt
35	*spring*	*sprang*	sprung
36	*blow*	*Blew*	blown
37	proofread	Proofread	proofread
38	broadcast	Broadcast	broadcast
39	keep	*kept*	*kept*
40	*lose*	*lost*	lost
41	*kneel*	*knelt*	knelt
42	lend	*lent*	*lent*
43	lie *(not true)*	*lied*	*lied*
44	lie *(position)*	*lay*	*lain*
45	*lay*	laid	*laid*
46	hear	*heard*	*heard*
47	*pay*	paid	*paid*
48	*say*	*said*	said
49	*seek*	sought	*sought*
50	sell	*sold*	*sold*
51	*shine*	*shone*	shone

52	*send*	*sent*	sent
53	know	*knew*	*known*
54	*cry*	cried	*cried*
55	*put*	put	*Put*
56	fight	*fought*	*fought*
57	*give*	gave	*given*
58	drink	*drank*	*drunk*
59	*draw*	drew	*drawn*
60	*burst*	*burst*	burst
61	*cast*	cast	*cast*
62	let	*let*	*Let*
63	*write*	*wrote*	written
64	fall	*fell*	*fallen*
65	*spread*	*spread*	spread
66	*mean*	meant	*meant*
67	deal	*dealt*	*dealt*
68	stand	*stood*	*stood*
69	go	*went*	*gone*
70	*shoot*	*shot*	shot
71	*meet*	*met*	met
72	sing	*sang*	*sung*
73	*set*	set	*Set*
74	*shoe*	shod	*shod*
75	*born*	born	*born*
76	*breathe*	breathed	*breathed*

EXERCISE 10

1. (called ... ... had)
2. (explained)
3. (explain)
4. (eat)
5. (sang ... ... played).

6. (has)
7. (had ... ... arrived)
8. (dancing ... ... came)
9. (speak)
10. (narrated)

CHAPTER 3

EXERCISE 1

The adjectives in the sentences are underlined.

1. Njala University is a <u>powerful</u> institution.
2. The <u>green</u> van is very <u>slow</u>.
3. The <u>outdated</u> truck has an <u>oversized</u> trailer.
4. Jainaba is so <u>dull</u> in class.
5. The bicycles were <u>new</u> two years ago.
6. Tuesday was <u>cloudy</u> and <u>humid</u>.
7. The <u>old</u> man is wearing a <u>blue</u> suit.
8. The workers are very <u>displeased</u> with their salary.
9. He is a <u>good</u> player of basketball.
10. The work was <u>hard</u> but <u>manageable</u>.
11. The campus has <u>excellent</u> water supply.
12. The <u>stupid</u> boy laughed uncontrollably.
13. The boy said he was <u>sad</u>.
14. The <u>mad</u> dog chased people at night.

EXERCISE 2

Proper adjectives are underlined in the sentences below.

1. Nowadays, the <u>Chinese</u> goods dominate the <u>African</u> markets.
2. Most <u>European</u> football clubs buy <u>African</u> players.
3. Many <u>English</u> teachers in the <u>Gambian</u> schools are foreigners.
4. <u>Sierra Leonean</u> writer from the <u>Mende</u> ethnic group has won a prize.

5. <u>Christmas</u> celebration will start on <u>Tuesday</u> evening next week.
6. <u>United Nations</u> secretary general is Paul Lyhai.
7. The current <u>American</u> present is very controversial and unreliable.
8. One <u>Nigerian</u> movie was launched in the <u>Bakau</u> stadium yesterday.
9. The <u>Gomez</u> families within the <u>Majango</u> ethnic group are religious.
10. I was born in <u>Islamic</u> faith but I grew up and I'm living in <u>Catholic</u> faith.

EXERCISE 3

All the pronouns function as adjectives in the sentences below are underlined.

1. <u>That</u> moment I saw them, <u>her</u> kid, Paulina, was in <u>their</u> car with <u>her</u> dull.
2. <u>My</u> little dog chased <u>their</u> car and <u>your</u> cat away from <u>our</u> compound.
3. <u>Her</u> father had gone to collect <u>another</u> wife from <u>her</u> family in <u>our</u> village.
4. <u>This</u> morning, I saw Mr. Lans and <u>his</u> children in <u>their</u> car.
5. We have finished <u>their</u> work for <u>this</u> academic year.

EXERCISE 4

The underlined nouns function as adjective in the passage.

There are many <u>street</u> children in the <u>car</u> park. They sit under the big <u>mango</u> tree near the <u>iron</u> pole in <u>Kissi car</u> park. These <u>government</u> children spend their days discussing <u>football</u> news. Some of them have <u>skin</u> diseases and <u>eye</u> infections. There is only one <u>boys'</u> room for all of them where they pass <u>Monday</u> and <u>Friday</u> nights. Two days ago, I spoke to Talk-in-Blues, their leader. He told me that most of the <u>garage</u> children have parents that care for them but they only love independent lives. 'They want to feel the reality of life of this wicked world.' He concluded.

EXERCISE 5

All the nouns function as adjective in the sentences below are bold.

1. The **bush** people who live near **Mamba** mountain are peaceful.
2. My **school** bag was among the things the **forest** fire destroyed.
3. The **mango** leaves and the **banana** leaves are common in the **forest** region.
4. Hers is a **street** boy; they meet behind Jokor Night Club.
5. The **forest** animals living in Luawa chiefdom are different from the **sea** animals.

EXERCISE 6

In the short passage, all the nouns are underlined and their modifiers are bold. The articles and the pronouns are not included.

During **moonlight** night, I sometimes decide to walk home after practice rather than traveling in the **overcrowded, noisy** and **smelling** buses. My **weak** and **lazy** friends sometimes decide to travel home in those **old rotten** cars. One night, I met a very **tall, huge** and **fearful** man standing in a **dark** corner of the road. He coughed and cleared his throat, and then called me. "You, **short** and **thin** man! Come here, or you stand and wait for me! "His **heavy** voice frightened me. I stood to attention like that **black** and **high** statue standing at Westfield. I looked at his **gigantic** structure, and then, at my **tiny** and **feeble** structure. I became very **timid**. I looked around me but there was no one around. I put my hands and head up and called my **dead** father. I prayed to the **great** saviour to come to my rescue. Just when I put my **shivery** head down, I saw a **white** effigy of the **legend** president with his **long** sword in his hand, about to redeem me. Then very **bright** light from a **latest brown-new black American** Hummer car flashed on me. My **poor** ghost went in **deep** trance. It was Mambu B. Sheriff, one of my **long-time intimate** friends that approached. With a **wide** smile plastered on his **shiny** forehead, he opened the **huge** door of the car and waved me in. My fear was gone ...

EXERCISE 8

Fill in the spaces with the appropriate comparative adjective.

1. c). bright,
2. a). fast,
3. b). round,
4. a). tall,
5. a). old
6. b). loud,
7. c). weak,
8. a). heavy,
9. b). rich,
10. a). happy

EXERCISE 10

Adjective	Comparative	Superlative
1. weak	weaker	weakest
2. difficult	more difficult	most difficult
3. fine	finer	finest
4. easy	easier	easiest
5. tall	taller	tallest
6. precious	more precious	most precious
7. sweet	sweeter	sweetest
8. lazy	lazier	laziest
9. strong	stronger	strongest
10. new	newer	newest
11. dull	duller	dullest
12. fat	fatter	fattest
14. heavy	heavier	heaviest
15. brilliant	more brilliant	most brilliant
16. fast	faster	fastest
17.effective	more effective	most effective

20. rich	richer	richest
21. quick	quicker	quickest
22. happy	happier	happiest
23. moderate	more moderate	most moderate
24. wicked	more wicked	most wicked
25. bad	worse	worst
26. far	farther	farthest
27. old	older	oldest
28. educative	more educative	most educative
29. foolish	more foolish	most foolish
30. light	lighter	lightest
31. rude	ruder	rudest
32. famous	more famous	most famous
33. serious	more serious	most serious
34. beautiful	more beautiful	most beautiful
35. little	less	least
36. ugly	uglier	ugliest
37. active	more active	most active
38. poor	poorer	poorest
39. playful	more playful	most playful
40. honest	more honest	most honest
41. funny	funnier	funniest
42. religious	more religious	most religious
43. deadly	more deadly	most deadly
44. stubborn	more stubborn	most stubborn
45. decent	more decent	most decent
46. short	shorter	shortest
47. good	better	best
48. long	longer	longest
49. small	smaller	smallest
50. cruel	crueller	cruellest
51. sad	sadder	saddest
52. notorious	more notorious	most notorious

53. smell	smellier	smelliest
54. slow	slower	slowest
55. high	higher	highest

EXERCISE 11

1. c,
2. b,
3. c,
4. c,
5. b,
6. a,
7. a
8. b,
9. c,
10. b,
11. c,
12. b,
13. a,
14. c

EXERCISE 12

In the paragraph below, the adverbs are underlined and the word each qualifies is bold. Note that adverbial phrases are not included.

I **saw** many people yesterday in our school compound. All of them were smartly **dressed**, and they **walked** quietly to the principal's office. The secretary, who **appeared** too busy, quickly **came** out and smilingly **showed** them seats. They patiently **waited**. Suddenly, the principal's car **drove** up and slowly **stopped** in front of the office. She worriedly **came** down from the car. She stood to attention and quickly **glanced** at the strangers. 'Why **are** you here and how long have you being here?' She surprisingly **asked** them. 'Our children invited us here to sign documents on their behalf.' One of the men timidly **got** up and responded to the principal's question. 'I **was expecting** you yesterday to sign those documents, not today. I don't believe if I have anything like that on my agenda today.' She angrily **told** them and boastfully **walked** into her office and slowly and proudly **sat** in her comfortable chair.

EXERCISE 13

1. late,
2. slowly,
3. quietly,
4. too,
5. suddenly,
6. quickly,
7. heavily,
8. aloud,
9. immediately,
10. seriously,
11. firmly

EXERCISE 14

The adverbs are bold in the sentences below.

1. The forest fire spread **rapidly.**
2. September mornings are **really** cool.
3. She did **rather** well in the exams.
4. He told us to talk **quietly** in the darkness.
5. The huge supporters of the president matched **across.**
6. The young woman drank the juice **slowly.**
7. It is **exactly** 3:00 in the morning.
8. The dog **quickly** pounced on the snake.
9. They marched **happily** through the garden.
10. Jinnah is **always** late for school.

11. Could you please leave her **alone**?
12. The green car is **extremely** magnificent.
13. She **seldom** did well on tests.
14. Green, white and blue are **definitely** my favourite colours.
15. He carried the bucket of water **very carefully**.

EXERCISE 15

1. on,
2. in front of,
3. to,
4. in,
5. between,
6. under,
7. on,
8. from,
9. towards,
10. through,
11. in,
12. behind,
13. below,
14. up,
15. above,
16. across,
17. on,
18. from,
19. off,
20. over,
21. into,
22. beside,
23. among,
24. behind,
25. on,
26. at,
27. around,
28. in,

EXERCISE 16

In the paragraph below, the prepositional phrases are underlined. Object of any phrase is bold.

My father sent a letter to **the chief** about **the complaint** the community people made to **him**. The people complained about the criminal **behaviour** of **the youths** in **the area**. The youths together with the young **adults** in the **area** have adopted the habit of **taking** drugs, armed robbery and prostitution. After he has read the letter, the chief called the community elders and put the matter across. In the elders' **meeting**, my father sat next to **the chief**. I was called to serve as secretary for **them**. Behind **me** was the chief's elder son, Kaliru. He was the head of the **Christmus Prayer group** that used both the Bible and the Quran. They claimed to be very prayerful and religiously holy, yet they were truly ungodly. Their meeting place was called ChurMosq Center; a place that was widely believed to be the meeting and breeding ground for **criminals and prostitutes**. In fact, it was believed that he, Kaliru, was the head of **one** of the notorious **group** in the **community**. He remained silence throughout the **meeting,** and from **time** to **time**, the embarrassment plastered on his father's **face**, showed up. Towards **the end** of **the meeting**, Kaliru made very little contribution that was not even necessary. He told the people that he believed that God is greater than any criminal and that the people should put their problems to **God** to fight for **them**. At the **end** of the **meeting,** we all decided to summon all the members of **community** into a general **meeting** to further deliberate on the **matter.**

EXERCISE 17

ADVERB	PREPOSITION
4, 7, 9, 10, 11, 12, 14, 16, 17, 19, 20, 24,	1, 2, 3, 5, 6, 8, 13, 15, 18, 21, 22, 23, 25, 26, 27, 28

EXERCISE 18

1. Both __ and,
2. Neither __ nor,
3. Neither __ nor,
4. Either __ or,
5. Either __ or,
6. Both __ and,
7. Either __ or
8. Neither __ nor,
9. Though ___ yet,
10. Both __ and

EXERCISE 1

In the short passage below, the noun phrases are underlined and numbered; the function of each phrase is stated against its number in the table.

(1)Our team won (2)the match that was played yesterday in (3)our village. (4)Every fan from (5)the surrounding villages was present and they were extremely happy for(6)the players. When (7)the final whistle was blown, (8) the jubilant fans jumped into (9)the field to embrace (10)the players. Even (11)my grandmother, (12)the oldest creature in (13)the village, celebrated (14)the victory. A week to (15)the match, everyone fervently prayed for (16)our young team to carry (17)the day. (18)Traditional worshippers too called (19)our ancestors to support (20)the team. If we would have lost (21)this match, (22)many heads in (23)the village sport committee would have rolled. Now that (24)the team has qualified to play (25)the district league next season; we must encourage (26)our young players, and we will try to get (27)few experienced players too. We hope to bring trophies home in time to come.

Subject	Direct object	Object of preposition	appositive
1, 4, 7, 8, 11, 18, 22, 24	2, 10, 14, 17, 19, 20, 21, 25, 26, 27	3, 5, 6, 9, 13, 15, 16, 23	12

EXERCISE 3

All the prepositional phrases are underlined and the object of each phrase is bold.

<u>In my **class,**</u> there are fifteen boys and twelve girls. Each seat is occupied <u>by two **pupils.**</u> Fatou Gibba, the girl <u>with the most admirable **character**</u>, sits <u>near **Abass**</u>, the prefect <u>of the **class**</u>. <u>Behind **them**</u> are Jarju and Kamara, the best <u>of **friends**</u>. The seat <u>adjacent the latter's **seat**</u> is occupied <u>by the two admirable and brilliant **twins.**</u> <u>Towards the left hand **corner**</u>, there the noise causing group is. <u>Above **them**</u> is the ceiling far. The crin-cran sound <u>from **it**</u> and the offensive noise <u>from this notorious **group**</u> make the class unpleasant when there is on teacher. <u>On the **wall**</u> <u>in front of the **class**</u> is our wide blackboard. Whenever the English teacher comes <u>into our **class**</u>, the pupils sit <u>on their **bottoms**</u> and listen <u>without **writing**</u>. He will clearly explain the concepts <u>for **us**</u> to understand; and writes the summary <u>of the **note**</u> <u>on the **board**</u> <u>for **us**</u> to copy. <u>At the **end**</u> <u>of any **lesson**</u>, he will urge us to either ask questions or to make contributions. Whether we ask questions or not, he will continually fire us questions <u>until the entire **topic**</u> he taught <u>within the **period**</u> is summarized and hammered home.

EXERCISE 4

The adjectival phrases are underlined; the word each modifies is bold.

1. The **books** <u>in the principal's office</u> are very new.
2. Plenty **novels** <u>among the books</u> were written by Africans.
3. Those **boys** <u>under the trees</u> sing aloud in our class.
4. There is a boy who narrates **stories** <u>about the forest devil</u>.
5. Some **teachers** <u>from other countries</u> do not speak our native languages.
6. The big **apples** <u>on the table</u> are not in good condition.
7. In the class, I sit behind the **girl** <u>with the black bag</u>.
8. There are different **kinds** <u>of fish</u> in the **river** <u>below the mountain</u>.
9. Several **children** <u>above the **age**</u> <u>of ten</u> are from low income earners.
10. Some of the **boys** <u>around the mansion</u> are the **strangers** <u>from the university</u>

EXERCISE 5

The adverbial phrases are underlined; the word each modifies is bold.

We **passed** <u>by the river</u> and **entered** <u>into the forest</u> to fetch some fire woods. <u>In the river</u>, we **saw** too many little fish **swimming** around <u>with few bigger</u> ones. A long black snake was **chasing** the bigger fishes <u>with full speed</u>. I **sent** my machete <u>in the water</u> to cut the snake, but I missed it. It **came** <u>out of the water</u> and **climbed** <u>up a big tree</u>. <u>On the top</u> <u>of the tree</u> **were** several birds and their nests. They all **flew** away <u>in the air</u> when they saw the black cobra climbing their tree. We spent time watching the drama between the snake and the birds. When it **reached** <u>on the top</u>, the snake started **searching** <u>in the nests</u> one after the other for eggs. <u>In one of the nests</u> where it found eggs, it **spent** more time. Few birds **flew** <u>on it</u> and **pecked** it <u>with their powerful beaks</u>. It was a serious battle we witnessed.

EXERCISE 7

In the sentences below, all participles or participial phrases are in bracket. The present participles or participial phrases are underlined and the past participles or participial phrases are italicized; the modifying nouns are bold. (pp=participial phrase, p=participle)

1. The (<u>talking</u> *p*) **parrot** is destroying my (<u>growing</u> *p*) **plants.**
2. The **kite** (<u>flying in the air</u> *pp*) will land on the (<u>waving</u> *p*) **leaves**.
3. It is the (<u>flowing</u> *p*) **water** that brought down this (*broken* *p*) **statue** of the king.
4. The (<u>caring</u> *p*) **parents** will treat the (*ill-mannered* *p*) **behaviour** of their children.
5. SLPP (<u>dancing</u> *p*) **group** won the (*advertised* *p*) **position**.
6. The (<u>governing</u> *p*) **APC party** won the (*cheated* *p*) **elections**.
7. The (<u>sailing</u> *p*) **boat** found itself in an (*unknown* *p*) **destination**.
8. Please bring me the (*broken* *p*) **chair** that is in the (<u>dressing</u> *p*) **room**.
9. The (<u>exciting</u> *p*) **fans** vigorously clapped for their (<u>winning</u> *p*) **team**.

10. (<u>Sleeping up the ceiling</u>, **pp**) my neighbour's **cat** cannot catch any rat.

11. Some **children** (*pampered and spoilt by their parents*, **pp**) will rudely behave in (*forbidden p*) **places**.

12. Your (<u>singing **p**</u>) **toy** scattered the **documents** (*edited and compiled by the secretary pp*).

13. The (*suspended p*) **activities** will resume on the first (<u>working **p**</u>) **day** of this week.

14. (*Running like a kangaroo*, **pp**) **the boy** will take the first position in the (<u>awaiting **p**</u>) **event**.

15. (<u>Sitting on the tree</u>, **pp**) **my parrot** plucked the (*easily destroyed* **pp**) **buds** on the tree.

16. (<u>Moving along the river</u>, **pp**) **Paul** sang a love song for his (*widely admired pp*) **Massa**.

17. **The old woman**, (<u>walking slowly</u>, **pp**) saw the (*lost and forgotten p*) **ring** in the grass.

18. The (<u>fast growing **pp**</u>) **economy** has no effect on the (<u>less and slowly developing **pp**</u>) **nations**.

19. **The boy** (<u>feeling uneasy to speak</u>, **pp**) waved vigorously to the (<u>loud cheering **pp**</u>) **spectators**.

20. (<u>Developing slowly **pp**</u>) in the sub-region, **Sierra Leone** will soon feed her (<u>rapidly growing **pp**</u>) **population**.

EXERCISE 8

In the sentences below, the infinitives are bold and infinitive phrases are underlined; then the function of each infinitive or infinitive phrase is stated against it.

		Function as
1.	<u>**To eat** with kings</u> is considered as special blessing.	a subject of the sentence
2.	He loves <u>**to move** about at night.</u>	a direct object
3.	<u>**To find** a life-changing job</u> is also a difficult job.	a subject of the sentence

4.	They are wealthy enough **to live** on few dollars per day.	an adverb of manner to qualify enough
5.	My Massa is a lady **to admire and copy** for her neatness.	an adjective to describe lady
6.	Humans are creatures **to study** carefully.	an adjective to describe creatures
7.	Are you ready **to pay** for it now?	an adverb of manner to qualify ready
8.	He laughed **to satisfy** everyone in the party.	an adverb of reason to qualify laughed
9.	I will pay **to eat and dance** for the rest of the day.	an adverb of reason to qualify pay
10.	Now is the time **to pray**.	an adjective to describe time
11.	We have come **to mourn** our grandparents.	an adverb of reason to qualify come
12.	The tradition demands us **to do** so.	a direct object
13.	We bring them **to entertain** us.	an adverb of reason to qualify bring
14.	**To do** hard work may be dangerous to your health.	a subject of the sentence
15.	They deserve **to win** the scholarship.	a direct object
16.	**To talk** like a parrot is what I admire.	a subject of the sentence
17.	He has come **to disturb** us today.	an adverb of reason to qualify come
18.	Tell them **to move** backward.	a direct object
19.	Mohamed has come **to see** us for his arrangement.	an adverb of reason to qualify come
20.	**To be** a man is not a day job.	a subject of the sentence

EXERCISE 9

In the sentences below, the gerunds are underlined and gerund phrases are bold. The grammatical function of each of them is stated against the sentence.

		Functions as
1.	Questioning is part of policing.	subject and object of preposition
2.	**Asking too many questions** helps to fish out the truth.	subject of the sentence
3.	Ansumana loves **reading romantic novels**.	the direct object
4.	**Keen listening and careful writing** make a journalist effective.	compound subject of the sentence
5.	What all coaches want is **winning matches**.	a predicate nominative
6.	I stopped **writing my examination** on Friday.	the direct object
7.	They started smoking when I was not born.	the direct object
8.	Dancing will make people famous in the society.	subject of the sentence
9.	He is paid for **teaching in two schools**.	object of preposition
10.	Gossiping is killing.	subject and predicate nominative
11.	**Laughing to people** is equal to **healing their wounds**.	subject and object of preposition
12.	**Lying to people** is similar to **stealing their belongings**.	subject and object of preposition
13.	Watching and peeping are part of his crime.	compound subject of the sentence

14.	<u>Drinking and smoking</u> are not part of fasting.	compound subject of the sentence
15.	She loves **singing for God and dancing in the club**.	compound direct object
16.	<u>Diving and swimming</u> are his best hobbies.	compound subject of the sentence
17.	Her best events are <u>running and jumping</u>.	a predicate nominative
18.	**Laughing the old man** put them into trouble.	a subject of the sentence
19.	**Finishing the race** was everyone's target.	a subject of the sentence
20.	**Bringing people together** is our aim.	a subject of the sentence

EXERCISE 10

In the sentences below, the appositives are underlined and appositive phrases are bold. The word (s) each re-names are written against the sentence.

1.	We met him, the prize <u>winner</u>, on our way to the school.	him
2.	The boy you told us about, <u>Jusu,</u> is in town.	the boy
3.	The subject matter, <u>condemnation</u> of drug abuse, is in place.	subject matter
4.	The two hills, <u>Maamba and Turgboo</u>, are in Sierra Leone.	the two hills
5.	We met him, <u>the principal</u>, on our way to the school.	him
6.	His autobiography, *At <u>Last</u>*, won him award in the 80s.	*At Last*

7. I want to spend the holiday with parents in my village, <u>Fandou</u>.	my village
8. 1975<u>, the year</u> I was born, was graceful year for my family.	1975
9. Paulina, <u>our prefect</u>, will be with our English teacher, <u>Mr. V. Bangali</u>.	Paulina, English teacher
10. The president visited two schools, <u>Methodist and National</u>.	two schools
11. The highest mountain, <u>Maamba</u>, is very close to my village.	The highest mountain
12. They informed the chief,<u> man </u>of the people, about our party.	the chief
13. In the book, <u>Simplify English Grammar</u>, grammar is simplified.	the book
14. *Cutting the Chain*, <u>a drama</u> written by Paul, is very interesting.	*Cutting the Chain*
15. We saw cobra, <u>the</u> worst tropical <u>snake</u> on earth, in the forest.	cobra
16. Mohamed Kallon, Sierra Leonean international <u>footballer</u>, is generous. Mohamed Kallon	
17. Baba Alpha, a very faithful <u>Muslim</u>, has become a born-again pastor. Baba Alpha	
18. Massa Sama, <u>the wife</u> of the writer, is very beautiful.	Massa Sama
19. Foday Sankoh, <u>the leader</u> of RUF rebels, died at the end of the war.	Foday Sankoh
20. He obtained a degree, <u>Bachelor of Arts in Education</u>, from the prestigious Njala University. a degree	

EXERCISE 11

The underline word groups are noun clauses, their grammatical functions are stated against them as they is used in the sentence.

		Function as:
1.	My parents have to decide <u>who should be my wife</u>.	the direct object of the sentence
2.	I was asked to choose <u>whom we should visit</u>.	the direct object of the sentence
3.	We saw the hole in <u>which he dropped the pen</u>.	an object of preposition
4.	You decide <u>how you want to spend your money</u>.	the direct object of the sentence
5.	The truth is <u>what you told me in the meeting</u>.	the predicate nominative
6.	<u>Where she spent the night</u> was unknown to all of us.	the subject of sentence
7.	Every Muslim must have faith in <u>whatever the Quran says</u>.	an object of preposition
8.	<u>What you told me about him</u> is fact.	the subject of the sentence
9.	Children will believe <u>whatever their teachers say</u>.	the direct object of the sentence
10.	The madman remembered <u>where he lived and worked</u>.	the direct object of the sentence
11.	<u>What I do with my money</u> is not your business.	the subject of the sentence
12.	The final is <u>what they agreed on in the meeting</u>.	the predicate nominative
13.	<u>The way Jesus cured the blind man</u> was a mystery to everyone.	the subject of the sentence
14.	Tom told us <u>what was the problem in the village</u>.	a direct object

15. They showed us the hole in <u>which the rat entered</u>.	an object of preposition
16. <u>Even if she fails</u> should not border you.	the subject of the sentence
17. <u>The way the case was judged</u> beat everyone's imagination.	the subject of the sentence
18. <u>Whatever you may need</u> should be taken along.	the subject of the sentence
19. People will talk about <u>whatever you do or say</u>.	an object of preposition
20. *Pass on the news to <u>whomever you meet on the way</u>*.	an object of preposition

EXERCISE 12

Sentences	Clause	Function
1. We walked through the farm <u>where they were working</u>.	Adjective clause	It modifies farm
2. They told us about the man <u>we met in the farm today</u>.	Adjective clause	It modifies man
3. The new phone <u>which you bought for me</u> cannot function properly.	Relative clause	It modifies phone
4. He said students <u>who failed the exams</u> have been sent off.	Relative clause	It modifies students
5. The woman <u>whom you were sent to</u> passed here this afternoon.	Relative clause	It modifies woman
6. The boy <u>whose pen you borrow</u> will call you tomorrow.	Relative clause	It modifies boy
7. This is the trader <u>that sold to us the stolen phone</u>.	Relative clause	It modifies trader

	Clauses		Names	Functions
8.	We showed them the street <u>where he lives</u>.		Adjective clause	It modifies street
9.	I got the phone <u>which you send for me</u>.		Relative clause	It modifies phone
10.	No one wants to see the murderer <u>who slaughtered the baby</u>.		relative clause	It modifies murderer

EXERCISE 13

In the sentences below, clauses are bold.

Clauses		Names	Functions
1.	The boy **who told me about you** has come.	Relative clause	It modifies boy
2.	Paul **who wrote this book** is my friend.	Relative clause	It modifies Paul
3.	We saw the hero **that saved the nation.**	Relative clause	It modifies hero
4.	The Lord **that lives for all** is great.	Relative clause	It modifies the Lord
5.	I saw the boy **we met in the library.**	Adjective clause	It modifies boy
6.	I've been to Fandu **where the hero was born.**	Adjective clause	It modifies Fandu
7.	We talked to the man **he told us about.**	Adjective clause	It modifies the man
8.	He showed us the house **where the writer grew up.**	Adjective clause	It modifies the house
9.	The girl **who attends NSSK** has won prize.	Relative clause	It modifies the girl
10.	The book **you bought** is very interesting.	Adjective clause	It modifies the book
11.	The greatest law **God made** is love for one another.	Adjective clause	It modifies law

12. I read the book **which was written by Paulina**.	Relative clause	It modifies the book
13. The man, **whose death was announced**, was very brave.	Adjective clause	It modifies the man
14. **What we saw** was beyond everyone's expectation.	Noun clause	As subject of sentence
15. We showed them the road **that was safer**.	Relative clause	It modifies the road

EXERCISE 14

The adverbial clauses are underlined and the word each clause modifies is bold.

1. <u>When the game ended</u>, we slowly **walked** back home.
2. I **have contributed** <u>though you did not inform me</u>.
3. We **worked** <u>as if we were slaves from North Africa</u>.
4. You **must respect** her <u>since she is your mother</u>.
5. <u>As soon as you finish the exam</u>, you **will be given** the ticket.
6. They **came around** <u>as if they were invited</u>.
7. She **can't do** it <u>because there is no money to pay her</u>.
8. <u>Before you and mother came</u>, they **had fought** twice.
9. She **must read** her book <u>even if I am not around</u>.
10. We **can go** <u>where they were working</u> last week.
11. I **am implementing** it <u>as it was planned</u>.
12. <u>If the people want you to come</u>, they **will call** you.
13. We **will vote** him out <u>when we meet next week</u>.
14. Let's **eat** the apple of wisdom <u>since we are alone here</u>.
15. **Spread** the mat <u>if you want the fruit of knowledge</u>.
16. He **did** the work <u>when I was sleeping</u>.
17. <u>Unless you show me the man</u>, I **will not give** you the message.
18. <u>Whenever they arrive</u>, the classes **will start**.
19. <u>While we are waiting</u>, let us **prepare** the agenda for the meeting.
20. He is a **good** coach <u>inasmuch as he can take a team from zero to hero</u>.

	NAME	FUNCTION
1	adverbial clause	It modifies the verb phr. 'were talking'
2	relative clause	It modifies the noun 'Ousman'
3	Appositive	It renames Isatou
4	noun phrase	It is use subject of the sentence
5	past participle	It modifies better-half
6	adverbial phrase	It modifies 'were touched and awoken'
7	participial phrase	It modifies teenagers
8	noun clause	As subject of the sentence
9	adverbial phrase	It modifies the verb 'told'
10	infinitive phrase used as adverb	It qualifies the verb 'going'
11	adjective phrase	It modifies 'Orga man'

EXERCISE 16

	NAME	FUNCTION
1	relative clause	It modifies the village
2	adjectival phrase	It modifies heroes &heroines
3	adverbial clause	It qualifies will become
4	noun phrase	Object of preposition
5	Appositive	It renames Pa Henwa
6	Appositive	It renames elder son
7	participial phrase	It modifies Njombobla
8	adverbial phrase	It qualifies entry
9	infinitive phrase (as adverb)	It qualifies use
10	past participle	It modifies the village
11	infinitive phrase (as noun)	It function as subject of sentence
12	noun clause	It function as subject of sentence

CHAPTER 6

EXERCISE 1

Classify the sentences below as declarative, imperative, interrogative or exclamatory.

1. Was Papa Nukwu a traditional worshiper or heathen?   *(interrogative)*

2. Papa is so strict that he hasn't mercy on even his father.   *(declarative)*

3. What fanatic attitude displayed by Papa in the book!   *(exclamatory)*

4. Is Papa's behaviour resembled a true Christian?   *(interrogative)*

5. Read the book written by Paul Lahai aloud for us to hear.   *(imperative)*

6. Bring me the food prepared by your mother!   *(exclamatory)*

7. There are more boys on the street than girls.   *(declarative)*

8. Where are the boys that came from Kenema for the game?   *(interrogative)*

9. Remember to feed the birds and the goats in the noon!   *(exclamatory)*

10. Tell them to wait for me when they come.   *(imperative)*

EXERCISE 2

Underline the simple sentences within the sentences below.

1. When I was in university, I had many friends.
2. Summa was very kind and hardworking, but James was unserious.
3. Hassan is very handsome and he is always smartly dressed.
4. Whenever there were ladies around, Peter appeared happy.

5. <u>Sheriff sucks the chest apple</u> if it is available.
6. <u>Female's apples are full of happiness and long life</u>.
7. Whenever Bangali was allowed to play the game, <u>he would pay money</u>.
8. <u>Bockarie banks his money in treasure hole</u>.
9. <u>Fana perpetually checks in the devil's hole</u> if he is alright.
10. <u>He</u> who keeps my laws <u>shall be prosper and safe on Judgment day</u>.
11. <u>Jekujar saw the hole</u> in which the snake entered at night.
12. <u>John is my friend</u> but <u>he does not visit me perpetually</u>.
13. <u>The holy men are God's friends</u> though <u>some will not see heaven</u>.
14. <u>The man</u> who is called Fomba <u>is the head of the institution</u>.
15. <u>We went to the farm</u> where they were working.

EXERCISE 5

The complex sentences in the short passage below are italics. The simple sentences are underlined and the subordinate clauses are bold.

*<u>Paul loves Massa</u> **because she is beautiful and mannered**. <u>He was not too happy</u> **when she did not positively respond to his proposal of marriage** <u>at the beginning</u>. **When she went to Kenema on holiday**, <u>he actually confessed to Moses</u> **that Massa's love was killing him**.* Moses was always with him to encourage him. Massa hosts Paul's treasures of comfort, happiness, peace and satisfaction. *<u>**If this angel did not love him**</u>, <u>he may become crazy</u>.* True love is good but sometimes it kills. Please honey; *<u>love Paul</u> **because he truly loves you**. <u>I pray</u> **that God will make and bless their love because God is love**.* Lovers have loved and lovers still love, but no one has ever loved his lover the way Paul loves Massa. *<u>**When their waters are put together**</u>, <u>it can produce angels</u> **that will rule the universe**. <u>**When the two bloods are mixed together**</u>, <u>it will be equivalent to precious holy water</u> **that heaven dwellers drink**.* So God, let it be your will to bring these lovers together so that they will make Paradise on earth.

EXERCISE 8

The complete subjects are underlined and the simple subjects are bold in the sentences below. Note that some sentences contain more than one simple subject.

Eg: The **stories** about his journey make his novel very exciting.

1. **Tamba Tengbeh** of 22nd July Academy is also a writer of a literature text.
2. **My** favorite **story** in that book is 'A Sound of Thunder'.
3. **The** main **character** in the story is called Mr. Taul Mahai
4. For five dalasis, **Mr. Dolington** danced and laughed like a mad man.
5. **The** only **woman** in the house is preparing food for the workers.
6. On the football pitch, **the trouble** within the team started.
7. Because of one mistake, **the laws** of our land were totally changed.
8. **The result** of the mistake affected the future generation.
9. In our school, two hard working **teachers** from university resigned.
10. With his wife, Kailahun's **hero** for this year, travelled for sixty days.
11. In 1975, **the** great **writer** was born in Kailahun district.
12. **Fodei** lived on forest birds and animals in Sierra Leone.
13. At the time, **this** short and tiny **man** was a refugee in Guinea.
14. **Kpanaa's father** was also a local tailor in Fandu village.
15. Not everyone, but **the** tall black **boy** will not enter here.
16. **The** old **Kachier** attended secondary school in Kailahun.
17. In Nyandehun, there is **a** tall **mountain** called Mamba.
18. **His** elder **brother** must be given a copy of the document.
19. **The** new green **book** contains Poems, essays and stories about angles.
20. **John Peter Moon** of The Gambia wrote about his journey.

EXERCISE 9

Underline the compound subjects in the sentences below

1. <u>The</u> national <u>park and the museum</u> are the tourist sites in Sierra Leone.
2. <u>The Macarthy Square and Buffer Zone</u> are places people visit.
3. <u>Water and</u> other natural <u>forces</u> are agents of erosion.
4. Last year, <u>Musu and Karim</u> were best of friends in our class.
5. This evening, <u>the</u> two <u>girls and</u> their <u>mother</u> were walking along the road.
6. <u>Sinners and non-sinners</u> are all made in the image of God.
7. <u>Days and nights</u> are part of God's arrangement of His creation.
8. All <u>the boys</u> in the village <u>and the girls</u> around are my fans.
9. <u>God and Satan</u> together started the creation of existence.
10. <u>To watch matches and to write stories</u> are my best hobbies.
11. <u>Musicians, footballers and drug traffickers</u> make much money.
12. <u>My father and</u> all the <u>families</u> are very happy about my performance.
13. <u>Farmers and teachers</u> are most often looked low upon in African.

EXERCISE 10

In each sentence in the passage below, the complete predicates are underlined and the simple predicates are bold.

(1). Papa Nnukwu, Aunty Ifoema and her daughter, Ameka, **have** <u>many things in common</u>. (2) All of them **love** <u>the tradition of their ancestors.</u> (3) The pressure from Papa **does** not **let** <u>anyone of them to deviate from the culture.</u> (4) Papa Nnukwu **refuses** <u>to adhere to Papa's promises for the sake of his traditional worship</u>. (5) Aunty Ifoema **studies and lectures** <u>African Studies in the university because of her love for tradition.</u> (6) Her love for the traditional music **shows** <u>that Ameka</u> **loves** <u>the African tradition.</u> (7) All the three characters **are** <u>also hard hearted.</u> (8) Amaka and her mother **are** <u>the most admirable characters in the novel.</u> (9) The writer **makes** <u>the two characters complete feminist in the story.</u> (10) Aunty Ifoema **refuses** <u>to become a reverend sister as Papa</u> **had wanted** <u>her to be before buying her a car.</u>

(11) Another issue to know **is** the importance of grammar (12) Grammar **plays** important roles in English language learning. (13) In 1870's it **was included** in the syllabus of English language. (14) During English classes in my days in school, we **learnt** a lot about grammar. (15) Many English teachers **ignore** teaching grammar these days. (16) School like Nusirat Senior Secondary, **does** not **test** the students on it; it **is** never part of their examinations. (17) Many a time, pupils **study** grammar without much understanding. (18) In the end-of-year exams, very few pupils **pass** the subject. (19) The best teacher for the subject **was called** Mr. Glammar. (20) After his death in the 1830's, the subject **was named** after him.

EXERCISE 11

The compound predicates are underlined in the sentences below.

1. Papa <u>disowned and abandoned</u> his father, Papa Nnukwu.
2. His father <u>believed and worked</u> for the traditional gods.
3. Ameka <u>drew</u> beautiful objects <u>and</u> then <u>painted</u> them magnificently.
4. <u>Have</u> you <u>heard or learn</u> about the football game?
5. Jaja and Kambili <u>spent</u> little time <u>but learnt</u> a lot of new ideas at Nsukka.
6. Chelsea <u>used</u> the best players <u>and won</u> the trophy in 2012.
7. Aunt Ifoema and her children <u>will laugh and sing</u> happily.
8. A relative <u>called and told</u> Aunty Ifoema about Papa Nnukwu's ill-health.
9. Papa Nnukwu <u>was loved and cared</u> for by his daughter.
10. Papa fervently <u>prayed and</u> strictly <u>disciplined</u> his children

EXERCISE 12

The predicate nominatives are underlined the sentences below.

1. Massa is a <u>queen</u> to that mad lover.
2. His happiness and satisfaction is <u>she</u>.
3. My mother and father are the <u>elders and</u> great <u>contributors</u>.

4. He and others are <u>the owners</u> of the nightclub.
5. Who told you that John was <u>our choice</u> for the leadership?
6. Peace and freedom is <u>what everybody wants</u>.
7. The secretary and the organizer is <u>my father</u>.
8. Charles Fowlis is <u>the first school</u> I taught in the Gambia.
9. I am the only true <u>choice</u> of the queen of the angels.
10. They were <u>my friends</u> from Njala University.

EXERCISE 13

The predicate adjectives underlined in the sentences below.

1. My wife is <u>short, black and beautiful</u>.
2. She looks <u>quiet, polite and</u> very <u>brilliant</u>.
3. Her father is highly <u>educated and religious</u>.
4. The rest of the family members are <u>peaceful and admirable</u>.
5. In school, she was <u>clever and serious</u>.
6. Besides her beauty, she is <u>strong and hardworking</u>.
7. Our wonderful God is <u>great and disciplined</u>.
8. My young daughters were <u>stubborn and playful</u> in class.
9. The Dalasi is <u>strong but hard</u> to get and keep.
10. The players of Kailahun United were <u>lost but found</u>.

EXERCISE 14

The direct objects are bold in the sentences below.

1. The old buffalo killed the young **lamb**.
2. That small boy insulted his **friend**.
3. We send our parents **some money** every month.
4. My little dog fought an **elephant** two weeks ago.
5. Our teacher narrated **the story** about Lovidovy.
6. A perfect gentleman must speak many **languages**.
7. Play the **game** let us see.
8. Did you take your **books** to school?

9. Do we need **them** for the work?
10. The world needs **peace and tranquillity** to prevail.

EXERCISE 15

The direct objects are bold in the passage below.

The first day I saw **Massa Sama**, I cherished **her** to be my better-half in future. At the time, I knew **nothing** about her. As time went on and I understood **her** better, I grew more **love** for the beautiful angel. Apart from her beauty and politeness plastered on her face, God displayed His wonderful **handwork** in her magnificent structure which she maintains with simple but very smart attires. Besides all, she loves and fears **God**, and respects **everyone**. When she smiles, she exposes the **gap** between her stainless teeth which resembles the path leading to Allah's kingdom. Her generosity cannot be under estimated. She is as kind as sun or moon that gives **light** to both foes and friends alike. Every morning, she takes **bath**, dresses up, collects **her bag** and moves to the highway to on board **vehicle** that will take **her** to her office. I love **no one** but **Miss Sama**. So help me God.

EXERCISE 16

The direct objects are underlined and the indirect objects are bold

1. Who bought **you** the <u>new bicycle</u> you rode yesterday?
2. My elder brother sent **me** <u>this bicycle</u> from America.
3. Are you talking about the one that you sent **him** <u>email</u>?
4. I am going to tell **him** <u>the story</u> you told **me**.
5. I don't have enough <u>credit</u> in my phone.
6. Then write **him** <u>a letter</u> of apology.
7. We can tell your **grandmother** few <u>words</u> of encouragement.
8. Please give **me** your <u>pen</u> so that I will draft <u>it</u>.
9. Sing **us** <u>the song</u> you learnt in school yesterday.
10. Play **Mujeh-mama** the latest <u>music</u> in town.

EXERCISE 17

In the sentences below, the direct objects are underlined and the objective complements are bold.

1. I will tell them the <u>incident</u> **relating Momoh.**
2. They elected <u>Mr. Fomba</u> **the president.**
3. Please tell your father <u>the message</u> **from your grandfather.**
4. Write <u>the story</u> **about the coat.**
5. They appointed <u>the flag bearer</u> **of the party.**
6. Write your uncle <u>the letter</u> **about change of plan.**
7. He called <u>the hero</u> **of the class.**
8. Tell <u>the driver</u> **of this car** to go to the market.
9. Peter, open for the guests <u>the door</u> **of the main gate.**
10. Have you bought them <u>the attires</u> **for the Easter?**
11. Did you tell them <u>the message</u> **from the head of state?**
12. Bring them <u>some water</u> **from the freeze.**
13. They played <u>the ball</u> **of the season.**
14. He won the club <u>the best prize</u> **of the year.**
15. We wrote the chief <u>our report</u> **of the investigation.**

CHAPTER 7

EXERCISE 1

The verb in the bracket agrees with the subject in each sentence.

1. Joseph and our father (is, <u>are</u>) happily singing in the car.
2. Fatou and the three boys (has, <u>have</u>) completed the assignment.
3. The men and that boy (was, <u>were</u>) quarrelling yesterday for a dalasi.
4. These girls sitting here and the boys (makes, <u>make</u>) dresses weekly.
5. The manager with some of his workers (<u>is</u>, are) going for a conference.
6. A cup of tea and a loaf of bread (are, <u>is</u>) my best breakfast.
7. BBC and CNN (<u>are</u>, is) the most reliable international media.

8. The chief and the secretary of Deagbormei (<u>is</u>, are) my father.
9. Each man and each boy (was, <u>were</u>) asked to come with the fees.
10. Joe, Paul and Amie (is, <u>are</u>) happy about me.

EXERCISE 2

Underline the verbs that best agree with the subject in the sentences below.

1. The family (<u>appears</u>/ appear) very generous to us.
2. The club (<u>is</u>/ are) not united on the appointment of their leader.
3. The family members (is/ <u>are</u>) coming from Togo and Foni for our meeting.
4. The spectators (was/<u>were</u>) cheering and booing at the artist.
5. The committee (<u>was</u>/ were) to make unanimous decisions.
6. The team (<u>has</u>/have) taken seats in the bus before the coach arrived.
7. The mob (have/<u>has</u>) set fire on three government buildings.
8. The staff in school (want/<u>wants</u>) the principal to resign next year.
9. The couple (love/<u>loves</u>) and (<u>understands</u>/understand) each other.
10. The staff (<u>has</u>/ have) agreed to throw party for the outgoing principal.

EXERCISE 3

Underline the appropriate verb in the bracket that agrees with the subject of each sentence.

1. The president with his family (are, <u>is</u>) coming to visit us.
2. The man and his wife (has, <u>have</u>) gone home for prayer
3. The owner of the school and the principal (are, <u>is</u>) Mr. Jones.
4. Each boy and girl (was, <u>were</u>) sent home for the school fees.
5. She or they (has, <u>have</u>) not being to London.
6. Either she or I (is, <u>am</u>) not eating a mango now.
7. That girl with her husband (go, <u>goes</u>) to church every Sunday.
8. Either the women or the man (sing, <u>sings</u>) in the church.
9. Neither the boys nor the girls (was, <u>were</u>) ready to accept him.

10. Either they or I (<u>was,</u> were) not given the ok to study in the library.
11. My sister doesn't (has, <u>have</u>) degree but she is happy.
12. Here (<u>is,</u> are) the family we saw in town.
13. You or I (<u>was,</u> were) not there when he came around today.
14. They or Peter (make, <u>makes</u>) him laugh always.
15. My father's driver and my husband (<u>was,</u> were) Pa Abou.
16. Here (is, <u>are</u>) the men that called you this morning.
17. Mr. Lahai with his family (eat, <u>eats</u>) mangoes most time.
18. The coach and secretary of the club (are,<u> is</u>) Bubacarr.
19. Neither Jarju nor the students (was, <u>were</u>) in school last week.
20. Horoja and her brother (<u>have,</u> has) bicycles at home.
21. Each man and woman (<u>has,</u> have) to pay the contribution.
22. Every boy and girl (<u>has,</u> have) the right to move about.
23. Neither our father nor our brothers (has, <u>have</u>) come around.
24. Massa, Paul or T-man (<u>has,</u> have) to come for the meeting.
25. Either my mother or father (<u>was,</u> were) in the graduation party.
26. Neimatu, either your friends or your sister (<u>is,</u> are) coming today.
27. Neither the chief nor his son (<u>has,</u> have) the right to control me.
28. Either the girls or the boys (was, <u>were</u>) ready for the job.
29. Either my father or Jusu and Tom (is, <u>are</u>) willing to pay my fees.
30. Either you or I (are, <u>am,</u> is) not hoping to repeat this class.
31. Fatou, Musu or Alice (<u>has,</u> have) to come for training.
32. The men or the boys (has, <u>have</u>) to clean the church.
33. The family members (<u>are,</u> is) coming from Basse, Bakau and Brikama.
34. (<u>Is,</u> Are) he going to school tomorrow?
35. Either the students or the teacher (<u>was,</u> were) not in class.
36. Neither my father nor my mother (<u>has,</u> have) being to Banjul.
37. Either I, Peter or you (was, <u>were</u>) to attend the party.
38. All the men in the club with a lady (has, <u>have</u>) gone to see them.
39. Either the players or their coach (<u>was,</u> were) not around for the training.
40. Fodei, Paul or Amie (<u>is,</u> are) not too known to us.
41. Neither my father nor my brothers (was, <u>were</u>) invited to the party.
42. Both the farmers and the teachers (<u>are,</u> is) less important in our society.

43. Neither prostitutes nor a criminal (are, <u>is</u>) allowed in the party.
44. Neither Muslims, Christians or a pageant (<u>has</u>, have) ever been to hell.
45. The ministers with their deputies (is, <u>are</u>) here for the meeting.

EXERCISE 4

Choose the appropriate pronoun in the bracket to complete each of the following sentences:

1. John plays with (him/<u>his</u>/her) puppies.
2. Amie demonstrates with (his/<u>her</u>) legs how to dance the style.
3. Joe and (him/<u>his</u>/ he's) sister collected (them/<u>their</u>) results.
4. Many people want (we/them/<u>their</u>) views to be recognized.
5. (<u>We</u>/ Our) are here for (my/<u>our</u>/me) book.
6. She loves (<u>her</u>/she) mother more than (<u>him</u>/he).
7. Joseph carries (them/<u>his</u>/her) bicycle to school.
8. Mary loves (I/<u>me</u>) more than (her/<u>she</u>) loves (they/<u>them</u>).
9. They are happy because (them/you/<u>their</u>) mother is here.
10. My plant drops (her/it/<u>its</u>) leaves every week.
11. Everyone has (our/<u>his or her</u>) own problems to solve.
12. Every man and woman will make (<u>his or her</u>/your) own contribution.

CHAPTER 9

ANSWERS TO EXERCISE 1

#	Voice	Doer
1	Active	**Tom**
2	Passive	**Peter**
3	Active	**Fodei**
4	Passive	**Mary**
5	active	**We**
6	Active	**?**

7	Passive	?
8	Passive	?
9	Active	**They**
10	Active	**sea man**
11	passive	?
12	passive	**stone**
13	passive	?
14	active	**Amie**
15	passive	?

ANSWERS TO EXERCISE 2A

ACTIVE VOICE	PASSIVE VOICE
God created heaven and earth.	*Heaven and earth were created by God*
Gossipers and sycophants murder people.	*People are murdered by gossipers and sycophants.*
I will do all the writing for God in heaven.	*All the writing will be done by me for God in heaven.*
We bought all that was needed for the party.	*All that was needed for the party were bought by us.*
Paul and Peter will take care of the class.	*The class will be taken care of by Paul and Peter.*
Our principal drove many students for fees.	*Many students were driven by our principal for fees.*
My mother prepares the delicious food.	*The delicious food is prepared by my mother.*
His wife gives birth to baby boy every year.	*Every year, a baby boy is given birth to by his wife.*
I will teach English Lang. in grade twelve.	*English language will be taught by me in grade twelve.*
Who is going to carry grandfather to heaven?	*Grandfather is going to be carried to heaven by whom?*

Exercise 2b	
The chief asked me to supervise the work.	I was asked by the chief to supervise the work.
Satan sent the devil to do what he likes.	The devil was sent by Satan to do what he likes.
Everyone I come across loves me.	I am loved by everyone I come across.
A Sierra Leonean wrote this book.	This book was written by a Sierra Leonean.
Peter carried her for treatment.	She was carried by Peter for the treatment.
They wrote this wonderful letter.	This wonderful letter was written by them.
God created everything on earth.	Everything on earth was created by God.
Joe has bought the little garden.	The little garden has been bought by Joe.
The compound owner drove them.	They were driven by the compound owner.
They and we put the old man into the trouble.	The old man was put into trouble by them and us.
They, you and we carry her trouble.	Her trouble is carried by them, you and us.

ANSWERS TO EXERCISE 3

'I was not around when you reached.' Tom said	Tom said that he was not around when you reached.
'You do not care for us.' said Farrah	Farrah said that you didn't care for them."
Binta said, 'My brother is going to punish me.'	Binta said that her brother was going to punish her.

Job said 'We tried to pay ourselves.'	Jobe said that they tried to pay themselves.
'We have come for our books and pens.' The boy said	The boys said that they came for their books and pens
'I am here with mine and for myself.' Said John	John said that he was there with his and for himself.
'Our boys are in the church for Easter mass.' He said	He said that their boys were in the church for Easter mass.
'I worked for myself.' Said Fatou	Fatou said that she worked for herself.
'They told us, but ours was not ready.' They answered	They answered that they were told but theirs was not ready.
'My team must win the prize.' said Sowe	Sowe said that his team had to win the prize.
'We paid for our own benefit.' The people said.	The people said that they paid for their own benefit.
'I am sure we must pass this exam.' Haja said	Haja said that she was sure that they must pass that exam.
'I was talking to her when you called.' Said Musa	Musa said that he was talking to her when you called.

EXERCISE 4

The answers are the underlined sentences.

QUESTIONS

"Where did you place my Bible?" Pa asked the boy
Pa asked the boy where he placed the Bible.

"What were you asked to do?" Grandfather asked.
Grandfather asked what I was asked to do.

"What assurance do you have that she will come?" asked the boy
The boy asked what assurance I had that she would come.

Peter asked whether we were happy with him.
Peter asked, 'Are you happy with him?'

The pastor asked if we actually believe in God Almighty.
'Do you actually believe in God Almighty?' The pastor asked

I asked Massa if she will marry me.
I asked, 'Massa, will you marry me?'

REQUESTS

"Bring me some cold water to drink." Father requested
Father requested or asked for some cold water to drink.

"Jue, please tell you father to call me." Mr. Jusu requested
Jusu asked Jue to tell her father to call him.

Father requested "Please let somebody bring me a chair."
Father requested for someone to bring or carry him a chair.

Massa, please show me some of your love." he requested
He asked Massa to show him some of her love.

Abu asked John to take his books home.
Abu asked, 'John, please take my books home.'

Massa told Paul to exercise some patient with her.
'Paul, please exercise some patient with me.' Massa told him

COMMANDS

Mama shouted "Get-up! Go inside and bring my cane!"
Mama commanded him to get-up, go inside and bring her cane.

"The last person will not be allowed!" he threatened.
He threatened that the last person would not be allowed.

Mrs. Lam ordered "All late comers should kneel down!"
<u>Mrs. Lam ordered all late comers to kneel down.</u>

He instructed Joe to take his bag to the car park.
<u>'Joe, take my bag to the car park!' He instructed</u>

Papa commanded the boy to walk faster with his food.
<u>'Boy, walk faster with my food!' Papa commanded</u>

Peter asked Tom to follow him from the market to home.
<u>'Tom, follow me from the market here to home!' Peter commanded</u>

EXERCISE 5

1	Hasn't he?
2	Am I not
3	Aren't we?
4	Do you?
5	Isn't he?
6	Are they?
7	Didn't they?
8	Am I?
9	Don't they?
10	Doesn't He?
11	Will they?
12	Haven't they?
13	Is he?
14	Aren't they?
15	Is it?
16	Is there any?
17	Aren't they?
18	Isn't she?
19	Have they?
20	Has she?

21	Is it?
22	Don't they?
23	Wasn't he?
24	Isn't it?
25	Aren't they?

CHAPTER 12

ANSWER TO EXERCISE 1

1) .

2) ?

3) .

4) !

5) ?

6) .

7) .

8) !

9) .

10) ?

11) .

12) .

13) .

14) .

15) !

16) .

17) .

18) ?

19) !

20) !

ANSWER TO EXERCISE 2

One hot afternoon, I accompanied my grandmother to the previous year farm. We went to brush her vegetable gardens. She planted many different crops on all the ant-hills in the farm my father cultivated. Her best crops were pepper, garden egg, tomato, bean and green. She planted them plenty. On one of the ant-hills, we saw a very big and long black snake. I saw the snake first. I pointed at it and shouted. "Grandmother! A big snake!" "Where is it?" She asked. Though she was an old woman, yet she was strong and brave. She advanced towards the reptile and threw her short machete at it and hit it on the back. The snake became mad and jumped at her. I stood by to watch the drama unfold. Grandmother was very lucky to catch the snake by its head and held it firmly. "Give me my machete!" She turned to me and shouted. I was afraid to go near them. "Don't be afraid; the rest you see is just a rope. I hold the real snake, the head." I timidly jumped, collected the machete and gave it to her which she used to cut off the head of the black reptile.

EXERCISE 3

In the short passage below, only the end mark punctuations are used. There are areas where commas, semicolons, colons, apostrophe and quotation marks are to be applied. Identify the areas and apply them appropriately.

My father, sitting behind his machine, called me this morning and sent me to the market in town. When I reached there, I saw many people in the crowded, noisy, busy and dirty market. Dr Madman, the famous crazy market crier, pointed his iron bar towards me and asked. "Why are you looking at me? How can you call yourself a perfect man when among your seven billion handworks in your own image, there is no perfect one? Tell me!"

I felt threatened and I jumped into an old woman's tray full of items. The woman held me firm by my shirt and shouted above her voices. "I can't take any beg but the money! Pay mi money!" Some the items destroyed were mirror, ear-rings, a tin of baby powder, a pair of eye glasses and three spray bottles. When I paid for the damage goods the old woman laughed, sang, danced and clapped for me.

When I turned to go, the mad crier again threatened me. "You perfect being with imperfect parts and ways! Stand and wait for me! Stand let me come and wage a holy war on your imperfect soul that will take you to Purgatory through the perfect hell." I was completely baffled about his philosophical statements; I let them go. I remembered the paper where I listed the items that I went to buy. On the list were phone, bread, milk, sugar and tea cups. Then I looked at my time. It was 10:10 AM. "Look at him going with a document dated 19th December, 1975 found in an old building in Fandu village, Kpombai section, Luawa chiefdom, Kailahun district in the Eastern province of Sierra Leone!" Again, it was Madman that was vibrating. I paid less attention to him; instead I doubled up my steeps and escaped from the scene.

EXERCISE 4

Mama Salone is circular in sharp. The northeast, north and northwest shares border with Guinea; the east and south borders with the south of Liberia; and the Atlantic Ocean locks the west and the southwest. It is politically divided into provinces and western area, districts, chiefdoms, sections, towns and villages. Kailahun, Kono and Kenema districts are in the Eastern Province. Bo, Moiyamba, Pujehun, and Bonthe districts are in the Southern Province; while Kpombali, Port Loko, Koinadugu, Kambia and Tonkolili districts are in the north. Freetown, the capital city and its environs are located in the Western Area. The staple food is rice; next to it are cassava, potato and yam. Coffee, caocao and oil palm are the major cash crops the people grow. The major activities are farming, trading, fishing, mining and education. The currencies are Leones and cents. There are many rivers and streams, swamps, low lands, savannah lands, forests, valleys, hills and mountains. Additional natural resources include diamond, gold, bauxite, retile, stones and crude oil. Green, white and blue are the colors of the national flag. There are Christians, Muslims, traditionalists and Christmus peacefully co-existing in this anthem of West Africa. Inter-marriages are common among the eighteen ethnic groups which comprise of the seven million and more peoples living in the country. The two major political parties are Sierra Leone Peoples Party and All Peoples Congress Party; Creole, Mende and Temne are widely spoken languages. Almighty God blesses my beloved country!

EXERCISE 5

The sentences below are correctly capitalized.

1. Joseph and Kaina are the only two sons of Mr. and Mrs. Kasilio.
2. Freetown and Banjul are among cities in West Africa.
3. When I was in America, i lived in New York.

4. Many African footballers play for Premier League clubs.
5. Jesus Christ and Prophet Mohammed are true messengers of God.
6. President Jammeh, the Gambian hero, will never be forgotten.
7. Torgbo and Mamba are tallest mountains in Kailahun district.
8. The boy, Jeneba and I went to see doctor Lahai.
9. United states of Africa is the dream of most African patriots.
10. She lived in Britain, Germany and France before he returned home

Printed in the United States
By Bookmasters